Roxana's Children

Roxana Brown Walbridge Watts, ca. 1850. Daguerreotype taken in St. Johnsbury, Vermont. Print, courtesy California Historical Society.

Lynn A. Bonfield and
Mary C. Morrison

Roxana's Children

The Biography of a
Nineteenth-Century Vermont Family

University of Massachusetts Press
Amherst

Copyright © 1995 by
Lynn A. Bonfield and Mary C. Morrison
Printed in the United States of America

LC 95-2417
ISBN 0-87023-972-4 (cloth); 981-3 (pbk.)

Designed by Dennis Anderson
Set in Bembo by Keystone Typesetting, Inc.
Printed and bound by Thomson-Shore, Inc.

Library of Congress Cataloging-in-Publication Data

Bonfield, Lynn A., 1939–
    Roxana's children : the biography of a nineteenth-century Vermont
family / Lynn A. Bonfield and Mary C. Morrison.
        p.   cm.
    Includes bibliographical references (p.   ) and index.
    ISBN 0–87023–972–4 (alk. paper)—ISBN 0–87023–981–3
(pbk. : alk. paper)
    1. Watts family. 2. Watts, Roxana Brown Walbridge, 1802—1862—
Family. 3. Peacham (Vt.)—Biography. 4. Family—Vermont—Peacham—
History—19th century. 5. United States—Social life and
customs—19th century. I. Morrison, Mary Chase. II. Title.
CT274.W375B66   1995
929'.2'0973—dc20
                                            95—2417
                                              CIP

British Library Cataloguing in Publication data are available.

Dedicated to the relatives of Roxana Brown Walbridge Watts. Their careful preservation of the family letters, diaries, photographs, and artifacts inspired this book.

Genevieve Rix Burrows, San Francisco (deceased)

Helen Watts Chase, Dunedin, Florida (deceased)

Charles (deceased) and Mary Jane Choate, West Barnet, Vermont

Elsie A. Choate, Peacham, Vermont (deceased)

Isaac Watts Choate, Helena, Montana (deceased)

Paul and Elvira Choate, Durham, New Hampshire

Chris Choate-Raible, Glendale, Arizona

Allura Cockley, Santa Ana, California

Elizabeth Rix Fairfax, Walnut Creek, California

Roberta Choate Gaudette, Mont Vernon, New Hampshire

Randall V. (deceased) and Hazel E. Mills, Ashland, Oregon

Helen Watts Richter, Wheaton, Illinois

Roberta Garry Trunzo, Allison Parks, Pennsylvania

Lyman (deceased) and Elsie Buech Watts, San Francisco

Jennie Chamberlain Watts, Cambridge, Massachusetts (deceased)

"my children all left home and some gone so far that I do not ever expect to see them again"

Roxana to her granddaughter Augusta, May 29, 1853

"we are scattered all over the world and writing is the only means by which we can communicate with each other"

Dustan to his sister Sarah, March 14, 1863

Contents

ILLUSTRATIONS

FIGURES

TABLES

MAPS

PREFACE

THIS FAMILY and social history has a parallel history running alongside it—a story of opportune discoveries and coincidences amounting at times almost to miracle and of many far-flung friendships that grew out of the work.

In 1972, in San Francisco, Lynn Bonfield found on the shelves of the California Historical Society Library "The Daily Journal of Alfred & Chastina W. Rix," a diary alternating entries by this husband and wife from their wedding date in Peacham, Vermont, in 1849 to their settlement in San Francisco in 1854. The journal had been donated to the Library in 1949 by the diarists' granddaughter Genevieve Rix Burrows. Her historical instincts stirred by the diary, Lynn asked her friend Annette Glabe to transcribe it, which she did with great care. Then Lynn began to use entries from it in lectures.

At about the same time, in Swarthmore, Pennsylvania, Mary Morrison was wondering what to do with a box of papers of her mother (Helen Watts Chase) that had come to her with the closing of the family house in Florida. In the end she sighed and put them away in a closet—six well-worn diaries and a thin packet of letters from her mother's father, Isaac Watts, a Civil War veteran and farmer in Peacham, Vermont.

Lynn's lectures brought some surprising results. At one, another granddaughter of Chastina's, Elizabeth (Betty) Rix Fairfax, approached her with the news that she had some family letters that might add to the story. Indeed she did. She had about fifteen letters written from California to Peacham during the 1850s. They had been saved by her father, Edward A. Rix, who had retrieved them from Vermont, and Betty later placed them at the Bancroft Library at the University of California, Berkeley.

Another lecture at a conference in San Diego turned up a relative by marriage of Martha Walbridge Gregory. Hazel E. Mills, widow of Augusta's grandson, Randall V. Mills, knew of some letters written to Martha and Hubbell Gregory and their daughter, Augusta Gregory Mills, in Michigan and Wisconsin. These letters, including eighteen written by Roxana, were given to the California Historical Society in 1976 by Allura Cockley, Randall's cousin.

Lynn had learned early that Chastina Walbridge was actually part of a large family composed of two families, the Walbridges and the Wattses. On her first trip to Peacham in 1978, she was greeted warmly by Louis Lamoureaux, town clerk, and Edmund A. Brown, president of the Peacham Historical Association. She intended to spend only a few days there, gathering material. But Peacham cast its well-known spell upon her, and she began to spend her summers there.

Meanwhile Mary, drawn by some ancestral homing instinct, had bought a few acres of land and made a summer home on a hillside overlooking a lake not far from Peacham. The diaries, still stored in a closet, weighed on her mind, and in 1983, she brought them north with her, intending to transcribe them during the summer. She hoped to find an appropriate permanent home for them in a library, but had not the least idea how to go about it. She typed them, growing more and more interested in the large and complicated family that she discovered in their pages.

In midsummer a chance word of Mary's at a party led to her first experience of serendipity, when word of her existence and that of the diaries reached Lynn. The next day we (that is Lynn and Mary) sat by the Franklin stove in Mary's camp and began our long exchange of information and enthusiasm concerning the Walbridge-Watts family.

We also began a long friendship that came, as time went on, to include more and more people, Lynn's friends and colleagues and Mary's family, which extended still more as she resumed a connection with her Choate cousins in West Barnet, which had fallen off since her mother's death. Charles Choate, the grandson of Mary's great-aunt Alice Watts Choate and his wife, Mary Jane, lived in the family farm, occupied by Choates for more than 125 years. The Choate's farmhouse was—is still—a magical repository of family papers, out of which something new still continues to appear at every visit, even after eight years of plumbing its depths. In 1986 Lynn and her partner, Karen R. Lewis, placed this material in acid-free folders and prepared an archival inventory, listing six boxes, including the original diaries of Alice Watts and her husband, Charles Choate, grandparents of Charles, who died in 1992. Paul and Elvira Choate and other relatives, including Roberta Garry Trunzo and Roberta Choate Gaudette, found valuable material.

With a history of miracles, we were not the least bit surprised when, in 1989, Edward B. Lee, Jr., wrote from Pittsburgh (having been directed to us by Edmund Brown) that he knew of a collection of Civil War letters from Dustan Walbridge. After Lynn contacted the collector of these letters, John W. Turner, she received, almost by return mail, copies of these and many written by Isaac Watts as well. A year later John wrote to tell us about a collection of Walbridge and Rix letters written from California during the 1850s, which he knew were for sale. We were able to purchase these letters along with a small collection of Vermont Walbridge letters from the 1840s. These will go eventually to the Special Collections at the Bailey/ Howe Library of the University of Vermont where Mary has placed her family material. John also supplied us with copies from the National Archives of the military records of Dustan Walbridge and Isaac Watts and with information on the Civil War, saving us many hours of research.

Another Civil War collector, Jack Barilla, later turned up twenty Walbridge-Watts-Rix letters in his files, which he allowed John Turner to photocopy for us.

In trying to track down information about Charles and Lodoska Watts, who went to Illinois, Lynn contacted the Piatt County Historical and Genealogical Society in Monticello, which provided copies of newspaper articles on the Wattses and put us in touch with Mary Alice English, a great-granddaughter. She sent us on to Helen Watts Richter, her second cousin, from whom we received a copy of a photograph of the Watts farm on East Hill in Peacham. Since this image was missing from our collection, we were delighted.

While researching the Minnesota wing of the family, Lynn was directed to the Smithsonian Institution's National Museum of American History, which had been given the 1860s furniture of Sarah Walbridge and John S. Way in 1964. On a trip to Washington, Lynn was able to follow the curator of the Division of Domestic Life, Rodris Roth, into the storage rooms of that grand museum to see the Ways' Victorian parlor set consisting of a sofa, an armchair, and matching side chairs, all upholstered in black horsehair with exposed frames of walnut. Useful historical material on the Ways was found at the Minnesota Historical Society, Carleton College Archives, St. Olaf College Archives, Buckham Memorial Library in Faribault, Rice County Historical Society, and Northfield/Rice County Genealogical Society.

For information on the education of Lyman S. Watts we were helped by the special collections at Middlebury College and Andover Newton Theological School.

Peacham, too, has good material in its historical collections and town office, easily accessible thanks to town clerk and archivist, Lorna Quimby. The Vermont Historical Society Library was the depository for some of the notes compiled by Jennie Chamberlain Watts and Elsie A. Choate for the official history of Peacham. Published in 1948, *Peacham, the Story of a Vermont Hill Town* by Ernest L. Bogart has been the most useful secondary source available to us. Unfortunately, many letters quoted by Bogart are not found in the collection at the Vermont Historical Society. The staffs of the St. Johnsbury Atheneaum, the Northeast Regional Vermont Library, and the Vermont Historical Society have consistently helped us.

We will not list the many photograph collections we have researched for this book because they are credited on other pages. We do want to thank all those archivists and family members who preserved the Walbridge-Watts visual history on copper, glass, tin, and paper. Many prints were duplicated in several collections and, whenever possible, we credit the original. Prints for this book were made by Professional Photography in San Francisco, and we gratefully acknowledge the good work of Edward and Elfriede Dyba. Often working from a faded and cracked original, including daguerreotypes, Eddie continually surprised us with the clarity of the prints he produced.

We also found letters, photographs, and other historical material at the Passaic County Historical Society in Paterson, New Jersey, Corcoran Museum in Washington, Radcliffe College Archives, Mount Holyoke College Archives, and the private collection in Berkeley of the late Mildred Maurer Brown, the granddaughter of Hale and Alice Locke Rix. Valuable information was given by Carolyn Long, who has preserved the California gold mine letters of her grandfather, Ashbel Martin; by Margaret Watts Bevens, a relative of Lambert Watts; and by Josephine Butler, a relative of Polly Watts Guy.

Other useful archival material has been the probate records, including wills, guardianship papers, and household inventories, of the Vermont counties of Caledonia, Lamoille, and Washington in the courthouses in St. Johnsbury, Hyde Park, and Montpelier respectively. We used additional public records from the Rice County Court House in Faribault, Minnesota; Piatt County Circuit Court in Monticello, Illinois; Vermont State Archives; and the Vermont town clerk offices at Barnet, Cabot, and Wolcott.

Cemetery records in California provided useful information, and we thank Terrence K. Baillargeon at Cypress Lawn in Colma and Betty A. Nelson at Mount Tamalpais in San Rafael.

Among the people who have assisted us are Jim Abijian, Bob Bean, Beppy Brown, Edmund A. Brown, Bob Buckeye, Mary Lynn Byran, Thomas Carey, Chris Choate-Raible, Jonathan Choate, Robert I. Choate, Beverly Bubar Denenberg, Mary Anne Easley, Bill Ferraro, Beatrice Blanchard Freeland, Connell Gallagher, J. Kevin Graffagnino, Alfred C. Harrison, Jr., Brigitta Hjalmarson, Harley P. Holden, Joe Illick, Ann Kelly, Lucy Kendall, Pauline Kilian, Gary F. Kurutz, Wilber Leeds, Doris H. Linder, Betty Hoag McGlynn, Kathy Marquis, Jeffrey D. Marshall, Linda Mihalic, Stephen M. Morrison, Reidun Dahle Nuquist, Sue O'Brien, Beverly W. Palmer, Jan Paul, Tom Paul, Catherine Mason Phillips, Daphne Craig Quimby, Frank Randall, Gregory Sanford, Leon Sompolinsky, Danila Spielman, MK Swingle, Margaret Walbridge, Chris Way, Robert A. Weinstein, Sue Wheeler, Lois White, Thelma White, Martha Kendall Winnaker, and the "Poets Walk In" at Kendal at Longwood. For kindly showing Lynn through the Watts farm, we thank Gregory Reynolds; the Stevens farm where Alfred Rix boarded, Shep and Marion Clough; the Choate Inn, where Chastina and Alfred first lived after their marriage, Charles and Ina Wallace; the Choate Inn Annex, where Ellen Boynton Watts and later Lucy Ella Watts Choate spent their last years, Nancy Bundgus. Neil Bradley let us see a gun from the Civil War period which he found in the Watts barn when his family owned the property, possibly the weapon Isaac Watts used.

We have been fortunate to have available a wide range of support services at San Francisco State University. These include the help of Richard Uchida and Jeff Ciminello at Rapid Copy; Joan Borrelli, Mary Kubo, and Kathleen Messer at Interlibrary Loan, Bill Brockett and Dori Palmer in the mail room, and Carol Taketa in the Library Administration office. We also wish to thank Olive James, University Librarian, for encouraging Lynn to take a year's sabbatical, and Susan Parker Sherwood, Archivist, who ably filled the gap at the Labor Archives while Lynn was away (1992–93). In recent months, Eric Solomon, Interim University Librarian, offered sound advice. All of the staff at the Labor Archives and Research Center and the neighboring branch of the California State Library, the Sutro Library, were unfailingly helpful.

Special recognition for their thoughtful reading of our original manuscript and their creative suggestions goes to historian Gerald McFarland

and senior editor, Clark Dougan. Also Pam Wilkinson, plying her copy-editing trade, improved the manuscript to our great advantage.

We have gained historical insight from many people who for years have listened to us talk about the Walbridge-Watts family and who have read drafts of *Roxana's Children*. We are grateful to everyone who was put in this position; in particular we want to thank Karen R. Lewis, Mary Jane Choate, Lorna Quimby, Philip P. Mason, Elsie Freeman Finch, Maxine Martin Long, and Dorothy Shaw. Carma Muir Berglund provided most of the technical assistance on the manuscript and has offered expert editorial advice for which we express warm appreciation.

We thank all who helped in our adventure.

LAB and MCM

Peacham and Cabot, Vermont

August 1994

Authors' Note

All quotes are given exactly as written including spelling and punctuation, except that periods are added silently at the end of quotes. Material in brackets has been added by the authors. In this family of stepchildren and half-sisters and half-brothers, each referred to the other as simply "sister" or "brother." Each called Roxana "mother" and Lyman "father" or "Father Watts." We continue this practice as we tell their story.

PART I

ROXANA AND HER FAMILY

Roxana Brown 1802–1862

married 1821
1) Daniel Walbridge 1796–1835

Child	married	Spouse	Grandchildren Who Lived Past Infancy
Martha Walbridge 1822–1846	married 1840	Hubbell S. Gregory ca. 1820–1879	Augusta Gregory 1843–1903
Chastina Walbridge 1824–1857	married 1849	Alfred S. Rix 1821–1904	Julian Walbridge Rix 1850–1903 Edward A. Rix 1855–1930
Sarah Walbridge 1827–1909	married 1849	John S. Way 1822–1909	Martha Way 1850–1877 Edgar Way 1851–1925 Clara Way 1857–1922 Alice Way 1866–1875
Clarissa Walbridge 1830–1917	married 1856	Russell Rogers 1827–1886	Nellie Rogers 1857–1945 Adelaide Rogers 1863–1934 Harry Rogers 1867–1924
Lyman S. Watts 1832–1872	married 1867	Sarah E. Chamberlain 1838–1870	Jennie Chamberlain Watts 1869–1941
Dustan S. Walbridge 1832–1864	married 1860	Abbie T. Hardy 1842–1917	Nellie Walbridge 1861–1950
Charles Watts 1835–1875	married 1858	Lodoska Spencer 1835–1918	William Watts 1859–1886 Charles Watts 1861–1942 Lena Watts 1862–1931 Harry Spencer Watts 1871–1923
D. Augustus Walbridge 1835–1881	married 1881	Marietta Clark Hurd 1844–1906	

married 1830
Esther Sargent 1803–1836
Lyman Watts 1801–1875

married 1840
2) Lyman Watts 1801–1875

Child	married	Spouse	Grandchildren Who Lived Past Infancy
Isaac N. Watts 1842–1881	married 1870	1) Lizzie Way 1845–1874	Meroe Way Watts 1871–1921
	married 1877	2) Ellen Boynton 1852–1889	Helen Watts 1879–1945
Alice Watts 1845–1882	married 1868	Charles A. Choate 1838–1902	David Choate 1869–1909 Charles (Chub) Choate 1871–1930 Elsie A. Choate 1886–1959
Lucy Ella Watts 1847–1915	married 1891	Charles A. Choate 1838–1902	Isaac Watts Choate 1882–1953

Roxana Brown Walbridge Watts (1802–1862)

The Mother Who Held the Family Together

THIS IS the story of an ordinary woman, a nineteenth-century American farm wife who in her lifetime traveled no more than one hundred miles from her home in Peacham, in the Northeast Kingdom of Vermont. Born Roxana Brown in 1802, she became through her first marriage Roxana Walbridge, and then, through a second marriage, Roxana Watts. Between the birth of her first child in 1822 and her own death in 1862, she raised twelve children—nine of her own, two stepchildren, and a grandson—six girls and six boys. Remarkably, in an age when the death of children was a common occurrence, all twelve survived to maturity. Some ventured away and returned to spend the rest of their lives in Vermont, close to home. Others migrated permanently—to Michigan, Illinois, Minnesota, and California.

A daguerreotype taken of Roxana Brown Walbridge Watts around 1850 shows her sitting beside a table with a small stack of books on it. It is a fitting image because Roxana believed strongly in the virtues of learning and made sure that each of her children, girls and boys alike, received a formal education. As the children grew up and moved away, the family kept in touch through letters, which they read and reread and circulated across the country. Nearly three hundred of these letters, along with more than thirty personal journals and diaries, have been preserved by Roxana's descendants. The content of these communications was often parochial: they were about health of family members, the local weather, the condition of crops; they chronicled the births, marriages, and deaths of neighbors and friends; they described daily routines, annual events, and local disasters. At other times they recorded developments of larger national significance: the cataclysm of civil war, the settling of the Midwestern frontier, the quest for higher education for women, the building of the transcontinental railroad, the rush for California gold. Taken together, the writings of Roxana and her children offer an intimate portrait of an American family over the course of a century of tumultuous change.

ROXANA'S OWN story has its roots in 1801 when six families including her parents, David and Olive Brown, left Charlestown, Massachusetts, in search of cheap, fertile farm land. They found it in Peacham, Vermont, a town founded in 1776 by people much like themselves—hardworking, God fearing, from English stock. By the time they arrived, Peacham had already grown to 234 households with a total population of 875 in its six-mile-square area. The inhabitants were mainly farmers, although town records from the turn of the century indicate the beginnings of specialized trades, listing a joiner, a blacksmith, a "taylor," a shopkeeper, a mill owner, and a physician.

The lives of the people of Peacham were shaped by two institutions that had been established before the Browns arrived: the Caledonia County Grammar School, founded in 1795, and the Peacham Congregational Church, organized in 1794. While the church provided the town with its spiritual center, Peacham Academy—as the county school for older grades was more familiarly known—gave it a distinctive identity that continues to this day. Even though it was a hill town surrounded by farms, Peacham became a place where teachers and students debated ideas, from temperance and abolition to revivalism and western expansion.

Town documents reveal little about the Browns specifically. According to the Peacham Grand List for 1801, David Brown purchased a farm of ten acres on Macks Mountain, northwest of the village. In 1809 David was given eighty-three cents per week by the town to provide support for a young girl, part of a system of bidding off the town poor common in New England at that time. Records also show that David Brown could write his name, but it is clear that Olive was not literate.

Information about Roxana Brown's early life is similarly sparse. She was born on May 5, 1802, the fourth and youngest child, and second daughter, of the Browns. Because she could read and write, it may be inferred that she attended the district school, which first began admitting girls in 1805. Although family letters reveal that she was a steady churchgoer and Bible reader later in life, there are no records indicating that she or any other family members joined the local church when she was a child.

On November 14, 1821, at the age of nineteen, Roxana married Daniel Augustus Walbridge of the town of Wolcott, forty miles away, and moved to his farm of one hundred acres. A variety of evidence suggests that the

Peacham Congregational Church, with horse sheds to right, ca. 1905. The Methodist church is across the street. Courtesy Lynn A. Bonfield.

marriage was a happy one, and over the next fourteen years Daniel and Roxana had five children. They were expecting their sixth child when Daniel died of "a Billious complaint" on March 1, 1835.

With the help of the close-knit Walbridge family, Roxana tried to maintain the farm, and she might have succeeded if her four older children had been boys who could work in the fields. In 1839 she was forced to sell the farm for three hundred dollars and she returned "with two cows" to Peacham, where she joined her brother Simeon's family on their parents' farm.

Comments in the family letters indicate that Roxana's mother, Olive Brown, was a difficult woman—"a trial," her granddaughter Chastina was to call her. For Roxana to bring her six children into her parents' household could not have been easy, but she had little choice. Her situation was precarious in every way. Years later, in a letter to her oldest daughter, Martha, she hinted at how she felt about losing Daniel and being widowed at the age of thirty-two: "[T]ell your Brothers wife I know well the loss she has sustained in the death of her husband no doubt she feels that the arm on which she leaned is broken and her comforts fled yes and she left alone to mourn for a time yet I trust she looks forward to that day when they shall again be reunited to spend an eternity together."

Lyman Watts, the father, 1867. Courtesy Mary C. Morrison.

Up on Peacham's East Hill lived Lyman Watts, a widower with two young boys, who was willing to take on Roxana's large family. In December 1840 Roxana and Lyman married. By all accounts it was an arrangement of dignified convenience rather than a spiritual or emotional match; but it was a solid marriage nonetheless. In nineteenth-century New England, a woman's identity and status within the community were defined by her marriage, and Roxana recognized her good fortune in becoming the wife of a respected and financially stable farmer like Mr. Watts. As she confided in an 1843 letter to Martha, who was by then married herself: "I have a good home for my self and Children and I esteem it a great privilege that they can live with me."

At the time of this marriage, the Watts farm, purchased in 1830 when Lyman married his first wife, consisted of sixty acres, two oxen, two horses, one colt, eight milking cows, two heifers, and forty sheep. Of the 275 property owners included on the Peacham Grand List of 1840, only 54 had larger holdings than Lyman Watts. Further attesting to his high social standing was his election to the board of selectmen in 1836, a position he held on and off for the next ten years, after which he represented Peacham in the Vermont state legislature.

Roxana brought five of her children to the Watts farm in 1840, her eldest daughter, Martha, having already married and moved to the Midwest: Chastina, then fifteen; Sarah, called Sally, twelve; Clarissa, called Clara, nine; Dustan, seven, and Augustus, four. There they joined Lyman Watts's two sons: Lyman, seven; and Charles, five. During the next seven years Roxana and Lyman had three more children: Isaac (b. 1842), Alice (b. 1845), and Ella (b. 1847).

To judge from her letters, although new babies began to arrive, Roxana continued to identify most closely with her Walbridge children. This is understandable. They were older, the children of her youth; the daughters in particular became her friends as they matured; and all of them formed a link to the life she had lost. Her comments about her younger children carried a note of detachment, as if the whole situation were somewhat unreal to her. "[I]t seems to me some like living my life over again to be taking care of little children again," she wrote shortly after the birth of Alice, "my babe is the most quiet child I ever had. little Isaac grows well . . . he talks verry plain and on the whole he is a pretty smart boy." When the last of the new babies, Ella, was born, twenty-five years after the birth of her first child, Roxana was forty-five.

Large families were common in Peacham at that time, with many

Roxana's second brood: Alice, Isaac, Ella, 1856. Daguerreotype, courtesy Roberta Garry Trunzo.

Watts farmhouse with Isaac's daughters, Peacham, ca. 1890. Courtesy Helen Watts Richter.

households numbering a dozen or so members. The Watts family occupied a cape-style cottage, twenty-eight by thirty-six feet, with an unfinished chamber on the second floor that was most likely used as sleeping quarters for the children, the boys on one side and the girls on the other. Town records show that in 1845 Lyman Watts built a barn; two years later he added "a shed" to the house and finished off a kitchen and milk room. This architectural style was common in northeastern New England in the mid-nineteenth century when farmers reorganized their detached house and barn arrangements into connected buildings. This vernacular architectural style was described in the popular children's refrain, "Big house, little house, back house, barn." The inside of the house they "plastered & painted as nice as a pin" and "got the parlour & front entry papered & some copperplate curtains up at the windows." The hand-hewn beams and granite front step still can be seen at the end of the twentieth century.

The new additions may have been necessitated by the unexpected arrival at the Watts doorstep of Roxana's parents in early 1844. David Brown had been ill for several years, apparently with prostate trouble, and needed constant care. He used a silver tube as a catheter, which he had had the misfortune to break off in his bladder, causing him such continuous pain that he had "to take a great deal of Opium to get any rest at all." Chastina described the situation in a letter to Martha written shortly after the arrival of her grandparents: "Sister what will you think when I tell you that Gransire & his better or w— half are now living at our house & you may think yourself well off for no one can tell the many hard hours work that he makes . . . I expect they will go to Canada as soon as it comes warm weather if they live and can you think that mother or any of the rest of the family can take much comfort of their lives tho you know Sister to well the character of our Grandmother to know how that will be."

"Canada" was family shorthand for Dunham, Lower Canada, now Quebec, where Roxana's older brother, Leonard, lived and practiced medicine. "The Doctor" would have been the logical family member to take responsibility for his elderly parents, especially when they fell ill.

A letter from Roxana to Martha, dated June 1844, told the rest of the story: "Well they staid here untill 6 of this month and we found it so much trouble and expence to take care of him that we could not keep them any longer we wrote to the Doctor and he was not willing to have them come there but we knew if they were there they would be taken care of and we thought they might be carried accordingly we set about it and procured an easy Carriage and had him laid on a bed Mr Watts went with him and took care of him he had another man to drive and they got along better than we expected they went through in two days and a half not with standing they were obliged to stop once in 20 minutes and help him . . . draw his water but they did not take him out of the Carriage only at night you cannot think what a burden it has taken of from us and place uppon them but you know that there is none of them that has lived with them as I have and I think it rite that all should have there share."

The respite allowed by David Brown's departure for Canada did not last long. Six weeks later he died "with great bodily sufferings but perfectly reconciled in mind." After his death, Olive was sent back to the Watts farm in Peacham, where she spent the remaining eighteen years of her life.

Caring for her mother was an obligation Roxana had no choice but to accept. In an age when sickness and death always stood close at hand, when medicine was harsh and prevention almost unknown, nursing was considered women's work. Not surprisingly, Roxana's letters were full of these matters. "[L]ittle Isaac grows well but he has had a good many verry sick turns," she wrote in 1845, "Sally went down . . . to work in the factory . . . and was brought home sick it proved to be the Billious fever she was very sick . . . Dustan and Clarissa were both taken with the same [thing] . . . I think you never saw such looking Creatures as they were they were as yellow as a piece of flannel from the crown of there head to the sole of there feet." Infections, which took many lives, were treated with such remedies as "cabbage-leaf" poultices. Diphtheria killed many, especially children, and whole families could be wiped out in the course of a week. Tuberculosis, or "consumption" as it was known, was common among adults, and shortened many lives. Women often died in childbirth or of childbed infections, and their new babies with them. "It has been verry sickly the last winter and continues to be yet in many places especially among that class of females who have had children," Roxana wrote in 1843 during a local epidemic, "there has not been more than one woman out of ten that have lived to get well . . . sometimes they live a week and some not more."

When she was not tending the sick, Roxana was occupied with other duties. As a farm wife, she worked most days from morning to night. For cooking and baking she had a wood stove—an important advance over the open-hearth fireplace of earlier generations. She made butter and cheese from the "small dairy," baked bread and pies, stewed pumpkins ("a most excellent parfum"), made sausage, dipped candles, and had "a regular New England house cleaning" every spring. She spun stocking yarn; she wove "flannell" and wool; she cut out shirts and trousers; she knit socks. She washed clothes "always on Monday." At night she sat by the fire and mended by the light of a tallow candle—the closest she came to relaxation.

Even Roxana's community activities involved hard work, as evidenced by her description of an agricultural fair in 1856: "[I]t was composed of 5 towns Peacham Danville Barnet Ryegate and Groton The display of oxen was very large there were 251 yoke of oxen besides 2 and 3 years old steers in abundance we gave a dinner to more than 2000 people free of any expense to those who ate. We all cooked and carried in victuals we set tables in the two vestrys to the meeting houses there was room for 550 to sit at once and the tables were all filled 5 times and more to but they did not *eat us out clean* for we had a great deal left."

To ease her daily burdens, Roxana assigned tasks to each of her children and directed them as they did their work. Her daughters helped with the laundry and other household tasks. As she reported to her married daughter, Martha: "Sally has done almost all of my spinning and she has wove one web for fulld cloth and has another in the loom," while Clara does "some spinning" and "takes care of Baby." She added: "[W]e have made between 4 and 5 hundred pounds of butter and a hundred and 50 of Chese from 6 Cows." Yet for the most part, Roxana took the daily housework of her daughters so for granted that she seldom mentioned it in her letters.

The boys helped with the outdoor work. They tended the "calves & lambs," fed the hogs, helped with the milking, "laid up" the apples, and dried potatoes. They boiled sap in the sugar house in March and April and hoed the garden in June and July; they helped with "the haying & harvesting," too, as they grew older. "The Boys all grow and have got to be a good deal of help," Roxana wrote in one letter, noting Charles and Augustus chopping wood "at the door."

Although gardening was typically women's work in mid-nineteenth-century Peacham, it was the custom within the Watts family for the men and boys to do all the outside chores, including gardening. The men were responsible for the farm animals, the farm machinery and tools, the care of the land including roads and fences, the upkeep of the barn, the privy, and other buildings, and the unending maintenance of the wood pile.

In an economy that relied little on money, the Watts family farm provided a minimum livelihood based on self-sufficiency and barter. Everyone worked, every day and at least six days a week, contributing what he or she could to the total domestic production. If they needed something they could not produce themselves, they bartered for it with their labor or excess goods, such as butter, cheese, or wool. Lyman usually handled these transactions at the local store, although occasionally he traveled to a market "down Country."

For most farmers, the chief goal was not prosperity but simply staying out of debt—an ongoing struggle that required an ability to adapt to ever-changing market conditions. "Mr W[atts] values his farm at about 20 hundred and we keep 2 horses 6 or 7 Cows and about 50 sheep with some young stock," Roxana wrote to Martha in 1844; "he owns some more then a hundred acres of land and it is as much as we can do with our family to keep along and keep out of debt." She added that "farmers in this country [are not] in so good a way to pay debts as they were a few years ago be fore your western produce of every kind was filling our markets to the overflow good horses and wool are the two best articles we can raise here at present Beef and Butter are low." Some years maple "sugar"—not syrup, which was not produced in quantity until the mid-1870s—was a market product, although the early spring weather had to be just right for good production.

STATISTICS FOR PEACHAM, 1840

People	1,443
Horses	373
Cattle	1,910
Sheep	9,229
Swine	1,055
Wheat	5,491 bushels
Barley	730 bushels
Oats	23,603 bushels
Rye	90 bushels
Indian Corn	2,377 bushels
Potatoes	67,816 bushels
Hay	4,001 tons
Sugar	21,180 pounds
Wool	17,786 pounds

Source: Thompson, *History of Vermont*, 1842, p. 138.

Goods moving in and out of Peacham traveled along the "Hazen road," originally cut as a military route to Canada during the Revolutionary War, or the Connecticut River, the main thoroughfare linking a succession of river towns—Newbury, Barnet, Ryegate, Peacham—to each other and the rest of the world to the south. With the completion of a railway line to Barnet, six miles from Peacham, in 1850, the local economy expanded further. "Business has been verry brisk," Roxana wrote that year, and by 1856 she boasted that "we raised 100 17 bushels of wheat on 4 acres of ground and first rate wheat it is." One winter Mr. Watts was "drawing Cord wood . . . when he gets throug it will be as much as a hundred cords." Occasionally there were apples to sell, although most were for home use, and one year "our little Plum trees hang just as full as they can." Butchering week came around Thanksgiving Day. It was always a memorable occasion, as Chastina recounted in an 1847 letter to her sister Sarah, who was then away working in the Lowell textile mills: "[S]o just imagine a dirty house. *hogs every thing's* all round, squalling young ones & I think you will not be much home sick."

Although the members of the Watts family spent most of their time working on the farm, they also remained active in the life of the community. Here, too, men and women tended to operate in separate spheres. While Lyman became deeply involved in politics, at first at the local level and later as a representative to the state legislature, Roxana's public activities centered around the church. She first joined the Peacham Congregational Church in 1842, two years after her marriage to Mr. Watts, and in the years that followed she regularly attended Sunday services. Her correspondence

Peacham Congregational Church with horse sheds, ca. 1905. Courtesy Peacham Historical Association.

reflects a strong faith in an all-knowing and benevolent God whose ulti-mate purposes lay beyond human understanding. "[M]an can appoint but God can disappoint," she wrote, commenting on a family tragedy. "[H]is works are mysterious and his ways past finding out." She did not fear death, believing that those who die go to a better place and are spared the woes and tribulations of this life.

In an age when highly individual interpretations of Scripture were per-mitted, even encouraged, Roxana's religious thought remained steadfastly conventional, as evidenced by her reaction to the Millerite movement which swept through New England during the 1830s and early 1840s. The Millerites were followers of a New York farmer, William Miller, who purported to have discovered Scriptural evidence of an imminent Second Coming. According to Miller, Christ would come to the world again "on or before 1843," inaugurating a reign of righteousness that would last a thousand years. Eventually this millenarian sect claimed an estimated 100,000 adherents, with its highest numbers in Vermont and upstate New York.

Roxana was decidedly not one of them. On April 16, 1843, she wrote to Martha: "You wished me to write something in regard to the Second advent of our Saviour coming on earth it is a theme that has been in every ones mouth for a year past and some have got so much excited with it that they have fixed on the day on which they were a going to be caught up yesterday was the day that many had got ready I suppose I say got ready Because they have entirely neglected every kind of employment except just enough to live untill the 15 of April their immaginations have carried them beyond every thing that has any kind of reason . . . in their unhallowed worship but we see that day has passed by and all things remains as they were." Adding to the same letter, a week later she wrote: "This day is another day set by the Millerites for the coming of the Saviour and while I write I feel a solemnity resting on my mind in view of the reality that he has and will come to many individuals this verry day . . . therefore it becomes us as rational creatures to try and lay our minds open to conviction and not put far away the thoughts of death and Eternity for sure we are that that day will overtake us whether we are prepared or not, but I realy think that Sinful weak minded man has no business to try to be more wise then our Saviour who said but of that day and hour knoweth no man neither the Son but the Father only."

In her maternal role as moral teacher, Roxana taught her character-istically practical Christianity to her children. She held the prevailing belief that hard work and good habits made for a good life and that proper social behavior was an expression of inner spiritual goals—an effort to please God. "[S]eek first the kingdom of God that all other necessary things shall be added unto you," she told her children, "the Lord knows what is best for us although we cannot always feel that it is right." Four of the children who remained in Vermont followed their mother's example and attended church regularly, while of those who moved west, only Martha continued to practice the religion of her youth.

Yet of all the values Roxana held dear, none exceeded her faith in the benefits of education. She not only made sure that all of her children learned to read and write; she also saw to it that they attended school at every opportunity, however intermittent, until they were into their twenties. At first they attended the district school, although the boys usually skipped in summer, or at least left early in July "as they commence mowing." In the winter of 1846, Roxana noted that "we send . . . 7 scholars to [the district] school about one fourth of the school."

All of the children except Martha and Sarah went on from the district school to Peacham Academy. In later years one stepson, Lyman, and a son-in-law, Alfred Rix (Chastina's husband), served as principals of the academy. Two daughters, Chastina and Alice, taught there as well. Of the twelve children Roxana raised, only Martha, Sarah, Dustan, and Julian did not teach at least one session in a district school. Two children, Lyman and Alice, went on to college—Lyman to Middlebury and Alice to Mount Holyoke. All of them were encouraged to think for themselves, to be engaged by ideas and in the world around them.

Roxana's concern for education extended to her grandchildren. After Martha's death, Roxana kept writing to her son-in-law Hubbell about her granddaughter's education, at first expressing the hope that Augusta would be sent home to Peacham for the good schooling there. Inquiring about Augusta's activities, she asked whether her granddaughter "has got so that she can read, or knit, or sew," suggesting her own order of priorities. Later, grandson Julian was sent from San Francisco to Peacham to benefit from a New England education.

Clearly, Roxana's unshakable commitment to education paid off; for as her children grew to adulthood and left home, some never to return, it was their shared literacy that kept the Walbridge-Watts family together. In her letters to her children, which they called "visits from home," Roxana expressed her hope that they were healthy, "content," and "had things comfortable." She wanted her grandchildren to be "scholars," and repeatedly suggested that all of her progeny return to live near her in Vermont. She

Letter of Roxana to Sarah and John Way, January 18, 1856. Courtesy Lynn A. Bonfield.

reported on the family's health, the current weather, the yield of the latest harvest—whether the crops were "backward" or "well."

Roxana's letters were also filled with local news: events at a nearby agricultural fair, the marriage or death of a neighbor, the birth of the newest baby, the latest epidemic of disease. Given how much time she spent at the farm and how infrequently she was able to visit others, Roxana's knowledge of the community seems remarkably extensive. In the nineteen extant letters she wrote from 1843 to 1856, she mentions 134 people. Even though a third of them were relatives, it is clear that she was acquainted with many local residents and knew much about their daily business.

In their letters to her, Roxana's children expressed abiding love and always mentioned missing home, especially "Mothers cooking," "Sunday evenings around the kitchen table," "a taste of new sugar," "having a ride . . . over those old hills," and "green apples" from the farm. One daughter living in California complained, "I can't make it seem at all like winter. I should like a sleigh ride now and then. It would seem real good." In the summer this same daughter wrote, "I should like a good eat of home blackberries [and] raspberries—they are much better than ours here, they grow so fast they are rather sour." Of a daughter in Minnesota, Roxana reported that she was "faring hard and being homesick into the bargain" and "did not know how to prize all the comforts she enjoyed while she was in Vt." Her children sent one another wishes of "prosperity and good health," and Roxana once told a son-in-law, "I hope your latter days will be strewed with flowers instead of thorns."

Roxana penned her letters late at night, sometimes noting that "the family are all a bed" and often ending with a homily, such as "keep up good courage and all will come round right." She mailed them at the post office at Peacham Corner, which opened in 1799 and continues today. Sometimes her family in California wrote their letters with someone standing nearby, ready to run "to the mail Steamer [before it] Sails." On one occasion a daughter, at home in Peacham, wrote: "[We] have each of [us] sat down with a sheet of paper at our *dining room* table, under the old clock, to inform you of some of the '*happenstances*' about home." A letter from San Francisco described an evening's activities: "The girls are very busy with their needles and have asked me to write while they dictate so here is a letter writ by me & thunk by them."

The women of the family exchanged "minatures," locks of hair, sewing patterns, and pieces of calico. "I will put in some scraps of [my child's] dresses & sack," one daughter wrote home, "& also a piece of my dress." One sister sent another "a braid of her own hair to wear on you wrist wear it and remember the giver."

Letters ended with excuses for not having written "much that will pay the trouble of reading" and pleas for more letters: "Write all the news you can think of" and "anything you write is of interest to me." "Expect to be very *lonesome*, so you must write often for letters cheer me the most of any thing."

The children who had moved west frequently expressed their longing to be reunited with their mother. "We would gladly dispense with all the letters and letter-writing," wrote one, "could we have the pleasure of seeing you." It was a sentiment Roxana shared: "O how I wish I could see you all and have the privilege of talking instead of writing."

Unfortunately, that wish was never fully granted. Although some of Roxana's children came back to Peacham, others never returned. Still, they continued to write, even after their mother was no longer able to respond. "I am growing old," Roxana wrote in her last surviving letter, dated 1858, "and I find my energies are failing me as well as my health." Three years later, in February 1861, Roxana's youngest daughter Alice reported that "Mother cannot write any this time—she has a good deal to do, and her fingers are old and stiff." A few months later: "Mother is unusually well this spring, only her limbs trouble her a great deal. She is growing old, was *sixty* yesterday."

Perhaps fittingly, it was by mail that most of Roxana's children learned of her death, in October 1862, less than three months after her own mother died. "Grandmother [Olive Brown] died July 27 after an illness of a week," Alice reported, "the day after the funeral Ella was taken with Typhoid Fever and was very sick for three weeks . . . At the end of that time Mother was taken sick . . . She was sick six weeks, suffering severely some of the time, when she too died on the 3rd of Oct. . . . Some of the time she thought she would not live, but the greater part of it, she talked [about] getting well again, and even after she was struck with death did not realize it until we told her. But she was willing to die and talked with us all about it."

Roxana died in the manner of her time—with family and friends taking care of her by day and "watches by night." The *St. Johnsbury Caledonian* buried her with dispatch under four words: "wife of Lyman Watts." That was far from being her true identity, and her children knew it. Dustan, then serving in the Union Army, wrote to his sister Sarah in Minnesota from his post in Washington, D.C.: "It is sad indeed to think of the changes that have taken place since we were at home—our Home our old Home is forever gone—for where *Mother* is, thire is home—and it is probable as you say that we shall never meete around the old fireside again—and if we ever should, it would not be home—it does not seeme as though I could have it so, but it must be, hers has been a life of much sorrow and anxiety. It is hard to loose such a kind good Mother as ours was, but I hope she is in a better, happier land."

It is not known what patriarch Lyman Watts felt, although in Dustan's view "for all there was never much love between them I think he feels Mothers loss severly." Lyman paid for perpetual care for her gravestone, as he had for his first wife, and placed the same epitaph on each of their stones:

> Farewell my partner, children, all
> For God, our Savior, doth me call
> Prepare to meet on Canaan's shore
> Where parting times are known no more.

PART II

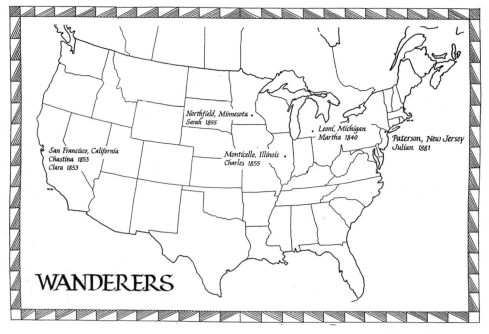

Northfield, Minnesota •
Sarah 1855

. Leoni, Michigan
Martha 1840

Paterson, New Jersey
Julian 1881

San Francisco, California
Chastina 1853
Clara 1853

Monticello, Illinois •
Charles 1855

WANDERERS

Thomas J. Carey

Roxana's Wanderers: The Children Who Left Vermont and Stayed Away

ROXANA'S LIFE spanned one of the most important and dramatic periods in Vermont, and indeed American, history. The great westward movement accelerated during these years, as tens of thousands of settlers migrated to new homes in the old Northwest Territory and into the trans-Mississippi West.

Many Vermonters—five of Roxana's children among them—pulled up stakes during the great westward movement and left their farms, stores, mills, and hardest of all, their family and friends, to seek a better life. The men experienced more gain than loss: they found a longer growing season, cheap fertile soil, an abundance of forest and game; and, once the land was cleared, a farming environment and style similar to what they had known at home. The women experienced more loss than gain: there was homemaking shorn of amenities, days and years filled with the grim drudgery of life in log cabins or worse, and the constant worry of raising children in rough country. For both men and women, resettlement meant hard work for many years before they obtained any civilities or ease of life.

By 1850 half of all those born in Vermont lived outside of the state. Emigration was nothing new to Vermonters. Almost as soon as the state was settled and its timber, game, and soil depleted, families began to pack up and leave for another chance elsewhere. The first to leave beginning in the 1810s went to "York state" and the western part of Massachusetts, but soon these areas offered few opportunities for cheap good farm land, and the migration to Ohio and beyond—what is now called the Midwest—became popular.

The picture of migration into the Midwest was similar to migration to Vermont in the eighteenth century. First the young Vermont men went off searching for a new settlement. They went on foot and later by stage, steamboat, and finally by railroad. They chose their wilderness farms,

23

POPULATION OF PEACHAM, 1791–1990

Year	Population	Increase/Decrease (from previous year)
1791	36	
1800	875	+839
1810	1,301	+426
1820	1,294	−7
1830	1,351	+57
1840	1,443	+92
1850	1,377	−66
1860	1,247	−130
1870	1,141	−106
1880	1,041	−100
1890	892	−149
1900	794	−98
1910	777	−17
1920	657	−120
1930	620	−37
1940	543	−77
1950	501	−42
1960	433	−68
1970	446	+13
1980	531	+85
1990	620	+89

Source: Bogart, *Peacham, the Story of a Vermont Hill Town*,
p. 22, and Peacham Town Records.

sometimes making a rough start clearing land and building a cabin, and then returned to Vermont to bring back, often in a wagon loaded with household goods, a bride or a young family. The desire to prosper and the optimism surrounding their move offset the pain of leaving their family and friends.

Still, most Vermonters made it a practice to settle where other Vermonters had gone. Relatives and former neighbors furnished reliable information on the chances of success in the places where they themselves were located and also provided opportunities for visiting, which helped the newcomers feel less isolated in their new place. Towns in Illinois and Minnesota where some of Roxana's children settled were so full of Vermonters that visitors from Peacham needed days, sometimes weeks, to see all their former neighbors. Throughout the Midwest new villages were given Vermont names as settlers tried to carry their memories of home to their new location.

By the 1820s, Vermonters were migrating everywhere—some to the growing eastern cities, others to Canada. Some Vermonters, looking for a milder climate, moved south. The bulk of Vermonters, however, were farmers in search of better land, and they went west. Not all the men were farmers; there were also ministers, missionaries, soldiers, and school-teachers who moved west hoping for a better life. Teaching became a steppingstone to the medical or legal professions, and the frontier offered plenty of openings for energetic young lawyers and doctors. Vermont artisans—carpenters, blacksmiths, shoemakers, printers, masons, coopers, and wheelwrights—made their way west by working a few days at various stops on their journey and earning money to move on. Every new community needed the skills of these craftsmen, and Vermonters prospered by selling their labor.

During the 1830s, Vermont began to experience its greatest exodus. Before this time, emigration had been continuous but casual, an almost unnoticed process. After 1830 it had a name—"the Western fever"—and became a concern for public discussion at town meetings, as Vermont's population decreased. Almost all Vermont families experienced the exodus as their sons and daughters went off alone or accompanied their spouses to new homes.

The part of the West which most tempted Vermonters by the 1830s was the virgin region of southern Michigan, northern Illinois, and southeastern Wisconsin. Travel to these areas became easier in the 1840s as the water route opened all the way to Chicago, and highways such as the Ohio-Mississippi route improved, opening up southern and central Illinois. By the 1850s regions farther west—Minnesota, Iowa, and Kansas—were the stopping places. Vermonters joined with other Yankees in re-enacting the frontier story—uneasy contacts with the Indians, bitter battles with disease and poor health, difficult land clearing with few tools, oxen, or horses.

Often before the wells were dug and the log cabins were replaced with more substantial structures, women pushed for the building of churches and schools in order to bring their New England civilization to their new home. Women also encouraged the reform movement of the second half of the nineteenth century, which resulted in the establishment of asylums for the insane, the blind, and the deaf. These new institutions provided job opportunities for men, but also for single women who began seeking paid employment in larger numbers than ever before. Women, like Roxana's youngest daughter, Ella, who may have taught in Vermont district schools, became administrators, housemothers, and helpers in these new institutions.

As part of the New England heritage, men and women took with them their Yankee traditions of hard work and frugality. The only thing they bought readily was acreage, and land speculation was rampant. New settlers often bought more land than they could use, hoping to sell the unneeded land for a profit in a few years. Although the early emigrants began by clearing land and harvesting crops, as if agriculture were their permanent calling, it was not long before they jumped at the chance to start a mill or a general store or a horse-breeding business in order to earn more money and free themselves from working the soil. Yankee ingenuity served them well as more and more Vermonters entered business and the professions.

At the end of the 1840s, California was the new destination for Vermonters. By 1850 eleven hundred Vermonters—mainly men going to seek their fortune in the gold fields—had actually reached California. They went by sea around Cape Horn or combined the sea route with overland crossings through Panama, Nicaragua, or Vera Cruz. Most tried mining, but it was usually only a matter of months before they were back at their old occupations—keeping store, running mills, building carriages, carrying milk, teaching school. By the time the California mining boom collapsed in the mid-fifties, at least a third of the Vermont forty-niners were back home in Vermont or settled somewhere in the Midwest. The others, numbering more than three thousand native Vermonters by 1860, stayed in California and sent for their families. Women who had never been to a city or traveled farther than a few miles from their home now made the journey to California, alone or with small children, in order to start a new life with their husbands. To them and others, the West offered a better economic situation than seemed possible in Vermont. Many women and men took advantage of the opportunity with high hopes, willing to work and carrying with them dreams of a better future for their children.

Change and loss were facts of pioneer life. Where is Sarah's log cabin? What is left of the rough Illinois town where Charles practiced law? Where is the house from which Clara watched the 1906 San Francisco fire? Pioneers came west to get ahead, and in the process they left behind and lost their past. They moved to regions which were changing faster than anything ever had changed in Vermont. The irony is that their early days in Peacham have been better preserved than their later days in the West.

Westward emigration slowed after Fort Sumter had been fired on in the spring of 1861 and more than thirty-two thousand young men from the hill towns of Vermont put on the blue uniforms of the Union Army.

Migrants to the Midwest

Three of Roxana's children settled in the Midwest. The oldest, Martha, left Vermont in the spring of 1840 as a young bride and went to Michigan with her husband, Hubbell Seth Gregory, who owned land there. In the spring of 1855, Roxana's third daughter, Sarah, left, crossing the Mississippi with her husband, John S. Way, and their small children to make a home in Minnesota. The last of the three to move to the Midwest, Charles, went to Illinois in the fall of 1855 to teach and decided to stay and buy a farm. He went back to Peacham to marry Lodoska Spencer and then together they made their lives in Illinois.

Like many other wives, Martha, Sarah, and Lodoska did not want to leave Vermont but they were "good wives," willing to go where their husbands chose to seek their fortunes. Every New England community suffered the loss of their young families going west. It was good that the migrants were young because their new life required much energy. It took them a month just to clear an acre and they also had to build barns, a house, and a privy and dig a well. Most families had new babies one after the other. Martha had three children in six years; Lodoska, six in thirteen years; and Sarah, who had two when she went west, gave birth to two more. Women were either pregnant or nursing their babes during most of the early years when they were establishing their new households.

Hubbell Gregory's family had been speculating in land in Michigan for ten years by the time he and Martha went there to farm. The couple lived near his parents and brother and went to meeting every Sabbath, but Martha still felt homesick for her Vermont family. Most weeks she was so overworked that she did not have the time to answer letters from her mother and sisters.

John Way was a wandering sort who had left Sarah, pregnant with their first child, in Vermont when he went to California in early 1850 to make his "pile" in the mines. Upon his return, John contemplated many adventures, including going to the Australian gold fields, but finally decided to move to Minnesota where farm land was cheap and the chances for economic success were promising. Once there he devoted his time completely to the land. It was more than ten years before he built a house for Sarah who suffered from the cold and lack of water in a small log cabin where their youngest children were born.

Charles, however, was anxious to settle down as he reached his early twenties, but he did not wish to remain in Peacham. He found good farm land in Illinois and established a successful law practice. Like many younger sons born in New England, Charles made a name for himself away from his birthplace.

All three of Roxana's "Midwestern children," born and raised on a farm, settled on farms not much different from those of their childhood. Farming continued to define their lives until their deaths; farming was in their blood.

Martha Walbridge Gregory (1822–1846)

The Bride Who Went West at Seventeen

IN THE lives of farm women, enduring household skills passed on unchanged from generation to generation. Spinning and weaving, cooking and sewing, bearing children and rearing them, feeding hungry men and sending them out to the fields, mothers and daughters worked together and knew no break in the lives they shared. Where temperaments were harmonious, they could weave a loving unity that amounted almost to a shared identity. Such was Roxana's good fortune and happiness with her oldest daughter, Martha.

Roxana was twenty when she gave birth to her first child on August 21, 1822, almost nine months to the day after her marriage to Daniel Walbridge. In those nine months, the young bride had moved from Peacham to her husband's farm in Wolcott, which was surrounded by farms owned by Daniel's father and brothers. The house to which she moved was to be her home for seventeen years, the happiest time of her life. She was young and married to a man she loved; they had five healthy children, and a sixth one was on the way when Daniel tragically died.

Martha's birth was followed by those of her three sisters, one almost every other year. As the oldest, Martha took on a large part of the responsibility in the house, teaching the younger ones and becoming her mother's constant helper. Of all the children, Martha was to grow closest to her mother. Theirs was a special mother-daughter bond, cemented by the shared crisis of the loss of a beloved husband and father.

Martha was thirteen years old when her father died in March 1835, and although the girls, as described in the journal of her sister Chastina, had "found imposed upon them very many tasks and hardships even in their youth, the death of the father caused these to be increased. The course of [our lives] was the same as that of most girls in the country—the daughters of farmers—That is, labor six days in the week, attend church on Sunday.

At home, mostly, summers and at school—the district school—winters."
No matter what the season, however, the girls had housekeeping skills to
learn.

Martha was impatient but quick and able at spinning and weaving. As
Chastina, only two years younger than Martha, explained again in her
journal, there was quite "the difference of disposition of the two girls
Martha and Chastina" when "scarcely tall enough to reach the spindle." In
drawing out the thread from morning till night . . . [s]ometimes the thread
would break." Martha then "would bite her lip, seize hold of her wheel and
give it a hearty shaking," while Chastina "would half say and half sing as she
was mending the break, 'Fush-fiddle-dum!' "

In 1837 when Chastina was sent to Dunham, Lower Canada, to board
with Roxana's sister and help care for a new baby, Martha stayed at home in
Wolcott, assisting Roxana with the other four children, including the last
two babies, both boys, Dustan, age four and a half, and Augustus, only two
and a half.

Three months short of her eighteenth birthday, Martha married Hubbell Seth Gregory, a man originally from Wolcott whose family was well
known to the Walbridges.

His grandfather, Seth Hubbell, was one of the original settlers in Wolcott and a legend in the area. In 1824 he published a history of his relocation
in 1789 from Norwalk, Connecticut, to northern Vermont, first making
the trip in February through deep snowdrifts. Later, in April he led his wife
and five daughters to their new home, snowshoeing eight miles to Wolcott,
"arriving with scant possessions during the 'scarce season' to engage in a
desperate struggle for survival." He detailed the perils and disasters he
and his family encountered again and again, from hunger, disease, natural
calamities, and overwork. Each time tragedy seemed eminent, "they were
helped out by supernatural means." At the end of his tale, he claimed he
"not once was . . . discouraged or disheartened," and he repeatedly gave
thanks to his "benign Benefactor." This pioneer's story of faith in God
was probably recounted to every Wolcott resident. In 1843 when Martha
and Hubbell experienced hard times, Roxana reminded them to "remember Grandsir Hubbells history when you get to feeling discouraged and I
think it will serve to assure you that a bad beginning will make a good
ending."

Seth Hubbell migrated to Vermont, and forty years later his children and
grandchildren headed west. As early as the 1830s they began to speculate in
land in Michigan, the new frontier. Among them were Samuel and Mary

Gregory and their sons, Hubbell and Harlow, all of whom bought land first in Washtenaw County and later in Jackson County. In July 1835, Hubbell puchased an eighty-acre section, and the following spring, he added another forty acres.

Lucy Stow Morgan, a young bride who moved to Ann Arbor from Connecticut, described this area of Michigan Territory in an 1831 letter to her father in New England: "The whole County is settling very rapidly. You cannot have an idea of the tide of emigration that is flowing into Michigan. There is a constant stream of movers going to the west of us and many who have here improved their farms. Some sell them at a small advance that they may go west and buy more land at the government price."

After their marriage in spring 1840, Martha and Hubbell moved to a town called Leoni, about forty miles due west of Ann Arbor. The 1840 census for Jackson County lists Hubbell, Martha, his parents, his brother Harlow, and Harlow's wife, Lavina. There is a checkmark for H. S. Gregory in the box for age 20 to 30 years old and for his wife in the box for age 15 to 20.

Martha's departure was Roxana's greatest loss after her husband's death. The child Roxana most relied on left the family. Mother and daughter kept in touch by mail and there are seven letters that Roxana wrote to Martha to draw upon. Often Chastina or another sister added a line or two or even wrote her own letter. Unfortunately, no letters written by Martha survive. All letters address Hubbell as "son" or "brother" (or were sent to both as "My Children"), report news of Hubbell's relatives and friends in Wolcott, and send best wishes to his parents and brother.

Roxana's first letter, written on April 16, 1843, two years after the Gregorys left Vermont, expressed her relief to "receive that long looked for letter [from Martha] on the 7 of this month and was verry much gratified to hear of your comfortable state of health and especialy Marthas safe recovery from her confinement." The name Roxana suggested for Martha's second child—William having been born in 1841—was Augusta Ann. Roxana went on to thank "God for his kind dealings with you."

The next letter, written in August 1843, mentioned a fire that had occurred at the Gregory farmhouse. It was limited but serious in that all their clothing and furniture were lost. Roxana praised the Lord for their "comfortable health," which was always her first priority. Then she rejoiced "to think the Lord has dealt in mercy as well as in judgment with you as it appears that he has shown you both that there is something on which to place your affections which is not of a perishable nature. Although you have been called in [by] Providence to meet with a verry severe loss in the first beginning of your days in regard to your keeping house yet I hope that you will yet live to see your loss made up to you . . . you aughht to be verry thankful that you had your little Children with you for if they had perished as many do your loss could never be made up in this world. I want to see you more then ever so that I could encourage you on your way both in a spiritual and temporal life and I feel verry glad that you both have chosen that good part which neither flames nor floods can distroy and remember that you have the promise that if you seek first the kingdom of god that all other necessary things shall be added unto you."

Immediately upon hearing about the fire, Roxana began preparing a box of household goods for Martha, wanting to help her recover. The big obstacle, however, was getting the box to Michigan. Roxana explained, "The Girls have already begun to make some things for the Children but it is like casting their Bread uppon the waters for they know not as they will ever reach you but if we do all we can we may leave the event in His hands who suffers not a Sparrow to fall to the ground without his notice." It was unusual to send packages long distances, especially when both route and transport were unknown. The next month Roxana wrote, "I received your last letter . . . giving directions how to labell a Box well according to directions we have filled one and it is now all ready to go and it will start for Burlington day after tomorrow we send it in care of Simeon Spencer as far as Detroit we shall pay the freight as far as that and if you get it I suppose you will settle . . . I send this letter by the same man as far as Detroit and he will mail it there as soon as you get the thing mail a Paper and send it with some mark that we may know that they have got there." The box contained "a Bed and a good many other light articles I think if you get them you would not be willing to take less than 20 dollars for them, but I could not send any heavy articles such as I could help you to if you were near me. I should send you some flannell for your Children but have not got it wove yet and so you might take the will for the deed."

The letter reported in detail on everyone's health and activities, and then Roxana added, "I have wrote all that I can think of about our temporal affairs and have said nothing about Spiritual things . . . I often think of you and especially on the Sabbath when I expect you are at meeting with your bretheren I hope that you will always have that privilege and enjoy your-selves in that way though ill luck should atend your excusions in regard to your temporal affairs . . . I hope you will not have any more bad luck and you will eventually regain what you have lost there is no need of cautioning you against being careless with your fire but one thing remember to not leave your little children as you know some do but take them with you or stay with them."

In September 1844, "ill luck" again struck Martha. Roxana responded to "the sollem news of the Death of your little Boy and your own sickness which we were verry sorry to hear but it was no more than I have expected to hear considering the sickness that we have had accounts in our [news] prints in the western States but was in hopes that it would have been your good fortune to have escaped as you have done heretofore. But the Lord knows what is best for us although we cannot always feel that it is wright no doubt but what you have had feelings like this many times arisse in your mind but try to be reconciled as much as you can and not give [in] to immoderate grief . . . but [keep] in mind that mourning will not recall those who are gone from us we may go to them but they cannot return to us I cannot tell your feelings as I could had I ever lost a child yet I know the ties that bind children to Parents and they are strong cords which when one is broken it seems as if all must break and we feel to cry out with the Patriarch of old I will go down to the grave with my Son mourning Little William no doubt was a promising Child and you antisipated great comfort in him and to have your fairest hopes thus suddenly cut off is hard to bear but he is taken away from a world of sorrow sickness and distress to be forever in the presence of him who said suffer little Children to come unto me and forbid them not for such is the kingdom of heaven."

Roxana closed her letter with one of her constant themes: "For myself I should be verry glad to have you come back to Vt if you think it is best to live if you could dispose of your property there so as to settle yourselves here on a comfortable farm Real estate is not worth so much here as it was when you left . . . when you write again tell whether you can sell your farm for any thing near what it is worth and what you value it at whether you have sold your wild [uncleared] land or not I think if you could get back here with seven or eight hundred dollars you might get a place that you could get a good living off of but to lay up much from such a farm you could not expect it."

And if Martha and her family could not return permanently to live close to Roxana, she hoped for a visit. "You must come next fall if you can at any rate and I hope little Augusta Ann will be spared you so that you can bring her with you."

But Martha and Hubbell's plans did not work out, and fall came and went without a visit. Roxana was "verry sorry on our part as well as yours but we are all liable to disappointments in this world and we all have our share that is allotted to us . . . let us . . . bear them with that resignation that would become us as Christians knowing that the Lord does not afflict willingly nor grieve his Children perhaps you may yet see causes to rejoice at your disappointment and I hope you may."

In this same letter written in April 1845, Roxana announced to Martha that she had another little sister, ten pounds at birth, whom they called Alice. "She looks the most as you did." Twenty-three years and seven children after Martha was born, Roxana still remembered vividly her first born.

After the crops were harvested and before the first snows, in fall 1845, Roxana again looked for Martha and Hubbell to make their way to Peacham's East Hill, but once more their plans were thwarted. Martha was in poor health. In January 1846, Chastina scribbled a long newsy letter requesting again that a visit be planned. "We want to know whither it is your intention as yet to come over next fall. we all feel very anxious to have you come over here, and I hope we shall meet once more. It seems a great while since you went from here and little did we think when you left that it would [be] 6 years before that we could see you again."

The next summer, the final heartbreak came. On July 24, 1846, Martha died during childbirth. Hubbell wrote the news and shortly thereafter a second letter, reporting the added sorrow of the baby's death. Maternal mortality as well as the rate of infant deaths at childbirth remained high until the twentieth century. Although Roxana gave birth to nine children, all of whom reached adulthood, she and all women of her times knew the tragedy of such losses as described in their letters and diaries.

It was several months, however, before Roxana could respond, and then she used no salutation on the letter to Hubbell. "It is with feelings of great commotion that I am obliged to address you in different language from what I used to when I could write that endearing title my Children but alas . . . God in his providence has ordered it otherwise. Not that my affections for you have by any means grown cold although you may perhaps think I have so long neglected writing since I received your letter that I have forgotten you but this is not the case I can assure you. I received your last the first week in Nov which gave some further particulars about Marthas Death and likewise the Death of your babe which I expected to here . . . I want you should if ever you come here bring some of Martha hair if you have got any of it and something that she used to were if it is nothing more than an apron . . . I had looked forward to this Thanksgiving day with a great deal of anxiety hoping that I should once more have my Children all with me but when I sat down to my breakfast table and thought of you and your departed wife my grief was uncontrolled and I was forced to give vent to a flood of tears." At age forty-five, Roxana had indeed lost a child, Martha, her eldest and the one with whom she felt a special harmony.

Over the next years Roxana was to transfer her feelings for Martha to Martha's daughter, Augusta. Twelve years after Martha's death, in February 1858, she wrote, "Now Augusta dont feel as if Grandma dont want to hear from you for *you* are *certainly mistaken*. I am ever glad to hear from any of my Children and such you are as the representative of your Dear Mother." Chastina had earlier expressed the same transfer of feelings: "I assure you we were all glad to hear from you [Hubbell], and the dear little Augusta. We feel much interest in her welfare, as she is all that remains of our dear Sister whom we never can in this life behold again. Does she look like her mother when alive? I hope she does."

In spring 1847, Hubbell remarried. Chastina graciously wished him "happiness and prosperity" and hoped that "she [who] has taken the place of my sister" will "be a Mother to Augusta." Then began a series of letters urging Hubbell to give Augusta a good education. In the fall Chastina sent "best respects to your wife & tell her for my sake to look well to Augusta, & see that she goes to school."

Unexpectedly in the summer of 1847 Hubbell moved his family from Michigan to Wisconsin, and Roxana was "verry sorry to hear you had gone so much farther from us without first coming to see us." In January 1850, Hubbell's move was finally explained. He had left his wife; she had contacted Roxana trying to locate him. Roxana wrote Hubbell that "I am going to take the liberty of writing to you although it is a long time since you have written to me . . . I was verry sorry to learn that you was in trouble and of such a serious nature as it appears to be although I had received a letter from your wife before yours. It appears that she expected you was here in Vt and she was verry anxious to hear from you she writes that she expected you would [stop] on your way here to Mich and see her and she appears to feel verry bad to think you have neglected her so long. Now Hubbell this is a verry serious affair. . . . I want to ask you if you think there could be no way settling your difficulties and live with her again . . . now Hubbell I think you had better sit down and write . . . I should think by her letters she was a woman of no inferior mind and talents but I know that one cannot judge by outward appearances always for many there are who may appear verry Beautiful without like whited sepulchers but within are full of all unclean things I hope this is not the case with her she speaks verry affectionately of Augusta says she is a bright child and she thinks a great deal about her and wants to see her verry much Now Hubbell I suppose she was the woman of your choice and the marriage covenant is in it self a solemn vow that we take uppon ourselves we are bound by the [illegible] of God and man to provide for each others needs as long as we both live and I am verry sorry that you had any trouble." Here is Roxana becoming involved in an awkward situation, which allowed her to expand on her views of marriage. Like Hubbell, she could compare her first loving marriage to her present marriage of convenience.

The figures for divorce began rising in the 1840s although they remained low through the century. Marital separation was more common, as can be seen by the increased numbers of notices in newspapers of "separation from bed and board," a public announcement that allowed one partner to disclaim any debts incurred by the spouse. Hubbell's separation is one of only two such events mentioned in the Walbridge-Watts letters. The other couple separated briefly and were soon, according to Alice, "reconciled and live together as they ought to now."

Roxana still harbored hope that Hubbell might return to Vermont with Augusta. "You wrote that you thought of selling your land and coming to this country . . . I hope you will be able to come here next summer there are a great many ways that one can get a living in this country if they have their health and as you are situated just as you are perhaps you could do as well here as there . . . I hope to see you next summer without fail if your health is spared you."

Hubbell must have written assuring Roxana that he was committed to Augusta's education, for in May 1853 Roxana replied that she "was glad to hear that Augusta is going to school and hope she will make a good scholar and she must be a good girl and learn to work and keep house for you if you have no other Oh how glad I should be to see her and hear her talk and tell me how she has got along without a mother poor little girl she little knew what a treasure she lost when her mother died I hope I shall yet live to see her here . . . I will put [in the envelope] some of the Childrens hair and likewise some of my own give them to Augusta and tell her to keep it and when she sees it think that she has got a Grandmother and one that loves her although she has never seen her but loves her for her mothers sake." That fall Roxana got her wish, for Hubbell and Augusta spent the winter at

Martha Walbridge Gregory's daughter, Augusta, at her high school graduation in Wisconsin, ca. 1860. Tintype, courtesy Elizabeth Rix Fairfax.

the Watts farm. After the visit, Roxana returned to addressing her letters to Hubbell as "Dear son."

During the visit Alice and Augusta became fast friends and continued to exchange letters until Alice's death. For years to come, Alice wrote Augusta about the people she had met in Peacham, regularly reporting marriages, births, and deaths. The letters written by Alice survive but there are none from Augusta. Alice often closed her letters with "Your reverend Aunt" and took pride in joking about being two years younger than her niece, Augusta. She was playful about other things too. In February 1861, with the Civil War in the background, Alice reported: "Elvira Sargeant has really *seceded,* left the *sisterhood,* committed matrimony, in short, with a Mr. Wesson from Danville. She was married at home, and then *we* went home with them—staid until 12 o'clock, then came home It was very bad going [in the sleigh], but no one *tipped over."* Augusta, too, was soon to leave the sisterhood, for that same year, at eighteen, a young bride like her mother, Augusta married a blacksmith, E. Alluron Mills, a widower with one young child. Alice wrote, "I am glad that you have a kind husband and a good home, and hope you may long live thus happily."

Augusta and Alluron made their home in Wisconsin where she gave birth to ten children, nine living past infancy. Her first child died as a baby and her aunt Clara in California comforted her in an 1863 letter: "I was very sorry to hear of your misfortunes your *own* sickness—and the loss of your babe—your first born—Truly you have tasted the bitter cup of affliction while you are yet young—and I deeply sympathize with you in your bereavement It seems but a short time since we heard of your little brother, Willie's death—Well do I remember how we all wept [twenty years ago] when we heard of it—for although we had never seen him we loved him for his mother's sake, and knew how hard it would be for her—in a land of strangers to part with her *darling* boy."

For Roxana, who never stopped remembering and mourning Martha, Augusta was a link with the beloved past; and for Roxana's children, the persistence with which they maintained this tenuous and fragile contact with Martha's child testifies eloquently to the strength of the family bond that they felt for one another, near and far, seen and unseen, living and dead.

Sarah Walbridge Way (1827–1909)

From a Factory in Lowell to a Minnesota Log Cabin

WEAVING IS a theme that runs through the life of Sarah (Sally) Walbridge Way. As a girl she wove at her mother's great loom. As a young woman she worked in the weaving mills at Lowell, Massachusetts. And as a pioneer wife and mother she wove a comfortable domestic life from the raw material of frontier Minnesota.

The third of the four Walbridge sisters, Sally took to the household chores easily. When she was sixteen, her mother noted: "Sally has done almost all my spinning and she has wove one web for fulld cloth and has another in the loom. she is small, does not weigh more than a hundred and 6 or 8 but she is a good girl to work."

It was common practice at this time for girls to be hired out to learn the "many useful branches of home industry" from a relative or neighboring farm wife, often for room and board only. In June 1845, Sally began to serve out her time in Peacham Hollow, at the household of Lyman Watts's brother. Roxana wrote: "Sally lives at the hollow with Isaac Watts she has been there 5 weeks and I expect she will stay a year she does not have much wages but the work is not hard and she works for herself a good deal."

By October 1845, Sally had left housework "to work in the factory," actually a weave shop that her uncle Isaac owned along the Peacham Hollow Brook. After only three weeks there, she became ill with "the Billious fever." Near the end of her recovery Sally assured Martha in Michigan, "I am a going back to the hollow to work again this week Jane Brown has worked in the factory this summer and Cynthia [also] is now at the factory." The weave shop was a thriving enterprise, employing Sally and her two Brown cousins, as well as others. And the pay must have been better than teaching, for Cynthia Brown had previously "kept school in Danville."

A change worth noting had come about in the lives of Peacham women. In the late eighteenth and early nineteenth centuries Sally's grandmother and mother had been an integral part of the subsistence farming—managers of the household, care givers for the children, and helpmates of their husbands. Although concentrating their work in the house, they connected closely with the produce of the barn and field, and they were familiar with all the tasks handled by their husbands, sons, and hired hands. In one area, however, Roxana may have expanded the role her mother played. Her butter and cheese, and maybe even her wool, had begun to be sold outside the home, the first steps toward a more commercial, modern way of life. Further expansion in the role of women took place in the Walbridge-Watts household in the late 1840s, as new economic opportunities outside of the home opened for young single women. Roxana's daughters Chastina, Sally, and Clara took advantage of these—Chastina and Clara as teachers, and Sally as a factory worker. Furthermore, these women had control over their earnings.

Although wage earning became acceptable in the 1840s for girls in their late adolescence, marriage was still their expected future. The Walbridge girls worked outside the home, but they saw this as a transitional stage before marriage. Statistics show that girls who worked for wages, such as mill girls, were as likely to marry as their sisters who remained on the farm. Chastina worried about becoming an old maid shortly before she reached age twenty, and Sally complimented her oldest sister Martha, who married at seventeen: "Sister has don very well to get maried so young as she is."

But although women could now work outside the home, the real possibilities were few. The most acceptable employment, recognized by family and community alike, was teaching, a profession that Chastina and Clara followed easily. As Sally was not a scholar, she could not take this path. She attended the district school and received a primary-level education, but she is not listed as a pupil at Peacham Academy.

If teaching was not an option, domestic service was an acceptable possibility, and until almost the turn of the twentieth century, it was the largest employer of female labor. Sally took advantage of the opportunity it offered. The pay, however, was low, the isolation must have been stifling, and the work was unrewarding. Sally did not stay with it long.

A third option, new in the nineteenth century, was employment in the factories that mass-produced products earlier hand made singly on the farm. Small factories shot up in most of the New England villages, especially along rivers which could be dammed for water power. And once a young woman like Sally had worked in a local factory, it was a small step to the larger factories at Lowell. As early as the 1820s, this new economic opportunity was opening for the daughters of New England farmers, but the major increase came in the 1830s. At that time the textile factories along the Merrimack River in Massachusetts were developing into the largest manufacturing center in the United States. Cheap, reliable labor was the key to their success. It soon became clear that rural farm girls living north of the factories could solve the labor problem. In order to entice these young women to leave home, however, the mill owners realized that they would have to provide living conditions to satisfy the farm families that their daughters would be well cared for and suitably chaperoned. They set up a system of boardinghouses where women workers were required to live under a strict set of rules, which included mandatory church attendance. The work was difficult, the factories noisy and hot, and the hours averaged seventy-three hours a week: thirteen hours a day, Monday through Friday, with eight hours on Saturday. The workday ran from dawn to 7:00 or 7:30 P.M., with half-hour breaks for breakfast and midday dinner. But despite what today seems like economic exploitation, the women workers themselves often felt stimulated, and even liberated from the isolation of their rural life, the constraints of their farm work, and the limitations of their small-village society. Most important, they earned cash. Monthly wages are estimated to have been from nine to thirteen dollars. Most factory girls, including Sally, experienced a new kind of power, which came with a salary they could spend at their own discretion.

Not all was positive, however, for there was certainly a stigma attached to working in the factories, as revealed in the family letters and in the comments quoted below from the Brown cousins and Peacham friends. Roxana, for instance, noted precisely the pay received when Chastina and Clara were teaching, but never wrote about Sally's wages. Also, she did not describe Sally's work except to say that she "has been to work in the factory about 7 months." One of the Peacham boys who went to California during the Gold Rush, learning of a former female classmate's decision to "go off to work in a factory," found it "strange enough."

The family had an additional reason to feel concerned and cautious about Sally's venture to Lowell. She was beautiful, a real "looker." When at twenty she was away at the Lowell mills, some cousins visited the Watts farm in the spring of 1848, and Chastina wrote to Sally of the occasion: "The boys would go and look of your miniature *once in a while,* but they thought it did'nt look near as well as you. By the way Albert says *you* are a very good looking girl, the best that he knows of. And that there will be a great deal more danger for you down there [in Lowell] because you are so handsome. The boys thought very strong of you going, and wondered why you went. I wanted to tell them that we had'nt a rich father. . . . Horace Brown made us a call [and] spoke of you and wondered why we let you go to Lowell—And said too that *he had heard how handsome you was.*" Chastina advised Sally to "take care of & for your *beauty.*" Beauty was highly valued; the unspoken reminder here was that it would help in attracting a husband, and the unspoken concern, that it would attract unwanted attention.

Unfortunately no letters survive written by Sarah (who from now on used her given name) or other Peacham girls who worked at Lowell. There are four letters written by Chastina to Sarah at the mills from the fall of 1847 to the spring of 1848. The first was dated in mid-October "early after your departure from Peacham," in which Chastina wrote: "We were glad to hear of your safe arrival at Lowell, & also of the prospect of your company, being so fortunate as to work so near together. I expect, you & Esther are rather *green* yet, in your weaving business. I want to know of your advancement. whether you are still considered as 'raw hands,' or can do your work alone." Sarah's expertise with home weaving and work at her uncle's weave shop might have qualified her for this more skilled and higher paid job. Weavers were known to take pride in their work and to feel self-respect, traits Sarah no doubt welcomed, being the third daughter who had never quite achieved the housekeeping skills of Martha or the scholarly accomplishments of Chastina.

While weaving advanced in the factories, home textile making continued at the Watts farm. Chastina reported to Sarah that "Miss Kittredge [a seamstress] remains with us yet, but I expect she will get through yet this week. last week [Clara] & myself finished the warp to the web. I spun twelve skeins. . . . Today I have cut Clarissa's calico dress, & tomorrow . . . I shall spin again. . . . Miss K. just cocked up her head in the bed, & said, 'are you writing to Sally?' answer yes. 'give her my respects then, & tell her I expect when she walks in the streets, her head is strait forward, but her eyes every which way' Exit under the bed clothes." Chastina ended the letter with the same theme: "I suppose all the family send their best wishes for your welfare. mind your health—keep a watch over yourself—knowing that there are snares for the unsuspecting." Even with all the assurances of the mill owners, families worried about their daughters. One cause for concern must have been simply the number of people in Lowell, thirty-three thousand in 1850 compared to fewer than fourteen hundred in Peacham. In Lowell's central district in 1849, one observer counted ninety stores; Peacham had three or four.

The letters reveal that Sarah was not alone at Lowell, for at least four other Peacham girls are mentioned by name. Both Chastina and Clara directed letters to the Peacham girls as a group, catching them up on gossip and sometimes teasing them: "My best to Esther, and tell her I should like to see her very much indeed. . . . love to Jane & Mary. Simon *hasnt got nobody to keep house for him yet.* He's in a pitiable condition. Tis leap year, & some of you girls ought to volunteer to go and keep house for him." Earlier Clara had written: "You must not work too hard so as to make your self sick now remember. Give my respects to Jane, Mary, Esther, Ann and all the rest of the good folks." Next spring Chastina wrote: "I suppose you enjoy yourself pretty well dont you. Do you think that one year at Lowell will do for you? or shall you want to go back when you get home?" As a postscript to the letter she added: "I dreamed the other night that you came home and brought twenty five hundred dollars home with you, I thought if that was the case I should go to Lowell." For the girls who remained at home, Lowell had a fascination, and also a reputation as a place to make a great deal of money.

It is not clear when Sarah left the mills for good, for there are no letters from the rest of 1848 or early 1849. She next appears in the Rix journal as accompanying Chastina and Alfred to the church for their wedding in July 1849. Among the guests at the reception were eleven family members and three friends, two a couple and one identified simply as "John Way."

John Way is the subject of a surprise journal entry written by Alfred two months later: "This day has been one of some interest. . . . Visit from Mother Watts, and learned from her that Sarah & John Way are to be married next Monday & that John is to leave for California." Two weeks earlier when Chastina was at the Watts farm, she had "helped Sarah quilt, on her pink & white quilt like mine," indicating that Sarah was preparing her fixings, the last stage of courtship. Now Chastina "went over to father's. Picked over the rasins for Sarah's wedding cake."

On October 16, 1849, Sarah Walbridge and John Way were married, only ten weeks after Chastina and Alfred's wedding. Chastina recorded the evening's events: "At six o'clock the appointed time; the guests began to arrive. When what a flutter we are in! the brides dress is not fixed yet, because the boys have but just come home from school, and were to bring fixings for the dress, & hat from Cowls shop for the *man.* So, I had to apply my fingers to the work . . . until the dress is done! And the bride is dressed. She looks neatly dressed in white muslin, with blonde lace in the neck & about the sleeves. A white satin sash about her waist. . . . Alfred & I stood up with them. . . . the pair did not seem much frightened, & did first-rate. Our refreshments consisted of tea, biscuit & Butter, doughnuts, cookies, tarts & two sorts of cake as usual. As near as I can remember, there were 33 there besides our family—which consisted of fourteen members after adding one new one." The next day "Mr. Way & his wife started for Dunham C.E." on the traditional wedding trip where they visited the Canadian Brown relatives.

Two weeks later Sarah and John returned to Peacham, where according to the November 3 entry in the Rix journal, "John is fixing up a room at home for Sarah" at the Watts farm. For the next few weeks the Ways visited local relatives, and finally on Sunday, January 6, the Rix journal in Alfred's handwriting reads: "After Service went over to the East Part, took tea with our folks and bade John S. Way, Goodbye." On the 7th: "The California Company started to day on their long & toilsome journey & labor. We have no hope that they will all, 18 in number, ever come back alive. But still we say, 'Success to ye! Bet you'll find more yellow things than gold—more blue one than the sky.'"

What we know of John Stephen Way comes from the few facts in *People of Peacham*. He was five years older than Sarah, making him twenty-seven at their wedding, and his father, Stephen Way, was a farmer in Barnet. A twentieth-century Way descendant said John's grandfather "had fourteen children by his wife and one by the hired girl; the latter event was known in the family as 'Great Grandfather Way's sin.' From this branch [is] descended" John Way, Sarah Walbridge's husband. There is no mention of John Way in Peacham Academy catalogs; perhaps, like Sarah, he was no scholar. He was, however, a good businessman, to judge from a letter Roxana wrote to Hubbell: "Mr Way Sallys man has gone to California . . . when she married him he was worth 15 hundred dollars in money but that did not satisfy and he must try his luck in C." It is possible that some of that bankroll was from Sarah's wages in the factories.

Seven months after the wedding, on May 18, a baby girl was born. Statistics show that the proportion of couples whose first child was born less than eight and a half months after marriage was at a high of nearly 30 percent in the 1780s, decreasing to about 20 percent by the 1830s. Therefore this scenario was not uncommon, but how would Roxana have reacted to it? In her letters from this period, she expressed no criticism but neither did she specify the dates of Sarah's wedding or the baby's birth. Whatever her personal feelings, she at last held a grandchild in her arms.

The baby was named Martha for her first-born, who by then had been dead for almost four years.

The story of the birth is worth telling; the following version is from the Rix journal written by Chastina who was herself six weeks pregnant:

May 17: . . . Came home [Watts farm] & found Sister Sarah feeling bad & weeping over the miniature of her husband.
May 18: . . . Awoke this morning @ 4 o'clock & found there had been a *mess* during the night. found some of the neighbors there. In short Sarah *was sick* & continued to be very bad, until about 10 minutes before 5 o'clock P.M. when She was delivered of a daughter. I took my place in the kitchen & there kept myself all day.
May 19: . . . The *baby* is a fine little plump thing—very pretty all getting along as well as could be expected. . . .
May 20: I have been sewing for the little *tot* nearly all day. Sarah quite comfortable.

Within a week Sarah "is not so well" and finally on July 6: "Dr Farr opened Sally's Breast," and the next day "She begins to feel better."

Full happiness appeared at the door on August 24 when John Way "the Californian was at home again—with his pocket full of Rocks." John had been gone less than seven months, and several of the letters he addressed to Sarah remain. On February 21 he informed her "of my safe arrival in San Francisco . . . 34 days from [New] york." His early appraisal of California was "I think that we have seen a little of the Eliphant in getting here and if I get gold Enough to pay me for Coming to California I Must be one of the lucky ones I think that California is the place to Make Money but not for enjoyment." He had not yet received a letter from home and was "most disheartened" about going to the mines without one.

His account of mail call in San Francisco described a situation common to most forty-niners: "The mails that come on in the steamer this time was sorted and ready to destribute on Sunday morning and there was more persons than could be served that day at the office door before sun rise they form in roes and each man takes his turn as he gets on the ground there is most order about it that I ever saw . . . sometimes a man will get within 8 or 10 [feet] of the door and sing out who wants to buy my chance they often pay an ounce of Gold for a mans chance and then they exchange places it is the most civil place I was ever in."

By June he wrote "about the Claim that we bot here Paid 830 dollars for the Privilege of four men to work with 14 others on the bar we since have bot out 3 . . . we should get it worked out by the 4th of July but it will take one month longer than that and perhaps more we Came in Possession of the last three Claims this morning." He had three "lucky" Saturdays; on one of them, four miners, including John "took out $1150.00 . . . but those strikes are few and far between the best weeks work I have made in California was last week my dividend was $334." John ended with words Sarah no doubt was waiting to hear: "I shall be at home next Winter some time if I have my health."

In this he succeeded. The Rix journal noted on September 21, 1850: "The Gold from California, dug by Way, [and other Peacham men] has come. John has got as much as a boy can lift all in 20s & 40s—he dont tell how much in value, but I gues it is $2700.00."

At the end of December, Roxana wrote Hubbell that "Mr Way Sallys husband has returned from California he done well while he was there he has bought a farm in Hardwick and is going to move onto it soon he pays 21 [hundred] dollars for it They have a fine little girl 7 months old and they call her Martha Sallys health is not verry good as she was sick all last summer."

With a customary wry humor, Alfred described the farm, which was about twenty-five miles northwest of Peacham, as being "situated on La-moille River—with a fair view of the Stream from the house. In front of the house towers Mount Pisgah & a little north Mount [Horeb]. The stream is filled with fine trout & gravel—one a great luxury, the other a small one. The buildings of the *Ancient* Order of Architecture—still they have an air of comfort, except in cold weather when the air is too cold for comfort—though even then, I suppose, it will bear the name of cold comfort. I think, on the whole, John & Sarah are very favorably situated for enjoying life." Their family grew, and in 1853 Roxana wrote to Augusta that "Sally and her man live in Hard wick they have two Children a Martha and Edgar little black eyed rouges as ever you saw Mr Way is doing verry well and getting a good living . . . Sallys husband made half a ton [of maple sugar]."

But Hardwick did not satisfy John for long. Although he stayed there until 1855, within three months of returning from California, he began to discuss with Alfred plans for going west again and at one time he even had "Australin fever." In the spring of 1855, Alice wrote Augusta: "John Way & John Martin and their families started for Minesota the 25th of last April. Sarah and Mrs Martin were awful homesick."

One of the striking patterns about New England families moving west is that they moved in groups. Diaries and letters reveal that families did not go alone and settle among strangers; they moved to areas where friends and family had already located, and they created communities with the spirit and culture of home. Such a place was Northfield, Minnesota, in Rice County in the Cannon Valley amidst rolling country and wooded hills. Within five years of the Ways' building their log cabin and clearing their land, at least five other Peacham families were mentioned in letters and diaries as living in the area, including both Watts and Way relatives. By 1867 when Isaac visited Sarah and John, it took him more than a week to see the people he knew from home, and even then he missed some.

The 1850s and 1860s were the years of the population boom in Minnesota, partly because land closer to Vermont had already been settled and partly because improved transportation—better roads, open waterways, and expanded railroads—made travel to Minnesota easier. In 1850 the U.S. Census listed only one hundred native Vermonters in Minnesota; by 1860 there were 4,208. Minnesota entered the Union in 1857, two years after the Ways settled there.

The first priority for pioneer families in Minnesota was preparing land for crops; housing was of secondary importance, and John Way proceeded accordingly. Roxana wrote to Augusta the year after the Ways left Vermont: "I got a letter from [Sarah] a few days ago she says they were in tolerable good health but she is not contented I expect they have seen some pretty hard times since they have been on their new place They have built them a log house and the winter was so severe that they *suffered* very much with the cold [John] has bought 100 and 60 acres of land has got in about 19 acres of seed corn wheat oats and potatoes but Sarah says it has been so dry that the crops did not look well at all She says they are on a road of a great deal of travel and they are trying to build up a town about a mile from them." The letter not yet sent, Roxana added a week later: "Sarah writes that it has been verry dry in Minesota and the prospect for crops were not very flattering I think it is rather a hard case for one to go from a cold Country to a *colder* one and have to suffer all the privations of beginning new faring hard and being homesick into the bargain as Sarah is she thinks she dont see anything there that is any better than in Vt and a good many things *worse* especially the *Snakes* she has to watch there to keep them out of the house and beds she says she killed as many as three a day for 3 weeks within 3 feet of her house. I dont believe she will ever be contented there John wont own but what he . . . has to work verry hard to get things so that they can live they had no water last winter only as they melted snow he has got a well begun but cant find time to finish it." Contented Sarah may not have been, but settled she became, despite droughts, severe winters, economic slumps, Indian attacks, the famous Northfield bank robbery, and even the grasshopper plagues of the 1870s. Two more children were born, Clara Ella in 1857 and, nine years later, Alice.

One cheery episode, Christmas in 1863, Sarah described to her sisters in Peacham: "Thare was quite a time in our town Christmas evning with old folks & young they went 15 miles after some pine trees & put them in a larg hall & had them hung full of every thing you can think of for presents fo[r] old & young that had been bought & put there by any one that wanted to give a christmas present . . . & they had someone drest up for Santa Claws (the worst way) that handed the presents as fast as they could get them from the tree & read the names I bought Martha a bible & she got it from the tree. . . . Every one makes a great account of christmas out here but when I lived in Vt I hardly knew when it was, do they make any acount of it there now! I got a new shawll pin but not from the tree."

Sarah returned to Vermont only twice, once in the summer of 1861 and again in 1882, when only two members of the family remained to greet her. Meanwhile, the rest of the family wore a path to her Minnesota door. In the fall of 1857, Dustan, fresh from California, went there with Augustus hoping to find work. After Isaac's return from the war, Father Watts went west and stayed the summer with the Ways, observing the horse stud business which had long been John's specialty and had become a key factor in the family's increasing prosperity. Sometime in the mid-1860s, the Ways finally built a "handsome" two-story frame house.

John, according to "old-timers" in the community, "bought the first Morgan stallion (Vermont Morrill) to Minnesota and made a great deal of money with the [stud fees]." Roxana would have rejoiced at Sarah's increasing comfort, and even more at the "contentment" that must have gone along with it.

A few years after the Civil War, Isaac ventured west, trying to decide what to do with his life. Upon his arrival he "found the folks all well and prospering." His activities in Minnesota, as described in his 1867 diary, included "draw sand," "went hunting," "riding around," "reading and tinkering around the house," helped put out a fire in a furniture store in town, attended "a meeting of the Y.M.C.A.," "went . . . to the woods after a load of wood," "butchering . . . slaughtered eight porkers," "helped . . . unload a car of lumber," "helped pick turkeys," "went to Sircle Lake fishing . . . only got twelve in all," "went to examination at the college," attended "prayer meeting," and went to church less often than he felt he ought, writing "I dont feel right about it."

Sarah Walbridge Way. Photograph taken by Ira E. Summer in Northfield, Minnesota, ca. 1860. Courtesy Choate Farm Collection.

One of the most striking things that Isaac saw was the "pile of bus[iness] done in Northfield. I never saw more business done anywhere than was done here last Sat. that is according to the place. It was one continual stream of humanity all day long. The business street was almost blockaded and the stores all full of customers. I should like to own either one of the eight or ten stores here, I know it must pay big."

Later, sister Clara and her family from California crossed the country by train in 1871 and spent a week in Minnesota before going on to Vermont. Sister Ella visited several times in the 1870s, staying many months to help Sarah, as maiden aunts in those days were supposed to do. In 1887, Ella found a paying job a short distance away in Faribault, the Rice County seat.

In 1882, when Sarah was fifty-five and John sixty, they moved (with their furniture) from their farm outside of Northfield into the town itself, marking what must have been a watershed of aging and retirement. From here John Way served as a state legislator for one term in 1883. Twenty-six years later they died within a month of each other, both recognized as pioneer settlers in the Northfield area.

In all of this, Sarah's voice is missing. Except for her three brief letters added to her mother's to other family members and the 1863 Christmas letter quoted above, there is little hint of her doings and feelings. The sisters and brothers who visited left few comments. Only three vignettes remain.

The first comes from Isaac's letter written to "Sister Alice" back in Peacham during his visit in 1867, in which he spoke of "Little Alice," Sarah's youngest child: "She is improving fast but cant talk yet. It took me about two weeks to get her tamed so I could play with her, but now she will play half a day at a time. She knows the most of any child I ever saw that couldnt talk." No other information is available on what must have been one of Sarah's hardest times—watching the slow development of this "worrisome" child, who died at nine years old in 1875.

One interlude in Sarah's life which must have been enjoyable was a trip to California in the spring of 1883 to visit Clara. All that is known of this comes from a brief letter written by Ella (who kept house for her in her absence): "She had a pleasant journey and did not get very tired."

Silent though she may have been in letters, Sarah speaks with a clear voice in another way. Shortly after the new farmhouse was built, she created a parlor for it. Parlors are a lost item in households of today, but once they were a social necessity in city mansions and rural farmhouses alike. Centers of peace and order closed to everyday family use, reserved for weddings, funerals, social visits, and other special occasions; quiet sanctuaries for the amenities and symbols of refinement, they were the only places in their lives that women could call their own. Sometimes a parlor came in for odd usage; Sarah's granddaughter "mainly remembers using it as a child to spread out platters of homemade candy to cool."

Thanks to photographs, a detailed description, and the furniture itself, now in storage at the Smithsonian, we can imagine Sarah's parlor: the door opens on a cool, dark room, its heavy curtains closed. When they are open, the room hardly seems lighter, for the only touches of color come from a vivid wall-to-wall Brussels carpet, the chromolith on one wall, and the gold-leaf inner panels framing it and two other pictures. Everything else is dark brown or black.

Along one wall is a magnificent cast-iron stove, polished to a gleaming black. A wide "settee"—what might be called a sofa if it were not so formidably uncomfortable—beautiful in its curving lines of black walnut and upholstered "tuft-style in black [horse]hair cloth" sits along another wall, with a large etching of a Bierstadt scene above it. In a corner stands a small round table, and over that a corner shelf with a bead-fringed lambrequin in needlepoint hanging from it, made for Sarah by her daughter. A Story and Clark parlor organ, with side chairs of the same black walnut and horsehair grouped nearby, fills the third side. The remaining wall space is occupied by two large armchairs, one with an upholstered back, with a large oval table between them and pictures overhead of two Greek figures in white against a black background.

This parlor as it stood inviolate through the years, first at the farm and then in town, was a symbol of the life of comfort and even elegance that Sarah wove out of her own hard work and the raw materials that she found in the new country to which she came.

One of the threads worked into the weaving of Sarah's life was the strong connection with Vermont that went and stayed with her. As late as 1889, Charles Choate wrote in his diary, "Sent 1 pail & 2 cans Sugar to John S. Way Minn."

Charles Watts (1835–1875)

A Surveyor, Lawyer, and Farmer in the West

IN 1855, at the age of twenty, Charles Watts left Peacham to live in the West. His career there provides an example of how easily young men in the middle of the nineteenth century could move from one job to another, and how casually they could acquire professional standing. Available records of his life show no formal training beyond Peacham Academy; yet he became a respected lawyer in Monticello, Illinois.

Charles was one of the two stepsons whom Roxana found waiting for her when she moved into the East Hill farmhouse, bringing her own two boys and their older sisters with her. They blended their lives and settled down together, and six years later Chastina wrote to Martha in Michigan: "Lyman & Charles are about the same size of Dustan & Augustus they are very good looking boys but I dont think that they look any better than the other boys. They all look enough alike to be brothers. All go to school."

Peacham Academy catalogs list Charles as attending from 1848 to 1855. After his last term, he took a teaching job in Monticello, Illinois, a town located midway between Chicago and St. Louis. It was not the cheap land that lured Charles west; mainly he just wanted to leave Peacham. It is likely he obtained the teaching position while still in Vermont. A schoolmate, Charles Choate, a few years younger than Charles Watts, finished his term at the academy a year behind Watts. With recommendations in his pocket from his teacher and pastor, Choate went west at age eighteen. In his diary for November 17, 1856, he wrote about the experience: "Comenced teaching school to day in Rock Island county, Ill. for 3 months and perhaps 4 for 23 dollars @ month for th[r]ee months and $25 for one." During the next four years he traveled through the West but in January 1860, his address again was Illinois—Chatham, in Sangamon County—demonstrating the wandering spirit of young men in the second half of the century. Charles Watts probably followed a similar path, writing communities in the

Charles Watts, ca. 1867. Courtesy Helen Watts Richter.

West for a teaching position and locating one in Monticello, Piatt County, where education was important to the early settlers who had built their first school by donations of material and labor. Teachers were paid by subscription of patrons, an unsatisfactory situation as told in his letter to Alice in March 1856: "I would never advise any one to keep school in Illinois—If you keep a summer school here you cannot get pay till the next April."

Why at age twenty would he have moved so far away? An answer may lie in the makeup of the Watts household at that time. His brother Lyman was there, in the first dedicated fire of a new religious conversion, and so was Augustus, who was sinking into mental illness, a worry to all. Charles's stern and fretful father ruled the family, and his overworked stepmother needed all her considerable competence to keep up with her tasks. At the other end of the scale were three children at just the ages to be of no interest to a brisk young man. Peacham was a place to get out of.

Beside all that, any bright young man would have felt a distinct sense of being in a closing trap. With the help of the remaining boys, his aging father kept the farm running. If Charles had stayed, he might have been expected to assume the main burden of the farm, for it was already clear that "Brother Lyman" was not to be a farmer. In any case, if Charles went west to avoid farming, he did not succeed. Almost immediately he saw that "Piatt Co. is one of the greatest stock Counties of Ill. and can show cattle which would look like great Eliphants beside the little rats of the common Vt. cattle." Charles liked Monticello and remained there the rest of his life, although he frequently visited Vermont, married a woman from Peacham, and maintained a strong connection to his native town.

In Illinois, he began to read law "when I can find the time" and did surveying "when it is convenient." Both Charles and Dustan maintained side careers as surveyors, perhaps getting the idea from Alfred Rix, who surveyed land around Peacham well into his career as head of the Academy. For Charles, being known as a surveyor would be an asset for becoming a specialized real estate lawyer.

Unfortunately none of Charles's letters has survived in its original form. Could he have mentioned the Lincoln-Douglas debates, for example? There are only short excerpts, showing his particular flair, made years later by his niece Elsie Choate from letters no longer in the family archives. After he became settled in Illinois, he wrote to the family in Peacham on November 24, 1856: "I am now staying in the office with McComas and diping into law a little now and then. I had my first case day before yesterday. I wrote two short speeches to the Jury, but what effect it had I dont know for I left before they had gaven in their verdict, as I had about twelve miles to ride and it was about dark when we got through." He learned the legal profession by working in an office with an established lawyer; no college education, simply an apprenticeship. This rather than college was the way nearly all lawyers were trained at the time.

A year and a half later he described the dangers of the lawyer's business in the West: "I was called to attend to taking the goods of a merchant on execution—when we went to levy on the goods the merchant drew a revolver and attempted to shoot a man that went with the Sheriff and myself. He made five attempts to shoot but was prevented by the Sheriff. We had him tried today for an attempt to kill, and he was bound over for trial. That is about the spirit of many of the citizens of the West. In that respect the county is not much like Vermont. When I first came here such conduct was very strange, but have become somewhat accustomed to it and now it does not seem very much out of the ordinary course of doing business." In Illinois, the practice of law depended less on reading law than on being gun savvy.

In 1856 Monticello had two lawyers advertising in the local paper, and by 1860 there were five, including Charles, listed in the census. From all accounts he became a successful lawyer, especially in real estate inventories. In 1862 Charles was appointed the attorney for the James McReynolds estate. McReynolds, a bachelor who had named the city of Monticello in 1857, had property valued at close to $100,000. Charles continued the practice of apprenticing young lawyers and several studied under his direction before passing the Illinois bar. Yet Charles never seemed to make a total commitment to being a lawyer. In 1865 he wrote that he was "doubtful whether I am lawyer, farmer, both or neither." He then added that "the farm paid very well last year" so a choice was not critical as he juggled them well.

Before moving west, Charles became well acquainted with Lodoska Spencer, the eighth child of a large family whose farm was located northeast of the Wattses'. Fourteen Spencer children are listed in *People of Peacham* although some did not survive infancy. Mentioned throughout the Watts writings are Lodosky, as she was called, born in 1836, and her younger sister Phebe whom Alice described in 1861 as "just as little and just as pretty as ever." In the summer of 1854, Lodosky worked as the hired girl for the Wattses, and Roxana found her "a first *rate good girl* . . . neat, industrious, modest and prety every way." So Charles had first-hand observation of Lodoska's housekeeping abilities.

There is a much-told legend explaining why Lodoska became a popular name in northern Vermont. It seems a Jewish peddler from Russia came through Peacham in the 1830s selling pots and pans. Once he arrived after the birth of a baby who had not yet been named. He said if the family would name their little girl Lodoska for his mother in Russia, he would give them a five-dollar gold piece. He struck the same bargain with other new mothers.

Charles and Lodoska's courtship lasted two years although as early as 1856 Roxana wrote that she expected Charles to "make a wife of her sometime." On November 22, 1858, the wedding took place in Peacham. This was a happy union. Both had been raised in large families, and they, too, quickly started having children, William, Charley, and Lena. Alice commented in 1865 that they had four children within six years—"Quite a family so soon." The fourth child, named Dustan Walbridge Watts after that much loved brother, lived only a year. The next child died at two years old—accidentally drowned in the wash tub. Harry, born in 1871, survived.

The Watts family used their relatives' homes in the West as a refuge when they needed a change of scenery, time to make a decision, or another chance to prosper. At different times both Dustan and Augustus went west to try their luck in the wheelwright trade. Even Father Watts made a short visit west in 1866, four years after his wife's death, relinquishing the farm, at least for a while, to Isaac's control.

Charles's younger brother, Isaac, also went west after the war, working the winter of 1868 in Charles's office "on his abstract of Co. titles," and finding that he was not suited for desk work. Isaac's diary and letters written during his stay report the full schedule kept by Charles—off to Champaign one week and to Chicago the next. Working in the law office with "tax books" and comparing "the collectors returns," Isaac helped at home in the evening with the chores. Finding one day too much like the next, he was relieved when court was in session and "times are some livelier." A lawyer's life in Monticello was busy, especially for Charles who was selected often to serve in public office. The history of Piatt County, Illinois, published about 1883, states that Charles was school and county treasurer "for a number of years"; was a trustee in 1872 when Monticello incorporated as a city with a population of 1,060; and became later a director of the Monticello Railroad Company.

In 1859 Charles and Lodoska moved into a farmhouse they had built outside the town limits, but by 1870 they had a new house in town at 217 South Hamilton Street. According to family legend, Charles decided against building on State Street where the wealthier people lived because he was county treasurer at that time and did not want people to think he "had robbed the till." The house, which still stands, was small—one story—

"unpretentious" with a porch off the front entrance and a second porch on the south side. Desendants remember a barn where Charles kept his horses which has long since disappeared, as have the apple trees he planted.

Visiting was not all one sided, and Charles and his family came east often. Lodoska returned to Peacham to have her second child in January 1861, and Charles came "after her in April." Later, in 1867, she and the three children visited for the summer, and Alice wrote that they "were here a good deal so we had little spare time." It was at the end of this visit that the fine photograph of the Watts family was taken. In October of the next year, Isaac wrote in his diary: "Bro. Charles came here this eve." A few days passed before "Lyman came up today so we three boys are all at home again this eve. Such reunions are not very common." In fact, it was their last time together.

Lodoska complained of homesickness, as Alice's letters revealed, but she was not alone in Illinois. Her sister Phebe appears in the census of 1860 living in Monticello, soon marrying Henry Bodwell, a local clerk. Through the years there is mention of "Henry Bodwell and family," and in 1868 they all "had a turkey dinner."

Sometime in the mid-1860s Charles began to experience serious health problems. He talked of wanting to move to Minnesota where he felt he might improve, and in October 1866, he did go to Minnesota for a lengthy stay with Sarah and her family. Family members wrote his "lungs were feeling quite strong again," but this was only a temporary improvement. In the 1870 census, Charles is listed as "retired lawyer." He was to live five more years in gradually worsening health.

In 1875 Charles's condition became so acute that Isaac, visiting in Minnesota, rushed to Illinois to be by his bedside. Charles died on February 4, 1875, just weeks short of his fortieth birthday. Isaac reported the death to his father in Peacham and wrote that the cause was "pnemonia of the right lung with a badly infected liver." A few days later Isaac wrote Sarah describing Charles's last days: "He died Thurs. morning at 8 o'clock. Up to Wed. P.M. he had taken his medicines, stimulants and such nourishment as beef tea, cream &c. very regularly and his strength held out remarkably well. Then he began to refuse almost everything, I think he could not swallow very easily, and he failed very fast from that time. He was delirious all the time and took but little notice of any one after dark Wed. He continued to talk wildly till five or six hours before his death."

The newspaper obituary described Charles as one of Piatt County's "most respectable and beloved citizens," and in his letter to Sarah, Isaac mirrored these sentiments: "Charles was respected by all and probably had as many friends as any man in Monticello."

Isaac also filled his father in about the rest of the family: "Lodosky's about worn out. She is one of the best women in the world. Henry & Phebe have been here all the time and have been a great help."

Lodoska lived a long life, staying sometimes in Vermont and sometimes in Illinois. For many years Charles had not collected his lawyer fees, and Lodoska took former clients to court but was slow in receiving payment. Isaac and Alice mentioned this in family letters, and a granddaughter verified Lodoska's court cases while going through the county records years later. Isaac lent Lodoska money through the hard times when the children were young. Baby Harry was not even four years old when his father died, and the oldest child was only fifteen.

Lodoska's widowhood was not totally unhappy; there were good times too. One was when Charles's niece, Elsie Choate, twenty-two years old, came in the spring of 1903 to visit relatives and friends in Illinois. She wrote of a play she and Lodoska's youngest son Harry helped put on and a party Lodoska's second son, Charley, held in her honor: "While I was [in Monticello], the young people gave a play, 'A Woman's Honor,' and went to a town about fifteen miles away to give it. It was a little one horse town and a little bit of a stage, so they had a great time adjusting them selves to narrow quarters. Harry took the part of a Cuban and was a villian also. His makeup was fine and he was doing his part all right on the stage when his goatee suddenly dropped off. He put his hand up to hide a laugh and then remembered that if he touched his face the paint would come off, so he stood there, mumbled his words and perspired like anything. The other players did all right and Harry did fairly, but not as well as he had when they gave it at home. . . . They all were ever so friendly to me and let me be on the stage with them, so I helped the girls dress, and enjoyed myself very much. They had to wait a long time at the station for the train [to return to Monticello], so some of the men who could sing well got together and sang ever so many songs, and it sounded quite fine.

"I think I told you that Charley Watts gave a little party for me the evening before I came away, Monday, and we had a fine time. I enjoyed the dancing much more than the cards, for I don't know anything about the latter and the first is *fun*. They had refreshments passed around by Charley's children, two girls and two boys, they are about the nicest behaved children I ever saw and seemed to know their place in company.

Lodoska Spencer Watts, wearing her needlework, ca. 1890. Courtesy Helen Watts Richter.

"The Monticello people said if I would come back that way they would
have a platform dance out under the trees. One of the men has a beautiful
home and has built a fine hardwood floor out under the trees on the lawn
with a place for the orchestra and all and the young people more than have a
good time." Did Lodoska dance too, or as an older woman, did she only
watch?

Lodoska was beloved by her grandchildren, one of whom, Rita, wrote
years later: "We were always delighted when Grandma came to stay a
while. So many interesting things to learn to do—tatting, hemstitching,
burnt wood, punched brass, and always the wonderful embroidery." When
Lodoska died at eighty-two in 1918, her obituary said she "was a woman of
lovely character and kind to her neighbors and friends. She took especial
pride in her needlework and embroidery, which she did beautifully, but she
was always generous with her work and no Christmas church bazaar was
complete without some of her fancy work." Three children outlived her.
Her oldest son, William, had died in Illinois in 1886, but Charles, Lena, and
Harry all lived into the twentieth century.

The static society of Peacham hardly allowed Charles and Lodoska to
make any kind of mark; but in the fluid social structure of the frontier,
their Vermont-learned skills and Yankee adaptability stood out. Charles,
the farmer, surveyor, and lawyer, and Lodoska, the fancy-work expert,
brought to their new setting what was needed for developing culture, and
left their mark in the court records and church bazaars of Illinois.

Migrants to California

In the early 1850s, many Vermonters, excited by the discovery of gold, traveled to California hoping to find their fortunes in the mines. A few were lucky, returning to Vermont with enough money to purchase a farm and settle into the lifestyle of their parents. Most, however, did not succeed in their quest for wealth; and of these, some chose to remain in California and start their lives anew.

In early 1853, Roxana's daughter, Chastina, joined her husband Alfred Rix, who after failing in the mines, settled in San Francisco teaching school. She traveled with her son Julian and her sister Clara by steamer down the Atlantic coast, crossing at the Panama Isthmus, and then catching a steamer headed up the Pacific coast. Like many women who remained at home while their husbands went west in search of fortune, Chastina had expected her husband to return to Vermont—if lucky, with pockets full of gold, or, if unsuccessful, with pockets empty. But like many men who went to California with every intention of returning home, Alfred was wooed by the mild climate and the excitement of opportunities afforded by the new settlement.

Once in California, both Chastina and Clara worked at jobs readily available to women—they took in boarders and did laundry and sewing. In the fall of 1853 Clara, returning to her former occupation, became a teacher at the first public school established near Mission Dolores. Both women adjusted easily to city life. Fashion, for instance, became a concern, and they spent hard-earned money on fancy cloth for dresses and capes. Single women in San Francisco were scarce and Clara had many invitations to participate in social activities including horseback riding, sailing, dancing, and the theater. Neither Chastina nor Clara attended church in San Francisco, a further indication of the gradual secularization of their lives.

Chastina never saw her Vermont home again. Like many displaced New

Englanders, however, Clara and her husband, Russell Rogers, took their children on a visit to Vermont after the transcontinental railroad was completed. They saw their relatives and friends, enjoyed riding in the green hills, and after a few weeks returned to California which had become their home.

Chastina Walbridge Rix (1824–1857)

From Teacher to Mother in Vermont and California

"SUNDAY, 29 July 1849. 1½ o'clock P.M. We, that is to say, Alfred Rix & Chastina Walbridge, *are married*—Therefore, according to custom & law the said Alfred Rix will retain his name and gain a wife, while the said Chastina Walbridge will lose hers and gain a husband—time and trial will determine whether one or both have got 'shaved' in this exchange. The World at large is Solemnly 'warned and notified' from this day forth to address us as Mr. & Mrs. and also, especially, to kick every dog that barks at us." Thus begins the journal kept by Chastina and Alfred for six years, in the early years alternating entries almost daily. On their wedding day in 1849, they were full of promise, proud of their accomplishments, and anticipating a bright prosperous future together.

Roxana described her second child, Chastina, as "a verry prudent economical girl and verry industrious." She shared her mother's respect for education and passed her teaching examination in 1843 at nineteen; she was to teach for the next five years. Her first school was "in her own district," but later she traveled to neighboring towns, once going as far as forty miles to take a school.

In the spring of 1841, only a year after Roxana remarried and the remaining five Walbridge siblings moved to the Watts farm, a young man, Alfred Rix, moved to the farm down the hill to live with Sarah Stevens, his maternal great-aunt and the mother of abolitionist Thaddeus Stevens, who was to play a prominent role in Alfred's life. Alfred had come to "fit himself" at Peacham Academy for the University of Vermont, known then simply as Burlington College, which he attended from 1844 to 1848 with money lent him by his cousin Thaddeus. After graduation Alfred returned to Peacham as principal of the academy.

"On the very important and ominous occasion of a quilting, at Mrs Stevens [Chastina and Alfred] were introduced to each other." As they

Chastina Walbridge Rix and Alfred S. Rix on their first anniversary, 1850. Daguerreotype taken in Danville, Vermont. Print, courtesy California Historical Society.

penned it, "the mutual impression was favorable," and "from that hour" when they first met, "each has not ceased to be of more importance in the eyes of the other than any other individual." An eight-year courtship began.

The delay in marriage came about because of his four years studying in Burlington, her poor health the year of his graduation, and the time she needed to prepare her personal clothes for the wedding and the linens for their early housekeeping days. The journal reported: "The spring & summer of 1849 Chastine spent in 'fixing.' And a hard time it was for her. Girls usually work themselves beyond what they are able in such times. It was so with C., her health was poor most of the time during the summer; and by the time she was ready to be married as the saying is—'She was poor as a crow.' "

The week before the wedding, Alfred slipped "a half eagle into the hand of the Rev. David Merrill," and on the appointed day made "ready with Horse Carriage," picked up the bride, her sister Sarah and brother Dustan, and "started for the church about two miles distant from her fathers. They arrived at the church in good time & quietly took their seats in her fathers pew . . . for the commencement of the afternoon services." At the appointed time "the bridegroom took his lady quietly by the hand & led her to the altar . . . & there amid this assembled congregation, they ratified the vows long before pledged to each other."

It is tempting to think of Chastina and Alfred's wedding as typical of rural nineteenth-century New England marriage ceremonies, but Chastina wrote that "a more than usual number had assembled, for a wedding in a country church is a rare thing." In fact, there is no evidence that any of the other Walbridge-Watts children were to marry in church. Following the Rix wedding, the couple "returned to her father's, where they met some of their friends invited to take supper with them. They had tables spread and a good wedding feast was neatly laid upon the cloth."

As a private honeymoon was not yet customary for newlyweds, Alfred and Chastina took the traditional wedding trip to visit family and friends. The morning after their marriage, they set off for Alfred's parents in New Hampshire, "with Mr Bruce's horse and Aunt Stevens' bran-new carriage," and stayed more than two weeks.

On a rainy afternoon several weeks after their wedding, Alfred wrote in their journal this description of Chastina, "our heroine." She was "of the ordinary hight—well proportioned—skin fair and clear save an inclination to moles." He continued: "Though laboring under the triple disadvantage of a neglected youth, poverty and almost constant ill-health, she yet, by her own efforts alone—clothed herself appropriately and even elegantly, and attained a good knowledge of the English Sciences and made considerable advancement in the study of the French language. . . . In addition to her natural prudence her circumstances have contributed greatly to make her economical—a thing too often wanting in the young wives of this day."

For their first home, the Rixes "boarded out," meaning they took rooms in a house located at Peacham Corner, across from the academy where Alfred continued to serve as principal. "We furnish our own rooms, do our own washing and pay 3.00 a week." In preparation for their new home, Chastina and Alfred "cut out our carpet & commence sewing it" at the Watts farm. Chastina wrote that Alfred "sews pretty well for a beginner." In addition, Chastina "spins stocking yarn with all her might—because her mother gave her all she could spin before she left." Once in their "new apartments," Chastina trimmed "her quilt," worked "on her curtains," and made "calls."

Soon it became apparent that the academy would be understaffed; and Alfred called on Chastina to prepare "herself to teach if necessary." She was needed for both geography and arithmetic, and the published catalog for fall 1849 listed "Mrs. C. W. Rix" among the teachers. It was uncommon but not illegal for Vermont married women to teach school. On New Year's Day, 1850, Alfred summarized their situation: "Our salary is $800.00 a year with all the tuition. From this there must be subtracted about 300 for wood, repairs and extra instructors leaving about 500$ for us to live upon." There is no payment noted for Chastina's teaching.

Theirs was a happy marriage, and six weeks after the wedding Alfred wrote that Chastina "is a very industrious & glorious young woman—and I know of but one reason for wishing I had not married with her, and that is, that *I cannot do it again.*"

Alfred discussed nearly all subjects of married life in their journal, but the most unusual for the times were his comments on sex, a subject rarely seen in first-hand accounts of New Englanders. Describing their first married night, he wrote "After life's fitful fever they slept well!" On September 12, 1849, Alfred commented: "This is warm weather and we are pretty well wearied out when we are done. GUESS." On the following day, Chastina wrote, "Alfred is as merry as a cricket these days, and it is more than I want to do to *manage* him. But as women are in *the habit* of doing so, I shall endeavor to do the best in my power." One evening they ended their entry with the words "GOOD NIGHT! GOOD NIGHT!" and one morning they began with "This morning we got up in good season."

Another little-mentioned subject which Alfred recorded in their journal was Chastina's menstruation. Almost two months after their marriage, he noted that they "had a visitor a certain nameless old lady—a friend of Chastina's and I think some way related to her—Heigh Ho! Heave oh! Who cares!" In October, he recorded that "Chastina's old friend called again to day & I met her at the door & bid her welcome—at this time we should be sorry to miss her visits—though we both hope we may soon come to that state of family independence when we can not only dispense with the presence of this old lady but even violently exclude her from our intercourse—meanwhile we shall take care that her visits are regular & of service and that she be not prematurely offended." At last it becomes clear that the "old lady" is Chastina's menstrual period, and although they wanted a family someday, they were not yet ready for the added responsibility. In November: "Another visit from the old Lady." In December: "Chastina's old *Acquaintance* came to day without giving notice. She was not expected these two days." In January 1850: "*The Old lady arrived.*" No

Chastina Walbridge, ca. 1844. Daguerreotype, courtesy Elizabeth Rix Fairfax.

mention until April 1: "Had *company.*" And finally on April 29: "No Visitor as C. expected!"

Pregnancy was another subject not commonly noted in diaries or family letters, with the baby's birth often coming unannounced even to mothers and sisters. Neither Alfred nor Chastina mentioned directly her condition after noting that they had no visitor in late April. Alfred wrote in early June: "We are now living in a *family way* and hope to prosper." Finally five months later Alfred recorded that "Chastina is making herself extremely busy now-a-days in prosecuting a certain branch of family manufacture. Winter will be likely to bring with it a necessity for a large amount of flannel garments. It is to supply such a contemplated want that Chastina's fingers are now so nimble." A few weeks later Chastina "got a loose dress started" and wore it two days later.

Chastina was one of those women who in the hours before labor experience a burst of energy. On December 29, 1850, "about 2 o'clock P.M. We got it somehow into our heads that if we had any thing to do 'twere well if 'twere done quickly. So Chastina goes about some little cooking which *must* be done. A couple of chicken pies and a pan of Nut-cakes were summoned forth in short order." Later in the day, Dr. Farr was called to attend. He and his wife walked up the path that Alfred had shoveled from the street, the weather being cold and snowy. "By invitation, at 1 o'clock A.M. Mrs Choate and Mrs Morse joined our circle." They were older women of Roxana's generation who had given birth—Mrs. Choate four times and Mrs. Morse, five. Because a medical doctor was present, they probably were not midwives but were there to provide female support. Finally on December 30, 1850, at "10 o'clock P.M. Chastina became the mother of a little Son, whose name is Julian Walbridge Rix."

Soon Roxana was "on the ground to aid us" and a hired girl was "engaged" at two dollars a week. Alfred wrote that although Chastina laughed and talked the day after the birth, "she has . . . been very sick and for a long time as the record of Yesterday will show. She thinks it is paying pretty dear for the whistle!" Almost three weeks later Alfred recorded: "The baby grows like a weed and makes all stir—he is an early riser & therefore a reformer in our family."

Alfred's life was changing too. In the fall of 1850, he gave up being principal of the academy, but continued teaching there three hours a day at sixty dollars a term. This allowed him time to study law, which for many years he had professed to be his goal. Three weeks before Julian's birth, Alfred passed the state examination. He went into partnership with William Mattocks, a noted Peacham lawyer, and in the spring, Mattocks and Rix took on at least a dozen cases, described in the journal.

Alfred also developed an active commitment to the abolitionist movement. Throughout 1850 and into 1851, Thaddeus Stevens had sent him speeches from Washington where Stevens served as a representative from Lancaster, Pennsylvania, his home after Peacham. The words of Henry Clay, Daniel Webster, William Henry Seward, and Thaddeus Stevens himself had fired up Alfred and many others in the country. In the first political matters found in the Walbridge-Watts letters and diaries, Chastina and Alfred commented on the Wilmot Proviso and the Fugitive Slave Law— they favored the first and opposed the second. On June 14, 1850, Alfred wrote: "About this time Congress is wide awake on the subject of Slavery & the admission of California as a state. We take much interest at this date in public matters especially such as are now transacting at the Capital. Chastina and myself agree remarkably well. We are both free-Soilers. We both are anxious to see by one means or another the territory of the country free from the *possibility* of slavery." That Chastina would align herself with a political opinion was unusual for women in the Walbridge family.

For some time Alfred had talked about going west. In the fall of 1851 a combination of events came together and encouraged his decision to go to California. He was well aware that Caledonia County could not support another lawyer in addition to William Mattocks; he was no longer needed at the academy; he felt alienated by the local hostility toward abolition which he strongly favored. Since he had Chastina and Julian comfortably settled in a two-family house owned by Mrs. Marsh, surrounded by friends and family, he "concluded to go." On October 4, 1851, Alfred left his wife and nine-month-old-son, and Chastina wrote: "Never Shall I forget our parting; if it be our last there is a sweet consolation in the thought that we were & ever have been the happiest of the happy in each other's society. He has gone!"

Accompanying Alfred were twenty-five men all listed by Chastina in the journal, including her younger brother, eighteen-year-old Dustan Walbridge, and Alfred's older brother, thirty-two-year-old Oscar Rix.

Chastina was burdened emotionally and physically by Alfred's departure. She went about her life in Peacham as if he would return in a few months, a year at the most. The days after he left were "long & wearisome," and almost every journal entry mentioned missing him. Sunday in particular "passes drearily away" as she nostalgically remembered their former "pleasant times reading & conversing together."

Late in the winter, which was to be a long cold one, Chastina went to the Watts farm to nurse her ailing mother. She decided to move there until Alfred's return. Women without husbands or fathers were dependent on the good will of neighbors and friends, as Chastina was to discover. On February 17 Father Watts went to bring the first load of her possessions from the Corner. Mrs. Marsh, was "full of wrath because I am going to leave her . . . [and] claimed rent for the year." Chastina became upset when she heard that Mrs. Marsh "talked very unchristian & very unbecoming" to Father Watts. For days she filled her journal with bitterness about this situation, knowing how vulnerable she was to public opinion with no husband to defend her. The seed was being planted which would open her mind to the idea of leaving Vermont.

Once on the Watts farm, however, Chastina focused her attentions on household activities and settled into a busy routine. It had been a long time since she made pies and doughnuts and bread on "so large a scale." On March 6 she made "nearly thirty" pies. Sewing took up a great deal of her time as she made a "fine shirt for Augustus" and "cut two dresses for the girls." She wrote of "twisting stocking yarn," making a mantilla, and doing "something I never did before, to cover a parasol." After a few weeks, she added that she "sewed some & done some of the forty unnamable things which belong to house hold affairs." On June 1 "we have had a regular New England house cleaning. Consequently I am very tired tonight."

One pleasure which Chastina mentioned often in the journal was reading. She and Alfred had read aloud to each other many evenings and Sundays. When he left, Chastina continued the habit of turning to books and magazines in the evening. Her reading time was "after I retire to bed. I place my candle upon a stand, where there is no danger [of] fire then I read about an hour," with Julian asleep by her side. On a regular basis she received from "the Reading Circle" *The Knickerbocker, Eclectic, Harper's, Sartain's Magazine,* and *American Journal of Science & Arts.* Reading Harriet Beecher Stowe's *Uncle Tom's Cabin* made a deep impression on her. "I hate slavery & always did. This Work although a fiction is calculated well to touch the feelings & enlist ones sympathies for this unfortunate race. A curse upon our country will surely come if men will presist in keeping these poor creatures in such a degraded condition aye & hold there own children in bondage too! It makes my blood burn when I think on it."

Alfred's letters were a tonic for her loneliness and depression. He wrote often, never missing the monthly mail steamer. The Peacham company had taken the Nicaragua route and he had "been sick all the way on the Pacific."

From San Francisco he went to the mines for a few months but had no luck. By April 1 he was back in San Francisco experiencing "sorry times" as "regards money matters. Thousands and thousands are there to catch at every opportunity of making any thing." Like many other disappointed miners, he turned to his former work skills, and in his May 2 letter, which arrived in Vermont on June 5, he wrote "he has the offer of a school . . . about three miles from San Francisco at the Mission Dolores, one of the first settlements of the country." He accepted, took up residence on a farm nearby, and began "taking lessons in Spanish." His wages were $150 a month, quite an increase from his earnings in Vermont.

Soon Alfred led up to inviting Chastina to join him in California. In the journal entry for June 5 she wrote "he thinks he shall stay two years from this month. I do not know about that. He has the offer of a school. . . . Wants me there. I wish I was there with him. But I can never go that journey without him." By June 30 the invitation was clear: "He wishes me to go there to him. He does not say I must come. But 'invites me to come.' "

Several things happened in June t6 help change her mind. Some of the men who had been to California returned to Peacham and their stories portrayed San Francisco as a civilized place. Alfred's own experience reinforced this impression, as Chastina wrote reflectively: "He is well & happy or would be completely so were Julian and I only there."

After she fretted about the situation for weeks, she finally recorded in August: "I may go. Time will tell, I cannot now." She neared a decision while visiting Sarah and John at the Way farm in Hardwick where she was reminded of the pleasures of family life. Finally on October 28, 1852, she wrote simply, "I have made up my mind to go to California as soon as I can go." Other things may have encouraged her decision at this time. Julian was now almost two years old and, after a struggle, had been successfully weaned. There is no mention of toilet training.

As matters turned out, Chastina was not to travel alone. Her sister Clara and Alfred's younger brother, Ira, both twenty-two years old, decided to join her. Following Alfred's directions, Chastina ordered a box from Boston and "put in *my all* that has cost me so many hard days labor—to first *earn* & then to make." In addition to her linens, she placed their journal in the box and sent it off for the voyage around Cape Horn.

On January 17, 1853, fifteen months after Alfred's departure from Vermont, Chastina, Clara, Ira, and Julian "bade adieu to our friends in Peacham . . . with sad hearts and tearful eyes . . . for a long time perhaps forever." Father Watts took them by wagon to Barnet where they caught "the cars" to Springfield and on to New York City where they boarded the steamer.

Chastina wrote three versions of her month-long trip to California. She kept a pocket diary, describing their daily activities in brief entries, and listing all the expenses on the trip in order of payment on a folded page in the back of the diary (her steamer ticket was $305 and, apparently, Julian did not need one). Also, she wrote three letters to her mother in Vermont, one from New York, one aboard ship, and one from San Francisco, describing some of their adventures. Third, once her box bringing their journal arrived in San Francisco, two months after she did, Chastina filled the pages with a detailed summary of the trip, emphasizing in this version her fears and the terrors she experienced, fully aware that Alfred would read these words and possibly appreciate how much she had to "endure" on the trip.

On January 20, they sailed from New York on the *Ohio,* a wooden side-wheel steamer with three decks and four masts and stateroom accommodations for 250 first-cabin passengers and permanent berths for 800 steerage. "Clara began to be sick the first night," Chastina noted in the small diary. For the next eleven days and nights on the Atlantic all of them were seasick off and on. Fortunately she "could sit up & go & vomit" and also take care of Julian. And intermittantly, she was able to appreciate her first experience of the sea: "The little ripples sparkle in the sunlight & look like sheets of silver studded with diamonds. The distant sails look like specks of gold with the sunlight gleaming upon them. Everything looks grand and beautiful. . . . Bubby [Julian's nickname] is charmed at seeing the 'big water' & running round on deck."

Another new experience for Chastina was seeing people of African descent. "We had an excellent dinner & I did justice to my No. at the table. I always had an idea that I could not relish my food when waited on by 'blacks.' But on the contrary, I have not such distaste toward them. I like them; they seem so kind & smart too. They are a fine lot of colored gentlemen. There is one Negro on board who is a passenger. He has been out to California & is on his return with his wife, a very smart looking couple they are not withstanding they wear the real wool on their heads."

A stormy night left her terrified, never having suffered "more with fear. The idea of being engulphed in the mighty sea is a terrible one to me." Another night, hoping to get a breath of air, she opened the window in their stateroom, only to receive "a shower of salt water directly in my face drenching me all over." Her final evaluation of the *Ohio* was that "it is a shame to the United States to send out such a ship, for it is unfit in its present state to accommodate passengers as they should be." She was at least grateful not to be in steerage where the passengers, including Ira Rix, "suffered greatly. . . . They do not get but two meals a day & not half enough of that."

The route was approximately sixty miles across the Isthmus of Panama from the Atlantic to the Pacific Ocean. They traveled by railroad and boat from Aspinwall to Cruces and finally reached the mountainous western part most "dreaded" by women taking this journey. Chastina wrote on February 2: "I had a mule with a side saddle so of course I rode as ladies do. . . . [I] almost got in love with him; he carried me so nicely." The Isthmus had its drawing power. "Such grand & wild scenery as one beholds is enough to make one in love with nature if they never before had a taste for such wildness."

Twelve hours and twenty-four miles later, they arrived at nine o'clock in the city of Panama and found for lodging "a place a most miserable one too at the American Hotel." Later she filled in the details in their journal: "*Such* a room & *such* beds. We took off the sheets for fear of disease. We went to bed and presently we heard such groans & cursing & swearing that it made ones blood chill. It proceeded from an adjoining room with only loose board partition. We tried to sleep in vain. We spoke to a man through the partition & found a man was sick & dying close to our heads. He called it the Panama fever. There was no window in our room & but one door, a stone floor & dark dismal walls. This was the first time I ever felt as though I was really imprisoned. Twas an awful night to us. Before dawn the poor creature had breathed his last. He was a young man from New York on his way to California & had fallen a victim to that pestilence the *Yellow fever—and* we were in the midst of it! We got away from this place as soon as we could in the morning."

Two days later they boarded the *Golden Gate,* which Chastina labeled "a palace compared to the 'Ohio.' " Once more the sea became rough, and they all were sick but, more ominously, they were surrounded by illness. Clara wrote to her mother: "From forty to fifty deaths occurred while on the Golden Gate. Most of them died with the Yellow Fever. . . . I watched [for a family] . . . the mother died one night and the girl the next. I was to have taken care of her the latter part of the night she died, and on awakening thought perhaps I had overslept myself when arose quickly and went to her state room and found three men sewing up the body in sacking ready to be thrown overboard." The Vermont newspaper, *Caledonian,* reported: "The steamer Golden Gate lost 23 of her passengers from yellow fever on her upward trip from Panama."

The trip on the Pacific took fourteen days. At its end Chastina wrote: "Feb. 19, at about six o'clock in the morning I hurried on deck for we were then passing through the 'Golden Gate,' a most beautiful sight. The sea was calm, the sun shining on the green hills, the morning mist & all looked so refreshing. Soon came the booming of the cannon [announcing the steamer's arrival]. Everywhere was bustle & preparation—beating & anxious hearts there were—as we neared the wharf of San Francisco. We are there."

Now the same tale from Alfred's view: "Last Saturday, Feb. 19, a friend tapped me on the shoulder and suggested that the Golden Gate had got into port and had a passenger or two who would be pleased to see me. Of course I clapped on a clean shirt and left. I always expected to feel pretty nice when the folks got here, but as their arrival at this time was rather unexpected I felt so much the better. Now and then Chance, Providence, or Fortune has shown me an acceptable favor, and I have felt thankful for it and happy in its enjoyment, but this safe transfer of my little family from the Eastern to the Western border of the continent is the 'kindest hit of all,' and gives me more satisfaction than anything else I could ask for." In this letter to Roxana, Alfred made "one complaint . . . of Mother and that is that she should let Chastina appear in California in such a shocking bad bonnet."

At first the Rixes and Clara lived at the mission where Alfred taught school, but within two months, they began boarding near the center of San Francisco, just off Kearny Street. "The girls," as Alfred called Chastina and Clara, worked for pay. They took in washing and sewing, and like many other women in the city, added boarders to their household. Chastina took on an order from a local church to cover eighteen dozen buttons on pew pillows, which kept her busy for weeks. Vermont "boys" stopped by on their way to and from the mines, allowing the Rixes and Clara to catch up on home news as well as the activities of Dustan and the others in the gold country. They greeted the monthly mails with excitement, and when a steamer came without a letter from home, Chastina was greatly disappointed.

Daily life in California differed greatly from Vermont. To begin with, Alfred was gone from the house all day—first as a teacher at the mission and later as a lawyer and justice of the peace, a position to which he was elected in the fall of 1853. Chastina was at home with "the work," engaged much more in wage-earning activities than in Vermont. Some weeks she rarely left the house. Occasionally she and Alfred "took a walk up on top of one of the hills in San Francisco" or went to "Tobin's and Duncan's," an auction house for Chinese goods, or "to Cal. St. Wharf & Long Wharf Saw five clippers & Gambling Dens & men fighting." Chastina and Julian visited Alfred's law office once he set up practice on Montgomery Street, and she "did some copying" for him there.

San Francisco was a booming town in the early 1850s with many new cultural and economic projects. Clara and her suitors often went to the "Metropolitan Theater," and even Chastina and Alfred "saw Hamlet played by Mr. Murdock." One evening in spring 1854, Chastina and Alfred "went to the Musical Hall to hear a lecture from Mr Winslow on 'The Preparation of the earth for the intelectual races.' " Chastina found it "a very scientific lecture, therefore good & interesting But it was hardly suited to the people of San Francisco." Alfred attended a meeting on the "great Pacific rail way," and he recorded in their journal the first telegraph service from San Francisco to San Jose. They went to an agricultural fair and described vegetables as "large as a mans leg."

Alfred's law practice was successful, although he did not describe his cases in the journal as he had in Vermont where Chastina knew all the characters. Soon the journal stopped. They were increasingly busy and their daily routines became more separate. In an urban center with close to fifty thousand people, their lives overlapped only at home.

They did not continue their Vermont pattern of attending meeting on Sunday. Chastina wrote that you had to be rich to be a churchgoer in California because those who attended wore expensive clothes. She and Alfred still recognized the day of rest on Sundays, although sometimes they recorded the fun they were missing by not breaking the Sabbath. Picking up their old habit of reading aloud, they were engaged by Dickens's *Bleak House* for several weeks.

In 1854 Alfred bought land on the north side of Market Street, between Kearny and Montgomery, and at the end of the year, they built a two-story frame house with a front porch and second-floor balcony. Chastina wrote with pride about "our house," and she had Dustan, who had abandoned the gold mines, draw the layout of the first floor both inside and out for Roxana. The backyard especially "is perfect—You see we women have a

Rix house on north side of
Market Street, between
Kearny and Montgomery,
San Francisco, 1855.
Daguerreotype at Oakland
Museum. Print, courtesy
California Historical Society.
Chastina Walbridge Rix and
Alfred Rix on left side of
porch; Oscar Rix on right
side; Dustan Walbridge,
Clara Walbridge, Hale Rix,
and Alice Locke Rix on
balcony. Julian and dog on
wooden sidewalk with
Edward in carriage made by
Dustan.

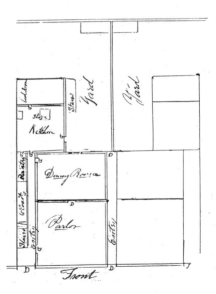

Dustan Walbridge's drawing
of the layout of the first floor
of Chastina's house on
Market Street, 1855.

good chance to 'gab' when we wish. Mrs. Plummer & Mrs Dagget come down the back stairs from their kitchens & I come out of my kitchen under the stairs."

A second son, Edward, was born on January 29, 1855, shortly after they moved into their new home and had discontinued their journal. Within a year Chastina was stricken with "her nervous disorder." She was sick off and on for a year and became bedridden the last weeks of her life. Roxana described "the particulars," as was the custom, to her granddaughter, Augusta, as follows: Chastina "was taken sick January 21 1857 her complaint was such as frequently happens to married women, she felt rather delicate about making it known, and I suppose she took cold and did not have the proper treatment that she should have had in the proper time, and her old billious complaint set in and she suffered very much from her stomach and Liver, but her Physician thought she would soon get up and they did not apprehend any danger untill the morning before she died, when there was a change came over her and the mortification set in and she died at half past 11 oclock that night February 23. She had her senses until a few hours before she died. She talked with her husband. She told him she was not afraid to die, but she wanted to live yet. Poor dear girl. She had a great deal to attach her to [life] with a kind husband two lovely boys and everything around her for her comfort so far as the good things of this life are concerned, but Oh it all could not stay the hand of death. She was called and she must obey the summons and be torn from all that she held dear on earth, and enter the untried realities of death. Her death was so unexpected that it fell on the hearts of her friends like an Electric shock. Clara took home her children to take care of while she was sick and consequently was not with her but little during her sickness."

Julian, now six and a half, returned to Vermont. Two-year-old Edward remained in California and was raised by his aunt Clara. Alfred continued his successful law practice in San Francisco and was appointed police judge in 1866. A year and a half after Chastina's death, he remarried.

Long afterward, three years before his death in 1904, Alfred wrote to his granddaughter about the importance of choosing the right husband. "If you read that old record of your grandparents' early life you will learn that it was a happy one, and just here I desire to impress on you that it was mainly due to the simple fact that we knew each other thoroughly—not only each others excellencies but also their defects and this had the means of meeting the mutual demands. Till now I have never had the opportunity to say what I have always wished to say to my progeny, to wit: that from the beginning to the end of our mutual life there never occurred between your angel grandmother and myself one single word or look or act not wholly harmonious and affectionate." Of Chastina he wrote: "She was a genuine lady—in the highest sense of that term." Although the passing years may have allowed Alfred to romanticize their relationship, their journal, written with an openness unusual for the period, reveals that they had a deep love and respect for each other.

Clarissa Walbridge Rogers (1830–1917)

The Yankee Schoolteacher Who Crossed the Isthmus in Bloomers

IN A region and at a time when household and farm tasks were rigidly assigned according to gender, the arrival of a fourth daughter in 1830 cannot have been viewed with complete joy by Roxana and Daniel Walbridge. Who would do the barn work? Who would help with the planting, the haying, the sugaring, the hauling of logs in the winter? Whatever her parents' feelings were, the child took her place in the family, and they named her, rather elegantly, Clarissa—soon shortened to Clara.

As the fourth daughter, Clara had a full supply of role models and she knew early what was expected of her. Her first "work," mentioned in one of Roxana's 1843 letters to her oldest daughter, Martha, was "to tend Baby," meaning Isaac, born the previous year. Roxana added, "Clarrissa is allmost as large as either of the other girls." The next summer, when both daughters, Chastina and Sarah, were working away from the Watts farm, Roxana announced that "Clarrissa is at home with me and she and I make out to get along with our work." At fourteen, Clara was her mother's only helper and had become skilled in all aspects of household work. By the end of September 1844, Roxana wrote, "Clarrissa and I have got along with our house work and some spinning we have made between 4 and 5 hundred pounds of butter and a hundred and 50 of Chese." Roxana seldom mentioned that in addition to the housework, she and Clara had to take care of the five boys, ages three to twelve. Clara learned child care skills that would prove useful throughout her life.

Early on Clara showed signs of being a scholar, and after attending the district school, she registered at sixteen at Peacham Academy. The following year, she began a ten-year teaching career. Chastina reported to her brother-in-law Hubbell in August 1847 that "Clarrissa is teaching this summer about four miles from home," on Penny Street, and when Clara's school term was over, Chastina summed it up: "She had very good success." At Thanksgiving that fall, Clara wrote with pride to Sarah working in the mills at Lowell, "I arrived home last evening from Cow Hill [the area around Penny Street in the western part of Peacham] where I am acting as *teacher* over some sixteen or eighteen young urchins, although some are not so very young either, say from 4 to 18, and that you know is pretty near up to my own age. I have kept a week and three days, I have one dollar and 25 cents a week for 4 months if I can stay as long as that, but sometimes I think that I cannot stay up there so long. I board at Mr R Craigs, It is but a short distance from the little *Knowledge box* as [cousin] Chester calls it. Mary Johnson had some difficulty in the school and she left and I took her place."

Mary Johnson was not the only teacher who had difficulty. Earlier Chastina reported on the local schoolmaster on East Hill: "Mr Joshua Gilfilen keeps our school three weeks, but he was taken with a very serious sickness and left his school his sickness was as every one though[t] because of his learning was not sufficient to keep the school for he recovered very quick after he went home."

The school on Penny Street, where Clara proved herself a competent teacher that fall 1847, became one of her favorite memories. Six years later in a letter from San Francisco, Clara sent her "love to all the folks on Penny street. . . . tell my scholars if you see any of them that although I am not there in *person* I often in *imagination* think I am still mistress of that little school room."

School teaching in those years was not as romantic as modern readers have been led to believe. In one-room schoolhouses the emphasis should be placed less on the "one room" and more on the "one teacher," who was expected to instruct "scholars" from age four or five to almost twenty. Keeping order under such conditions was not easy, and discipline problems often disrupted the whole class. But seventeen-year-old Clara was taller than either Chastina or Sarah and must have had a physical presence that was an asset in the classroom. Chastina wrote from her teaching assignment in Topsham: "Tell Clarissa I wish she had about a score of my little rogues. I doubt some whether *her eyes* could look them into good behavior."

Teachers had more to do than instruct the "scholars," as students were called then. In winter the wood stove needed constant stoking; in summer there was stifling heat. No matter what the season, however, teaching ABC's and numbers was the main job at hand. As to living conditions teachers most often "boarded about," sleeping and eating at one or another of the scholar's houses, moving from one household to another nearly every week. In the small houses, everyone lived in close proximity, often sharing beds with comparative strangers (of the same sex, of course) and all shared one privy. Standards of cleanliness probably varied as much as the food on the table.

Women began to teach school in Vermont at the beginning of the nineteenth century. At first they were assigned to summer schools where the students were mainly girls and young boys, since older boys were busy in the fields. Gradually women began to teach during the regular school year, especially in districts that did not want to meet the higher wage-scale male teachers commanded. According to the state's first school statistics, by 1844 the majority of Vermont teachers were female, and teaching became classified as "women's work." A quarter of all New England–born women taught school sometime in their lives between 1825 and 1860.

The work load could be heavy. Chastina described it well in letters written in the summer of 1847 when she was employed in a school "about 17 miles from home" in Topsham. "In all I have had 54 scholars, the oldest about fifteen the youngest three. However, forty is my general number. Now I can assure you there is some worke in even trying to take care of all these, without any thing else to do. I have Arithmetic Grammar History 4 kinds of Geography, besides numerous spelling book lessons, seven classes in reading, & the same number in spelling. You will not wonder then that I do not get through until nearly one in forenoon, & five in afternoon. . . . My school is very noisy, & tis impossible for *me* to keep them still. Sometimes I have some less than half a dozen sitting on the floor, around me, when I am hearing lessons, so to keep them as still as possible. However I like [the school] very well & have had no trouble that's serious."

Until 1845 Vermont teachers were not certified, and even after the state law required examination by school superintendents, many uncertified teachers continued to hold jobs. Both Chastina and Clara were examined for teaching in Caledonia County. It is unclear what rules of reciprocity prevailed at the time, but there was evidently no obstacle to the nineteen-year-old Clara teaching at Batavia, New York (where her father's younger sister lived with her family) the summer after attending school there for a term. The next year she went to teach in Littleton, New Hampshire, a job that Chastina's new husband, Alfred Rix, helped arrange. He had grown up in that area, and as principal of Peacham Academy, his recommendation carried weight. Like most women in the classroom at that time, Clara received two dollars a week as wages. In 1851, however, when (as Chastina reported in her diary) "Mr. Bickford of Cabot came to hire Clara to keep school," Clara asked for ten dollars a month. "After much talk he agreed . . . if she did well."

Chastina knew of this because Clara was staying at the Corner with her for a few days. Alfred had gone to California in October 1851, leaving his wife and son in Peacham. The Walbridges and Wattses took turns visiting Chastina; Clara in particular often staying a few days each week. She assisted with baby Julian, gave a helping hand on wash days, and tried to keep Chastina from spending every minute worrying about Alfred. During this time together, the two sisters began to rely on each other in ways that would last until Chastina's death. For pleasure they read the magazines and books borrowed from "the Reading Circle," an arrangement similar to present-day libraries although the reading material was delivered to the homes—presumably by the previous reader. In 1852, reading in turn, they agonized over *Uncle Tom's Cabin,* which was at the peak of popularity, having sold over half a million copies. They discussed their hatred for slavery with such fervor one night while visiting on East Hill that Father Watts had to scold them "because we disturbed him."

Among their other shared interests, Chastina and Clara were fashion conscious. In 1847 Clara at seventeen and Chastina at twenty-three requested Sarah, working in Lowell where there were many shops, to purchase for them "something fashionable & pretty" to wear "over their cloaks and around their necks . . . [we] tried to find something here at the stores but cant get anything. . . . We send you two dollars to get them. [Clara] says she cant afford to pay more than that. . . . Dont get cheated now." The significant fact here is that the sisters had their own money from teaching and were willing to pay a week's salary for a scarf!

Although in 1852 it had taken Chastina six months to decide to go to California to join her husband, Clara made up her mind within a few days of hearing of Alfred's proposal to have her accompany Chastina on the trip. And it was on that trip that major differences in the two young women began to emerge. Crossing the Isthmus of Panama, Clara donned bloomers and "rode astride" a mule using a Spanish saddle, while her more ladylike older sister stuck to her skirts and rode side-saddle. Clara explained, "Many [women] were so modest that they preferred side saddles, but I thought of the safety of the thing rather than the looks. . . . the road some of the way was so muddy that my dress and feet would drag right through the mud even though I tried to avoid it as much as possible and where there was no mud there were rocks and stones and places where it did not seem possible to get along, but let the mule take its own course and it will be sure and bring you out right side up."

Roxana described Clara's financial condition at the end of the trip: "It cost the girls about 9 hundred dollars to go and it will take some time for clara to earn four hundred and fifty dollars [for the return trip] and take care of herself beside." And Alfred described Clara's physical condition upon arrival in San Francisco: "as plump and gay as one could possibly expect. Clara has of course lost flesh, but is otherwise perfectly well. She went to church with me this morning and I could not help thinking she is a very pretty young lady. She is at this moment entertained by an excellent Spanish family [for a few weeks the Rixes boarded near the mission]—she's bound to be a favorite."

Six years younger and not so committed to domestic perfection as Chastina, Clara became a source of frustration to Chastina when the family set up its own home. Chastina wrote in her journal on July 28, 1853: "Clara tells me she does not take any comfort living with me, I find so much fault with her. If I am all wrong I am sorry for it. I own that I have talked pretty plain *but* I have said to her this morning 'here is an end to those things. You may rise when you please & do as pleases you. I will say no more.' " Earlier Clara had explained in a letter to her brothers and sisters in Peacham her philosophy about cooking and its consequences: "I do wish I could have some new sugar—C. [Chastina] and I would get along very well in our cooking could we have your [Roxana's] store house to go to, but I have such extravagant notions in my head that she does not think it best that I should do much of the cooking, for if I can find an egg or a little cream on the top of our *quart* of milk I *will* put it in, and this you know cannot always be afforded by poor people." No doubt it was Chastina who defined her family as "poor," although by standards of the time, they must have been thought comfortable. Chastina was simply more frugal than Clara.

Unencumbered by marriage or motherhood, Clara soon began to look for a teaching job. By that time Alfred had decided to leave education for a full-time law practice so he recommended Clara for his teaching position at the mission. Successful in her application, Clara was offered $100 a month, the usual reduction by one-third for a woman teacher from the $150 Alfred earned. Clara wrote to Peacham "[School] is somewhat different from schools in which I have formerly taught on account of its being composed of Spanish children mostly, still I find no serious difficulty." The pupils— and there were forty-one in total—may not have been difficult, but the transport to and from school was another matter. The road from the city to the mission was often flooded during the rainy season, so Clara boarded near her school for a while. Once the new plank road (now Mission Street) was completed in November 1853, Clara returned to the comfort of the Rixes most weeks. Like Alfred before her, she started Spanish lessons.

At the end of the term in December 1853, Alfred wrote to the Watts farm: "[Clara] is about to leave her Mission School and take her place in one of the larger schools in town." During the year both Alfred and Clara attended "the Teacher's Monthly Conventions" and occasional social events for teachers. On March 5, 1854, the Rix journal says, "Clara is at her school yet & makes about fifty dollars a month clear of all expenses," so she was able to save about half her salary. By 1855 Clara is listed in the newspaper again as "the teacher of the Mission School" and has "34 boys and 28 girls." She must have progressed well with her Spanish.

For the next few years Roxana's letters to Hubbell indicated that she hoped to see Clara and her younger brother, Dustan, return to Vermont. This hope may have been fueled by Clara who wrote enthusiastically about California but always added a phrase to temper her comments. "As far as I am concerned I like [California] quite as well as I anticipated for I did not, like some imagine it a Paradise. . . . I like the climate here very well; although we are having very heavy rains about these times which is not very *agreeable*. We are of course deprived of many privileges, and some of the *comforts* of life we can enjoy at home [Vermont] yet we have plenty to make us *comfortable* here and I cannot say that I regret the step I have taken, although it may not be for the best." Here was a balanced assessment of California—both good and bad.

For more than three years Clara lived in San Francisco with the Rixes in quarters they had rented on Geary Street "3 Doors above Kearny," paying them eight dollars a month rent. At first she slept "on a *bunk, cot* or whatever you call it in the dining room It is separated by a curtain from the rest of the room." Gradually they must have taken over more rooms of the "large two story white house," for in December 1853, Alfred wrote in their journal, "all went a shopping & purchased a work stand for Clara's Room." In January 1855, they moved to their newly built home on the north side of Market Street between Kearny and Montgomery where Clara had her own room "on the 2nd floor . . . in front 12 X 12 with casement opening upon the piazza." Alfred wrote Roxana that "Clara's room [is] a perfect beauty," although "she is now boarding at the mission, but comes home once a week or so."

Clara had never suffered for lack of suitors. From Peacham in 1846, when Clara was sixteen, Chastina wrote to Martha in Michigan: "I supose you would like to know whether Sally or Clarrissa has any beaux or not. none that I know of in particular, though there is a young Blanchard that walks home with Clarrissa whenever she goes out and comes home so he can wait on her though there is nothing in it I supose." A year later, Chastina wrote to Sarah, "Clarissa has just come in after 11 o'clock—been out to a bee." Earlier in the letter she had described "the present rage [of] 'Pareing bees,' 'apple pareings,' 'apple bees,' and all such kind of things that are amusing & delightful to attend. last friday night I attended an 'apple pareing' at Mr Franklin Varnums. We had a delightful time Such an assembly of *fine young gentlemen* are not to be met with every day. . . . We pared about twelve bushels, about thirty there. . . . Thus you see the young people have enough to employ themselves about evenings." Clara herself noted later in the year, "I have not heard as there is any thing going on to *day* but I should think that there was a party this *evening* [at the neighbors] by the way the *beaus* are riding *by* our house (but not one has called)." Social life in Peacham picked up in the fall when there was a slack in the field work.

Once in California, where the ratio of men to women was six to one, there was a line of suitors at Clara's door. Only three months after her arrival, Clara wrote to her brothers and sisters in Peacham: "I like the climate and country here very well indeed, but one must be possessed of considerable *change* in order to enjoy it, for you of course cannot walk out much, on account of the wind and sand, and teams are very expensive here. If it was not for the kindness of a few *young men* we should not have many rides. I went last week down to the old *fort,* and coast We found plenty of strawberries. I sat on my horse while my *gallant* picked strawberries for me to eat! By the way I did not want to go with *him* but could not well avoid it, however we had a very pleasant ride we went about fourteen miles and I was so lame the next day I could scarcely walk."

It is difficult to compare courtship in rural Vermont to that of urban San Francisco because Clara was younger in Vermont, and the group outings she attended such as bees and parties would have been appropriate entertainment for her age. Once in California, being older and more experienced with social situations, she often went to events with only her male escort. This was not unusual, as young Americans had traditionally enjoyed unsupervised activities. Beginning in the second half of the nineteenth century, however, middle-class families, especially in the Eastern cities, began to require adult supervision for their unmarried daughters. There is no indication that the Walbridge-Watts family had ever heard of this idea of chaperons for there is no mention of them.

On New Year's Day, 1854, at least eight men called at the Rixes and were served "cake and wine," which Chastina wrote in their journal was "the *fashion* in San Francisco." Other times Clara was "at the theater," "out sailing" or "out riding," and "not yet home." Certainly all "the boys" from Peacham, going either to the mines or returning for the next steamer, stopped by the Rixes. Some must have been calling on Clara, and two or three visited every day the week before catching the ship back east. In February 1855, Chastina wrote her family that Clara "dont care for any one that I know of."

Among the special social events that both Clara and Chastina enjoyed were the Pickwick Assemblies, public dances for which the sisters made new dresses and learned to dance. They also enjoyed themselves at dances and parties given at the Spanish colony around Mission Dolores. Having lived in the area and taught at the mission school, Clara and the Rixes were well known to the Spanish-speaking settlers. On January 3, 1854, Chastina described in her journal a party they all attended: "This evening we are invited to a ball at the mission. Donna Carmel gives the ball in honor of her new house She is a rich Spanish lady. So at seven P.M. Alfred, Clara & I put on our *fix up* & went out in the *Buss.* We had a perfect jam most of the ladies spanish. Clara & I got upon the floor twice each as for our dancing that remains for the spectators to relate. Suffice it to say 'we didnt get home till morning.' " Next month, they returned to the mission for "a ball on the eve of Washington's birth day." Chastina wrote they "had a very good time," and again they did not come home until morning. The commitment Clara and Alfred made to learning Spanish opened the doors of hospitality between these Yankees and the Spanish families at the mission, an inter-cultural relationship unusual at that time.

A year after Clara was settled in San Francisco, her mother wrote asking if she "would advise Margaret Blanchard to come here [California] or not." Clara replied, "I do not know whether it would be a good idea or not—If she would like to be *married* I presume she would have numerous *offers,* but many girls who are married here, are married to anything but *men*—they wear the *human form* to be sure but one is obliged to run the risk of *character* unless they knew them before, or have evidence here of their moral conduct." She added a common theme among young women of the time: "[California] is yet a good place to make money but a still *better* place to spend it."

Clara Walbridge, San Francisco, dressed for Pickwick Assembly, 1854. Ambrotype, courtesy Choate Farm Collection.

Clara purchased fine cloth for dresses and cloaks with her teaching money. Her letters are filled with descriptions of clothes she and Chastina were making. In May 1854, she described to Roxana their latest project: "We have just made us some black velvet capes to wear over us They are large and cut a half round—with collars pointed and a *tussel* on the end of the point. I presume you have seen them cut the same fashion. I do not dare to tell you how much they cost for fear you will think us *extravagant* but they will last a long time and it is so cold here that they are worn the year round." Bonnets were another item Clara regularly described to her mother: "You wanted to know whether I had a new bonnet or not. I have, it is white shirred satin with white plume and face-flowers. the price was fourteen and a half dollars. It distressed me very much to pay so much for it but I could do no better, and I had got to stay at home from the school picnic on *may* day or have a new bonnet, for my old one was so dirty I would not wear it." This attention to fashion reflected the adoption by Clara, and to a lesser extent Chastina, of urban life styles where wages were spent primarily by the wage-earner rather than contributed to the family as would have been expected in Vermont farm life. Individual interests were replacing Roxana's communal values. A move toward secularization and materialism had begun.

Clara married on August 9, 1856, at age twenty-six. Her mother learned about the marriage from a San Francisco newspaper article sent her with no note attached. "Mr. Russell Rogers married Miss Clarissa B. Walbridge at Alfred Rixes." Roxana wrote her granddaughter Augusta, "They have never given me the least hint of it . . . Rogers went from this place [Peacham] we were well acquainted with him he was Clerk in I Watts [Lyman's brother] store 4 or 5 years he has been in California 5 or 6 years and for the last 3 years he has been at the same City where the girls are." No doubt Roxana was hurt, having received no personal letter, but ever the optimist, she added, "[They] have not written to me since I dont know what to think of it unless they are coming home soon as I always have told them I did not want them to let me know when they were on their way as I should worry so much about them."

There is little known about Russell K. Rogers. As a caller listed by the Rixes in their journal, they always spelled his name as Rodgers. His first call is noted on July 2, 1853, followed by five more visits that month, and in September he called twice, followed by single visits in October, November, and December. By February 1855, he was part of the group that Chastina reported on when writing east. To her family she wrote that Russell had a team and was "doing first-rate."

Unlike Clara, he was not a scholar. The one surviving letter written by him is void of punctuation and does not identify the receiver. It was dated June 23, 1852, from Placerville, El Dorado County, where he was working and explained: "I have been mining seven days made five dollars a day shall stay here about mounth and then go on to the river twenty or thirty miles from here I like mining as well as any work I coud do it is hard enough but it gives me a good apitite and I feel as well as I ever did . . . [there is] any quantaty of Vermonters round here."

Two weeks after moving into their new San Francisco house, Clara wrote Sarah: "Our house is situated on Pine St. *high up* on a sand hill but when one has once safely landed there they can have a fine view of the Bay, Mission and a large part of the City. We have five rooms in the house, besides various closets, cupboards, &c. two rooms, a kitchen and dining room below, and a parlor & two bedrooms above. When the street is graded we shall have a parlor finished below. Our parlor furniture chairs, sofa and easy chair is covered with hair cloth, the other furniture is similar to that you had when you went to keeping house. The rooms are all carpeted, the parlor with Brussels—very pretty I think—I will mention what few articles of silver I had, and the price that you may see how much more we have to give for things in California than home. 2 table Spoons 2 dessert, and 1 Doz. tea spoons a butter knife and sugar shovel—cost fifty dollars—so you see poor folks can't have a great quantity here. I have 6 tablecloths 1 Doz napkins, 1 and ½ Doz. towels, 6 pr of sheets and 10 pr. of pillow cases. I made three tacks [mattresses] and bought 2 Marseilles quilts one of my bed is a single bed, because the room is so small it would not hold a double bed. . . . Last night some one was kind enough to take eight, out of our flock of ten hens, and to day Russell is building a new hen house, where *thieves can not break through nor steal.* I am cooking a Shanghai rooster to day, and it reminds me of the one I cooked for you in Hardwick once—I commenced boiling it yesterday, and I think the delicious odor must have attracted the thieves to the hen-house."

The birth, seven months after the wedding, of a daughter named Nellie, explains the quick marriage. The date, March 31, 1857, is missing from the letters because the tragedy of Chastina's death in February 1857 became the focus of all letters. With Chastina ill, Clara and Russell temporarily took in her two sons, Julian and Edward. In June, Julian returned to Vermont. Two-year-old Edward remained permanently with Clara.

Meanwhile, Clara's health was poor. She "had a long confinement" and "could not nurse her babe," Roxana explained in a letter to her grand-

Clara Walbridge Rogers, ca. 1865. Photograph taken by Edward Cobb, San Francisco. Courtesy Choate Farm Collection.

daughter. "They tried to bring it [Nellie] up with Cows milk but it was sick all the time and when it was 5 months old it did not weigh but 8 pounds. They thought it could not live but a few hours when they got a nurse and put it to the Breast and it soon began to revive . . . they have to pay their Nurse 40 dollars per Month and she does nothing else." Clara wrote sadly to Augusta in 1858, "I am very lonely since Chastina died although little Eddie her youngest boy, and my own little Nellie requires much of my time and attention." Now Clara had no immediate relatives in California.

In 1858 the Rogers family moved to Petaluma, thirty-seven miles northwest of San Francisco, where Clara explained to Augusta "we keep cows and make butter but do not cultivate much land—as it is better adapted to grazing where we live—Our home is quite small, only three rooms and we live in regular country style." One February day in 1859 Clara wrote again to Augusta, "We have been having a regular California *rain storm*. it is exceedingly *muddy* and he [Eddie] has amused himself today out of doors *digging worms* for the chickens, is as animated as though he were digging *gold*." Clara missed city life and to use the family word was not "content" in Petaluma. She added to the same letter: "With the blessing of Providence, I hope [we] will not be [here] many years. I do not like it here so well as in the City—we have so little society—Our neighbors are not very distant, but like myself are confined at home with little children." Clara and Russell had five children (two of whom died young), plus Edward to raise. "My life and interest has been at home with my children," she wrote years later.

Russell struggled to support his family. From Petaluma the family returned in 1860 to the outskirts of San Francisco. Their children attended the mission grammar school where Clara had taught only four years before. In early 1863 she described their situation: "We live . . . for the past three years . . . on a milk ranch Mr. Rogers has been to town every day with milk, for over three years—we keep one hired man—and have three children Eddie (Chastina's boy) and our two girls [their son had not yet been born]—So you see I have quite a family to take care of."

Five years later they left the ranch and "now live at the Mission in a small cottage. We have a pleasant little place, convenient to school, church, and the cars, when we want to go to town, and I do not have so much hard work to do as I did, so that I enjoy myself much better. . . . Russell still continues his business he keeps two men now, one to drive, another to milk a few cows."

Guarded optimism mixed with concern about Russell's ability to earn a living shaped family comments through the years. Alfred wrote in 1860 to

Roxana that he saw no reason why Russell should not succeed. Two years later when Clara's brother Augustus went to California, he reported, "I think Russ is doing very well now. I heard him say he thought he had cleared about $200 the last month. There is a family boarding with them now and probably will all summer . . . Clara has to keep a girl on their account, but they probably get well paid for their trouble." But the most revealing evaluation of Clara's life with Russell came from Dustan in a letter to Alice dated spring 1864: "Russell dont use her right." These few clues are all that is available. Through the years, Russell was a store clerk, miner, drayman, farmer, and dairyman, but never a success.

Almost ten years after Roxana's death, the Rogers family and Edward Rix visited Peacham in the summer of 1871. The transcontinental railroad had been completed, and Edward had graduated from the esteemed San Francisco Boys High School. In the fall he was to enter the University of California at Berkeley to become a member of their first class in mechanical engineering. The entourage stopped at Northfield, Minnesota, to see Sarah and John Way and near Milwaukee, where they spent a day with Augusta Gregory Mills and her family. (On the return trip they went to Monticello, Illinois, to visit Charles and Lodoska Watts.) After a quick stop at Niagara Falls, they arrived in Vermont, where they first stayed with Russell's mother in Boltonville. A few days later they took a buggy north to Peacham where they were met by Father Watts, Lyman, Isaac, Alice, and Ella. Edward kept a journal of the trip mainly for Julian who had returned to San Francisco three years earlier. He carefully recorded the number of miles traveled—7,520 miles on eleven different railroads—but unfortunately wrote little about the relatives he was meeting for the first time. Able to go off to Wolcott, Cabot, and Canada for visits, Clara enjoyed the trip. But Peacham without Roxana must have seemed bitter-sweet to her.

No letters survive dealing with Russell Rogers's death in October 1886, at age fifty-nine, so Clara's reactions and feelings are unknown. Ten years later, Clara warned her niece Augusta, "A mothers anxiety is not at rest, I know, when her children are grown, and especially is it the case with me." She went on to describe "the small house on our lot" she had built in the Mission district for her youngest child, Harry, and his family. His wife "does not really know that she ought to economize . . . and she is not at all domestic buys most of their food at the bakers and takes life easy as possible. . . . I never saw a woman who was so little interested in *home* . . . and I don't know what the children would do were it not for us to help them." At sixty-six Clara had become as "particular" about housework as Chastina had been and, ever the teacher, was now helping with the upbringing of her grandchildren.

The Spanish-American War brought a strong response from Clara in 1898: "Isn't this a terrible war? I suppose you do not hear so much about it as we do, being where there are so many soldiers encamped. They are only a short distance from us being near the park and the family with the exception of myself often go there, and usually take something for them to eat I have fried doughnuts and they have carried cake bread, fruit &c to them of course when they get settled they do not care so much for their food, but after their long journey they are tired and hungry but the ladies have been very kind—Several have died, and a great many are sick, measles and pneumonia have been very prevalent.

"At this time of year it is foggy and windy, and of course there was no good place for so many where the sewers would carry of[f] the refuse and there has been some fever & diptheria but the serious cases have been sent to hospitals and had the best of care, and those who have died were buried with military honors at the Presidio. . . . I don't like to see so many young very young men ready to enlist in such a hazardous undertaking even if they are not killed in battle many will die from the change of climate and I know many would be glad to get home again—"

No one living in San Francisco in 1906 experienced the earthquake and fire without feeling its effects. Clara's oldest daughter, Nellie, wrote to her "Aunt Sarah and Uncle John" in Minnesota that "it was wonderful how Mother [Clara] stood it all She was calm through it all but suffered from cold for a couple of months before we could get the chimney repaired & inspected." On the morning of April 18, Nellie, living a short distance away from Clara, found "the house began to shake" and "dishes & ornaments began falling around . . . like a ship at sea in a gale. . . . we spent the rest of the day on the hill watching our dear old city go to ruin. . . . At night we bunked on the floor The yard & [my] porch were full of refugees, some had saved nothing, but most had bedding & they were camped down anyway. It was so hot & the fire coming near & nearer The ashes & cinders fell like rain & covered [my] flowers & garden inch thick. It was as light as day." Fortunately the fire was stopped four blocks from Clara's house. At the time Edward Rix and his family lived on Russian Hill where they "dug a big pit & put in all their valuables [including his parents' journal] & then left the city, but their home was safe too, tho but seven houses on the top of the hill were left." Nellie continued: "Bricks were plenty everyones chimney had fallen & all quickly made little camp stoves & went to cooking . . . [I]

Clara Walbridge Rogers in her living room. San Francisco, ca. 1890. Courtesy California Historical Society.

cooked out on the bricks for five weeks before gas was put on again." Once again Clara had reason to suffer from the wind and dampness in San Francisco. From her windows she looked out at the fog, and she had no means to warm the inside of her house either.

In the same letter written four months after the earthquake, daughter Nellie wrote: "I have just been up to Mothers & found them sitting around the parlor contemplating a new carpet. Mother grows more feeble in walking about, but keeps up busy at something all day long . . . a cousin schoolteacher is boarding there." How Clara must have enjoyed comparing stories of her own teaching experience fifty years before with the young school teacher!

Clara lived a long life, dying in 1917 at age eighty-seven. She merited an obituary in the *San Francisco Chronicle* of two paragraphs including the words "native of Vermont," but there was no mention of her teaching career.

Two contrasting photographs of Clara reveal much about her life. One taken in the mid-1850s shows a portrait of a lovely young lady at the height of her beauty, dressed in a black dress draped off the shoulders, which she and Chastina had made. The second was taken about forty years later, in her San Francisco living room. She is seated in a Mission-style chair next to a large brick fireplace with Indian baskets on the mantle. Her hair has turned completely white, and her face is wise and content. The Yankee school-teacher had become a Californian, surrounded by Western artifacts.

TO AND FRO

ROXANA'S GRANDSON, Julian Walbridge Rix, crossed the Panama Isthmus three times before he was eighteen years old. From then until his death in 1903, he crossed the country at least three additional times by railroad. There are few primary sources describing the lives of small children who went to California in the 1850s. Some, like their parents, returned to their native states and told stories of their early life in California. Many were raised in the West, some making notable contributions to their communities, often attributing their ambition, fortitude, and work ethic to their New England pioneer parents. A few became bicoastal and traveled back and forth for business as well as pleasure.

Julian spent a total of seventeen years in California. For the last twenty-two years of his life, however, his address was Paterson, New Jersey, where he maintained a studio near the art market of New York City. Like many painters of the West, most notably Albert Bierstadt on whom Julian may have fashioned his life, he crossed the country to San Francisco, using his former home town as a base as he camped up and down the Pacific coast, inland up the Sacramento River and on to Yosemite, sketching from nature.

Julian retained his Vermont accent throughout his life, and whenever people met him—in California, New York, or Europe—they were aware of his birthplace.

Julian Walbridge Rix (1850–1903)

The Artist

BY THE middle of the nineteenth century, child-rearing practices had begun to change from strict discipline and molding of children to gentle guidance accompanied by a sentimental image of children's innocence and purity. The role of parents became one of protecting children from bodily injury, temptation, and worldly contamination and encouraging their natural intelligence, sensitivity, and creativity. Into this new world was born in Peacham on December 30, 1850, Julian, first child of Alfred and Chastina Walbridge Rix and fifth grandchild of Roxana. As in many New England families, the first-born son became Bub or Bubby, a nickname used for Julian until he went to school.

Julian's mother and grandmother had been born in farmhouses where routine chores were performed by children beginning at an early age. There was little thought given to allowing the expression of a child's free spirit when stove wood needed carrying, lambs needed water and food, cows needed milking and pasturing, and fields and gardens needed tending. Unlike his mother and grandmother, Julian was born in a village in what today is called a second-floor apartment. His mother's full-time energies were devoted to meeting his needs, and his father, beginning his law practice, was able to drop into the household to see Bub throughout the day.

Baby Julian's parents recorded his daily activities in their journal. He "grows like a weed and makes all stir," his father wrote on January 19, 1851, three weeks after his birth. A week later Alfred reported: "Our little 'responsibility' has come on at the uniform rate of 1 pound a week—7 lbs. to begin with—now 4 weeks & 11 lbs." Later he wrote: "We have pretty good times with our boy—only I have to spend a little too much time with him to the evident neglect of some of my older clients."

From the baby's birth until early March, Chastina had not written in their journal, but finally she took up her pen: "I am busy all day & accomplish but very little. The little Julian is quite cross & grows so fast that it tires me all out to take care of him." On March 16 Alfred wrote: "Playing with Baby. By the way, the Boy is growing old so fast that we can scarcely keep track of him. He began about the middle of last week to know folks so as to laugh & play—he is now giggling like a clown. He kicks his father & strikes his mother & makes mustard paste by the acre."

When Julian had a boil on his buttock, the "Doctor called to see him." At six months he "has got the chicken pox on him—most horribly—broke out in forty thousand blotches." This was such a hard time that Grandmother Roxana came to help.

This recounting shows that Julian was a well-loved baby, bringing both joy and concern to his parents. Very few parents have left a daily account of the growth of a child. From this period only the child-rearing practices of Bronson and Abigail Alcott are well known. In 1831 their daughter Anna was born in Germantown, Pennsylvania, and Alcott began his "Observations on the Phenomena of Life, as Developed in the Progressive History of an Infant, during the First Year of its Existence." Alcott did not stop at the end of the first year, however, but continued this record for at least five years at which point the manuscript filled nearly 2,500 pages. Chastina and Alfred's journal does not compete with Alcott's detailed account, but their comments imply a great deal about child rearing in midcentury New England when urbanization and professionalism were on the rise, bringing middle-class values to parents who had themselves been raised in a rural lifestyle.

The journal indicates that Alfred took care of the baby—once when Chastina went to church and another time when she was busy on wash day. But the primary care, as expected in nineteenth-century New England, came from Chastina.

At about six months, Julian began to show his independence. He went from a "pretty good boy" to a "little Scamp," "full of fun & pranks," learning "some new roguery every day." For one thing he "tore his mouth or rather throat with a long comb & was unable to nurse for the most of the day." Chastina described Julian's next achievements when at eight months he "has got two teeth, begins to creep & get up by things."

Julian was nine months old when his father left Vermont for the gold mines of California. Alfred missed Julian's first haircut on November 1 and his first steps alone on December 8—within a week he was walking "half across the room." By his first birthday he "got so he can run pretty well." On March 13, 1852, Chastina wrote that "he has his little book & he begins to tell the pictures already, knows several—& begins to say a good many words." Whenever he heard his uncle Charles sing, Bub "sings do do," and he watched the younger Watts children—Isaac, Alice, and Ella (ten, six, and five)—with delight. By August, he was learning to talk and when Chastina asked him "where papa is. He says 'Fannyforny.' 'Horse & Wagon' are the two first words he attempted to put together."

As the weeks go by, Julian became "more company" to his mother, who was lonely, missing Alfred and feeling overwhelmed by the responsibility of caring for her child alone. When Julian was so sick that they sent for a doctor, who "gave him an emetic," Chastina described the trauma: "Sat up with him all night. The litle dear how sick he was. O how much would I gave could Alfred only be here. But that cannot be. If our litle boy should die how should I live alone, & *he may die too!*"

While Julian became Chastina's constant companion, she feared that "he will be spoiled" and felt he "needs" his father, echoing the prevailing assumption that men were stricter disciplinarians than women. For the first time in her writings, Chastina reached for her religion. She feared that "I shall not do by him as I ought, & that he will not be so good a boy. . . . May I be directed from on High to do as I ought & do my duty to this our child" Of course, she was not alone, as her mother and brothers and sisters were close by, and in February 1852 she and Julian moved to the family farm on East Hill to live until Alfred's return.

In April she "begin to wean bub, though it is hard to resist the little fellow's pleadings." For the next few weeks he was "real troublesome" and on May 12 Chastina wrote: "Bub real hard for me to take care of. He cries after me whenever I leave him. He is greatly attached to me. Wants 'MaMa' to do every thing for him." While at the store, "Bub cut round & flourished the yard stick" making Chastina feel "real ashamed of him. Hope he will improve for he has not been out much yet." On a visit to the neighbors, "Bub fell upon the stove & burned his little hand badly. Poor little fellow he took on for a hour, in a dreadful manner." It was hard for Chastina to discipline Julian and Roxana must have raised her eyebrows to see her daughter be so permissive. "Bub has been cross, & caused me a great deal of trouble . . . I ought to spank him & make him behave, I suppose. But this time I thought I would not mind him & let him cry it out." When Chastina was a child, the older children looked after the younger ones, but at the

Watts farm, Chastina felt that the influence of the Watts youngsters was not all good, as she wrote: "bub is getting to be so funny. He talks so cunning and sad to say he is beginning to say many naughty things which he learns from the children. I feel sorry for this but cannot help it now."

Chastina had other things on her mind. Alfred had asked her to join him in California, and after weeks of indecision, she agreed. Early in November, she wrote of "making bub's clothes. . . . There are a great many stiches to take in these little clothes." A week later Chastina "went to the Corner to get Bub vaccinated." Preparations complete, Chastina and Julian started off for the West in January 1853 with Julian's aunt Clara Walbridge.

Although it was not uncommon for young mothers to travel alone with their children at this time when families were separated, it is rare to have a daily account of such a trip. The first part of the journey by railroad to New York "Bub enjoyed . . . pretty well, did not cry except for water." At the "Eastern Pearl Street House" in New York City where the Vermonters spent the night before embarking on the ocean voyage, Chastina wrote: "My little boy is as good as I am, nevertheless they did not wish him to sit at the table with me, but he made such a fuss they were obliged to let him." Once on the steamship *Ohio*, Julian was sea sick and "vomited several times," but when he "got over his sickness," he became as "hearty as a little pig" and "is charmed at seeing the 'big water' & running round on deck." Crossing the Isthmus of Panama, Chastina and Clara rode on mules for the last miles on land, and Chastina "hired a native to carry Bub, paid him fourteen dollars for taking him across the Isthmus. Dear little fellow I pitied him so—to go on the native's back away from me. Though he seemed after a little to enjoy it very much. It was perfectly astonishing to me how he would go to the boy & from me too, to have him carry him." There was much sickness in the city of Panama and on the steamship *Golden Gate* going up the California coast, but Chastina and her party fared well, arriving mid-February in San Francisco where Alfred met them.

Alfred's first letter to Vermont written on February 27 exalted: "All here safe and well!" He described Bub "as plump and gay as one could possibly expect" although he did admit that "Chastina had [a] hard time with bub . . . the result is that she is thinner than when she left you."

At first Chastina and Alfred lived as boarders near the mission but they soon set up housekeeping in their own quarters in the center of San Francisco. Chastina stayed at home and took care of the housework and Julian while Alfred went every day to the mission to teach school. Julian's progress continued to be recorded in their journal and in letters written home to the Vermont folks. In April Chastina wrote attributing her own homesickness to Julian: "There is hardly a day passes without [Julian having] something to say about *Gamma's* good *gavy*, or *do nuts*, or pie or something of the kind. When he starts to go any where he wants to go and see Gamma, &

Julian Walbridge Rix, San Francisco, ca. 1854. Daguerreotype, courtesy Elizabeth Rix Fairfax.

Alice Ella & *Iker* & Gampa & so on This is the order he usually begins & goes through the family, always putting Olive among the rest. He talks pretty well now all but his lisping." By August "he has got to be a good deal naughty there are so many children in the [boarding] house—seven now in all & he is the youngest—." Anticipating the goodies of Christmas, Alfred wrote his usual amusing description of Bub: "Dont Bub go into the fruits & candies? Instead of having one sweet tooth he has a jaw full of them."

Leave it to Aunt Clara, however, for telling the full story of Julian's behavior: "Julian is very fleshy and full of fun as can be. He made his first attempt at shopping to day, which caused his mother quite a fright. She was busy about her work to day, and Julian came in and asked her if he might go and buy her some candy—she of course said no and thought no [more] of it until some time after, when she missed him, she looked all about the house & he was not to be found. She then ran up to Kearney street which is a short distance from here and went on a while until she saw his light dress away some distance from her, but she caught him—he did not seem to be in the least alarmed, he had not found a confectioners shop—but he told her he 'saw some *medicine* some eggs and some *beautiful brooms*' She would not have been so worried about him but Kearny street is constantly thronged with Carriages drays &c of every kind and there is no sidewalk in this part of the City." Clara goes on to say that Chastina rarely went out without Alfred but Julian had not learned his mother's fears of urban streets.

A game Julian and Alfred played entertained them both for hours. "I wish from my heart," Alfred wrote to Roxana, "that you could come in & find us all at home on a Sunday or an evening—five happier humans [Chastina, Alfred, Julian, Clara, Dustan] never lived under the same roof— but if one is happier than the rest & even glorious, it is Julian, & especially when he plays 'Bubby' with me—that is when he is father & I am his small boy, Julian. He will make me promise to mind him & mother & be a good boy and offer to let me go to his office with him some pleasant day—to ride to the Mission—will buy me candy & will chop every Chinaman & Grisly that offers to hurt me."

When the family visited a farm near the mission, Julian "enjoyed himself highly with the chickens ducks & pigs." The Rixes counted among their friends the Spanish-speaking people at the mission, but they held the prevailing prejudices against Irish, Chinese, and Indians.

Chastina described Julian's activities later in August: "Julian is well and is as fat & dirty as you could wish to see him. He wants to play in the sand all the time. He wears out a pair of shoes every month. We get them for a dollar a pair. Children do not or cannot go barefoot here. The sand is completely filled with glass & everything to get into their feet—besides it is either burning hot or cold enough to freeze—"

Early in 1855 the Rixes moved into their new house on Market Street. Julian had his own swing to play on, but this was little compensation for the other changes that took place when his younger brother, Edward, was born at the end of January. Chastina wrote of the sibling rivalry: "Julian thinks a good deal of his little brother, but he thinks it rather hard if he cant have the same attention from his father that he did before. He has always slept with us, and it comes the hardest for him to go to bed any where else—The other night Julian came in crying loud as he could & awoke the baby whom I had just got to sleep. of course I scolded at him—. He sat down and pouted awhile, then he broke out—said he '*that is what makes me sick of him*' I asked him if it was because he could'nt make as much noise as he wanted to? of course he answered yes."

In February 1857, when Chastina died, Julian was sent back to Peacham accompanied by his uncle Dustan to be raised by his grandmother and receive a New England education. Roxana wrote that "he has seen to much of the world for a child."

Chastina and Alfred had always thought that they would return to the East to educate their children, both valuing New England schooling. When Chastina was on her death bed, she might have reminded Alfred of her wish that Julian return to Peacham. Dustan was anxious to go back himself, so it worked out well and uncle and nephew traveled east together. Julian's younger brother, Edward, just two years old, remained in California. Roxana described the situation to her granddaughter, Augusta: "Mr. Rix broke up housekeeping pretty soon after his wife died. He and little Neddy Board with Clara and little Julian is here with me. He came home with Dustan last June. He is now 7 years old his Father pays Mr. Watts 100 dollars a year for keeping him. He stood the journey well and has been well most of the time since he has been here. He is a sterring fellow and a good deal noisey. Yet he is a bright Child and I hope he will be a good boy . . . His father knew it would be better to have him brought up in the Country than in such a place as Sanfrancisco." Roxana later called Julian "restless & uneasy." It must have been quite an adjustment for him to move from being the center of his parents' life in an urban household to being one of many children, all expected to do their share of the farm work.

The two surviving letters that Alfred wrote Roxana after Chastina's death discussed Julian's education. He first went to the local district school on East Hill. As he grew older, he attended Peacham Academy where he had an undistinguished career although he is listed in 1867 as editor of *The Students Record*. Two drawings attributed to him from this period exist: one a girl riding a cow and one a rose.

In the fall of 1862, Roxana died after a short illness. Julian's great-grandmother Olive had died only nine weeks earlier. The Walbridge-Watts family soon became concerned over the future care of Julian. Dustan wrote from the Civil War that he felt responsible and would write Alfred, but no such letters are extant in the family archives and Julian's life did not change. He stayed on the farm with his aunts Alice, only seventeen years old, and Ella, now fifteen, his grandfather Lyman, and his uncle Ike who worked the farm at age twenty. Another blow came when Dustan died from wounds suffered at Cold Harbor in June 1864. Three people—Chastina, Roxana, and Dustan—who had cared for Julian were now gone, and he was only thirteen years old.

Julian went on to finish the academy in the spring of 1868, and his aunt Clara sent the money for his trip to California. Once more he made the sea voyage—this time alone—with a crossing of the Isthmus, arriving in San Francisco in June. He lived with his father, who had remarried, and his two younger half-brothers. Edward left Clara and Russell's house and came to live with his brother and father. The previously light-hearted Alfred had turned, surprisingly, into a somber self-centered man. A year or so after Roxana's death, he stopped sending money to Lyman for Julian's care. He kept his distance from Clara and never introduced her to his new wife. He had ignored Edward, rarely seeing him and contributing little to his care.

Five months after his arrival in San Francisco, Julian evaluated the situation in a letter to Ella: "The Step Mother is always finding fault with Ned & I. She never says one word to me—but does to *Ned*—Father pays no regard to the Sabbath. Last Sunday he made Ned work on his new house plastering up holes on the walls all the forenoon—I aske him if Ned might go to Sunday School—No he was to work and had to get over all such silly notions. He dont make me work for I tell him plum out that I wont, so he dont press the matter. Ned he does. If it wasnt for Ned I would leave but he will not get along alone—so I stay. Now don't think that I get mad and talk back, for I haven't since I have been here And always treated Step Mother as well as I knew how."

When Julian went to visit his mother's grave he had trouble finding the site "for the Cemetary is so large that it is difficult to find anything unless

Julian Walbridge Rix, Peacham, ca. 1868. Tintype, courtesy Peacham Historical Association.

you are well acquainted." He added, "Father has never put up a stone or done anything except put a rough Board fence around it . . . If it could be improved and I hope it will be if I live, there will not be a prettier place in the whole Cemetary . . . When I get money enough I hope with Russel to make that one of the best lots in the Cemetary, not for the show but it seems almost total wicked to think that my father has never paid what the poorest are willing to pay—respect for their dead."

At first Julian worked in his father's office, but he did not do well in copying work, and within weeks Alfred apprenticed him to Charles Hopps & Son, a local sign and decorative painting company. From here on, all facts of Julian's life come from newspaper clippings rather than family letters, of which there are few from this period. At Hopps he painted scenes on safe doors but soon graduated to canvas. In 1872, at the Snow and Roos Gallery, he exhibited an oil painting which, according to the local newspaper, "has great merit for a first attempt from nature and gives promise of talent," his first public acclaim. An interview with Julian just before his death has it that when Julian declared his intentions to be an artist, his father refused to help him but his brother encouraged him as best he could. And when Edward graduated from the University of California as a mechanical engineer in 1877 and began his own business, he helped Julian financially. In return, Edward was given a number of Julian's landscape paintings.

Although no record of a meeting is found in family letters or newspaper accounts, it is possible that Albert Bierstadt, the well-known painter, served as a mentor for Julian. Alfred Rix's younger sister Adeline married Albert Bierstadt's brother Edward in 1849. Before coming to California Alfred had visited his sister in New Bedford in 1850 and in Providence in 1851 where Edward Bierstadt worked as a photographer and printer. From biographies of Albert Bierstadt, it is known that the Bierstadt brothers worked closely together throughout their lives, with Edward often taking photographs of subjects which Albert later painted in his studio. In the early 1870s, both Albert and Edward Bierstadt were in San Francisco—Albert made his base there from July 1871 to October 1873 and Edward with his wife came sometime in 1872. Julian surely knew his aunt and uncle, and probably the famous artist too.

Both Julian Rix and Albert Bierstadt were landscape painters, and both applied oil paint in a similar manner. Julian did not paint the large exhibition works so familiar to Albert Bierstadt; nor did he achieve Bierstadt's grand reputation. Julian did receive acclaim as a fine landscape artist. He participated in the thriving art community of San Francisco, was an early member of the Bohemian Club, and made his living as an artist from the early 1870s until his death thirty years later. Julian traveled and sketched the California coast from Monterey to Oregon—and also took his easel around Marin County and the Sacramento area. In 1874 he crossed the country— by train. A diary his aunt Alice kept noted his Peacham visits over a five-month period which included a day fishing with Charles Choate. Newspaper accounts have him sketching in Maine and New Hampshire at this time and family documents put him "working," to use Alice's term, in Vermont.

Upon his return to San Francisco, a new painting with New England as a subject inspired this report printed in February 1875: "There is a picture of a Winter scene by Julian Rix, in Schwab's store on Post street, which is worth looking at—the rugged, hard, New England scenery, intensified by freezing Winter's breath. The sky is a-flame with one of those gorgeous sunsets of mingled orange and crimson, mocking with its fervent glories the shivering, ice-bound denizens of such a clime. The boy whose pencil spread this bit of nature's cold shoulder on the canvas, has improved his time. Not more than two year's since he was working away in our old friend Hopp's establishment, on Sansome street."

A year later the "Art Notes" of the *San Francisco Chronicle* reported on another Rix painting but also touched on a subject which was to haunt Julian and all young artists: "At Morris & Schwab's gallery, Rix's 'Day in Autumn' is the principal attraction and is universally admired as a picture of more than ordinary merit. If it only had the name of some older artist down in the corner, it would probably sell at sight for a large sum; but the idea seems to be prevalent that an artist's merit must necessarily be in proportion to his age, and a young artist finds it difficult to dispose of his works, no matter how excellent."

As he gained increased recognition through the 1870s, the *Chronicle* described him at age twenty-six: "Julian Rix is known among his brethren as 'the Adonis of the Profession.' Not undeservedly is he thus designated. He is in appearance and manner a thorough gentleman, and understands to perfection the art of making himself agreeable to the fair sex. His fine, light-colored side-whiskers give him a decided English aspect, but his accent tells the story of his New England birth, too unmistakably to allow him to be long thought a Britisher. Mr Rix's forte in painting is landscape. Nature's garb he has studied thoroughly, and the skill with which he contrives to transfer some of her most beautiful places to canvas is really wonderful." Other accounts label him a "raconteur," "irrepressible," and "bohemistic in his tastes."

In the 1870s in San Francisco there was a remarkable group of artists; intimate friends sharing studios, socializing together, enjoying "a little masculine fun," and learning the techniques of painting from each other. A fellow artist, identified simply with the initials, L.P.L., illustrated a note on August 23, 1878, to an art student in San Francisco while he was sketching on "a trip to Glenwood Magnetic Springs eight miles from Santa Cruz." Among his line drawings was one of "Mr Rix, the landscape painter, and I have a sociable game," with the two men playing cards and smoking cigars. Julian seems to have been closest to Jules Tavernier, French-born, six years older than he. They shared a studio in 1879 on Montgomery Street, and the

Julian Walbridge Rix, San Francisco, ca. 1872. Courtesy The Bancroft Library, University of California, Berkeley.

press implied that this friendship encouraged Rix's bohemian reputation, as Tavernier was a known eccentric, wild spender, and beer drinker and had a penchant for nude sunbathing, which shocked the city's art community.

After New York, San Francisco in the 1870s attracted more talented artists than any other American city. Even Albert Bierstadt wrote in 1877: "San Francisco, though only a little over twenty-five years old, already has its academy of fine arts and its life school and during the gay season, its art receptions."

In this decade Julian came to maturity as an artist. The newspaper announced in March 1879 that "Rix has sold his 'Summer Morning' . . . for $400." He was on the way to financial success; but just as his future seemed assured, many art buyers of San Francisco in the early 1880s switched their tastes from local painters to European artists, decorating their lavish new homes with art work from across the Atlantic.

In 1881 Julian left for the East; he could no longer make a living in the San Francisco art market. He was encouraged by a businessman, William T. Ryle, who, like his father, had made his money in silk manufacturing. Ryle became Julian's art patron, not an uncommon practice at the time, especially in New York, and Ryle loaned him approximately six thousand dollars. Establishing a studio at Ryle's summer estate near Paterson, New Jersey, Julian later opened a studio in New York City as well.

He did not completely sever his relationship with San Francisco. He continued to send pictures for the annual exhibitions, many of which received favorable accounts in the newspaper. In 1883 he sent sixteen paintings by prominent New York artists with a letter published in the newspaper—full of his frustration at the San Francisco art scene and showing the wit his father used to display: "You must understand that most of the men I send have a ready sale for their pictures, and it don't pay for them to send *good pictures* so far and miss the other exhibitions, when there is a chance, at least, of people buying. . . . I am sorry to say it, but the San Francisco Art Association is the only place in the United States that pictures are *not* bought, as a general rule, during the Exhibition, and people do not seem to grasp the idea that that is what they are there for. It is a humiliating fact, but nevertheless true, that artists are forced to eat. As to paying rent, they never were known to, unless on a lease. So, for those unfortunate beings called landlords it would be better if more pictures were sold and less taffy were given. I think the most unfortunate of beings is what they call a 'young and rising artist.' God only knows why people call them such, and he won't tell."

The only remaining family letter from this period is one Julian wrote to his aunt Clara in June 1885 on stationery printed with his Paterson, New Jersey, address: "You are very much mistaken if you think it was through neglect or carelessness that I left Cal. as I did.—I felt when I left very blue & disheartened and I did not know I was going until up to almost the last moment. . . . I did not want to see any one. so I quietly slipped away.— Another thing I did not believe I would stay but a few months and expected to go back on a trip for Harpers. but we could not agree on the price, & they sent someone else in my stead ('Joe. Strong'). Dont think for a moment for you will do me a wrong that I intentionally hurt your feelings or would I have you believe that I ever forget the Kindness that you & uncle Russ have always shown me." He went on to describe what would appear to be a failed love affair with Nellie Hopps, a painter well known in the art colony who sometimes took sketching trips with Julian: "In regard the Hopps affair—Nell [Nell Rogers, Clara's oldest daughter] will give you the particulars—She [Nellie Hopps] is happily Married to a man she told me she loved.—I hope she does, and is correspondingly happy.—I am sorry to break in on any sentiment you may have for the young matron But I assure you it is thrown away. During the time that she was whooping up S.F. with her broken heart [over me] she was quietly carrying on a little love affair with the gentleman she married. I was aware of it all along and because I refused to make an idiot of myself I am looked upon as a very bad young man. I have had some experience in this world, have found that as a general rule, that young ladies who smoke cigarettes—Eat late suppers at dubious French Restaurants—drink cocktails 'ad lebolurn' are not condusive to domestic bliss, I assure you I have none of it in mind. Hence I remain an old Do Do.—And believe me I have yet to *wrong* in any *way or cause* an *unhappiness* to any *young lady* I ever knew. that is the truth, and I smile when I hear the stories that I am sometimes regaled with. I would like your good opinion very much, and would not forfiet it for anything I have been knocked around so much I suppose I have grown callous in a degree and appear cold hearted and all that. But many a time I have grieved over my misfortunes & wasted opportunities, when if I had felt a guiding hand, would have saved me many heart burnings, and sorrow."

Photographs of the landscape around Julian's New Jersey studio are reminiscent of Vermont with its rolling hills and stone boulders. He added in his letter to Clara: "I am living quietly in Paterson and am doing well. I am getting a good reputation. I do not drink have given up smoking and am trying to make up for some few wild oats I have scattered by the way."

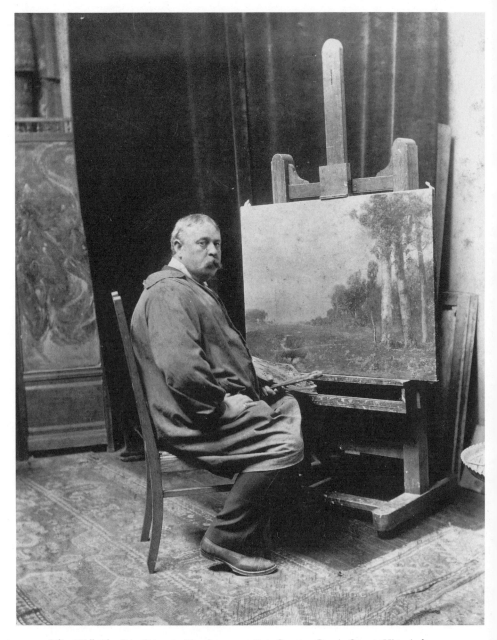

Julian Walbridge Rix, Paterson, New Jersey, ca. 1890. Courtesy Passaic County Historical Society.

Over the next twenty years, Julian gained great recognition in New York and limited fame in Europe where he visited at least once. His paintings were hung at New York's National Academy of Design almost every year until 1894. In addition to oils, his watercolors, pastels, and engravings were in demand. Like many artists of the time, he made good money illustrating for magazines, especially *Harper's,* and in 1889 he contributed to *Picturesque California*. According to one New York newspaper account, Julian Rix "got rid of his sideburns and acquired a great girth and a heavy pocketbook."

More important, Julian found in William Ryle, only five years older than himself, a lifelong friend, whose wife, Susan, considered him family. Julian became godfather to their daughter, Margaret Rix Ryle. Among the photographs of the Ryle estate at the Passaic County Historical Society in Paterson is one of Julian walking the grounds with Susan Ryle in a relaxed manner with a natural intimacy. In his will, according to the newspaper, Julian bequeathed to the Ryles about twenty-thousand dollars. The Ryles had become Julian's family.

Julian, "not in the most robust health," made his last trip to California in 1901. He went off on sketching trips but made his base at the Palace Hotel on Market across from his former home, where he had lived with his parents and brother almost fifty years before.

Only one letter written by Julian exists from this time. It was dated February 5, 1903, and was sent to the Corcoran Gallery in Washington in response to their request for biographical information after purchasing a painting: "I was born in Peacham Vermont December 30th 1850 My schooling & Education continued their until I was 17, When I went to San Francisco California Commenced painting when I was 22 as a Sign & Decorative painter After 3 years I opened a Studio in that City afterward came East I never studied under any body. Never took a drawing or painting lesson in my life. All I know was found out working out of doors from nature." Perhaps this brief letter, which includes no mention of his having been to San Francisco as a child, accounts for the many erroneous biographies of Julian's life. Newspapers have him born in California, raised by an uncle, educated in New Hampshire, among other inaccuracies.

Julian died on November 24, 1903, at the age of fifty-two following a kidney operation in New York City. His father died the next year and his brother lived until 1930.

Julian was buried in his patron's cemetery plot in Cedar Lawn Cemetery in Paterson with a large granite stone engraved with the words: "In Memory of Julian Rix Beloved Friend of William Ryle." According to an article in the *New York Times* reporting on his estate, Julian had asked art connoisseur Thomas B. Clarke to examine all his paintings and destroy and burn any which, in his judgment, were not worthy of the artist's name. Paintings were left to several friends and one family member, his brother, Edward A. Rix. His "fishing rods and sporting articles," a reminder of his love for the outdoors, were left to a friend.

The final evaluation of his art is given in the *New York Times* in his obituary: Julian Rix's "landscapes were said by artists to be ambitious and strong, often pronounced in color, too seldom atmospheric but revealing a real love of natural scenery." That love of nature—he would camp while he was sketching—no doubt began with his Vermont years; as a baby, Chastina carried him through the fields and Roxana held him in the wagon as they traveled through the countryside; as an adolescent, he worked with Isaac on the land, went raspberry picking with Alice, and joined school friends in fishing at Henderson's Brook. No specific view of the Peacham area has been identified in Julian's paintings, but certainly he was inspired by the hills of Vermont in the four New England seasons.

Today the paintings of Julian Walbridge Rix are sought after by major galleries and museums. He is recognized as one of the finest late nineteenth-century landscape painters.

PART III

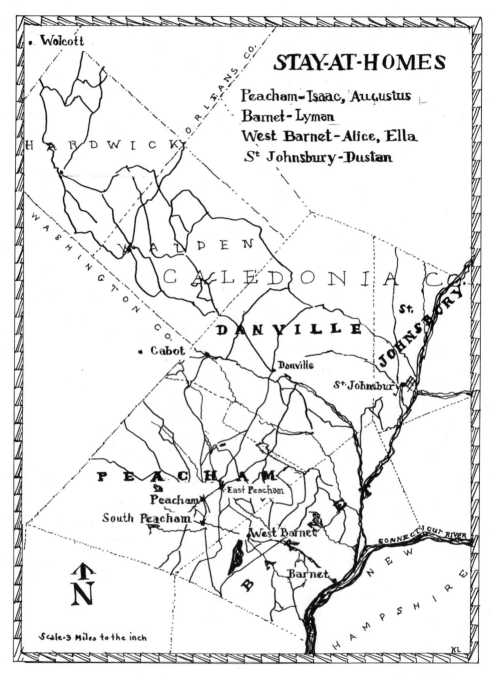

STAY-AT-HOMES

Peacham–Isaac, Augustus
Barnet–Lyman
West Barnet–Alice, Ella
St Johnsbury–Dustan

Karen R. Lewis

Roxana's Stay-At-Homes: The Children Who Made Their Lives in Vermont

PEACHAM CEMETERY sits on top of a hill, closed in by a white post-and-rail fence from the road that climbs up through Peacham Corner. It is a beautiful spot, snow covered and lovely in winter, green and lovely in summer, dotted with tall white single gravestones and granite monuments marking family plots. Great old sugar maples and white pines shade it; saplings or young trees in the time covered by this account, they are now, one by one, making their own gravestones of huge stumps, beside which young trees are springing up. A serene place, it calms the mind of anyone who walks in it; but like all graveyards it buries many sorrows and joys.

The Wattses and Walbridges never established a family plot but are scattered here and there within the old part of the cemetery. Father Lyman purchased a grave site upon the death of his first wife, Esther Sargeant, in 1836; his white stone stands next to hers, with Roxana's beyond, on a slope of the hillside that looks south, out over the Barnet hills—"these great land waves," as a letter writer of that time described them.

All of Roxana's children who remained in Vermont are buried here. Dustan's handsome gravestone, with its crossed flags and elegant scroll-work, stands just inside the fence facing the road. Beside him, in a line descending down the hill, are his brother-in-law, Charles Choate, Charles's two wives, the Watts sisters, Alice and Ella, and the small stones of the three children whom Alice lost as babies.

Lyman has a small stone beside his wife in the Chamberlain family plot with its big monument. Isaac and his two wives have three tall stones near the footpath gate, and a sugar maple grows close by their heads. Augustus's stone stands nearby in a group of three that includes his wife of only two months and her first husband.

Across the road, by itself at the west end of a large grassy plot, stands the Peacham Civil War monument, a simple granite column with the names of

Peacham Civil War Monument, erected 1869. Photograph, 1994, John Somers.

those who died cut into its four sides. Isaac campaigned vigorously for this monument against stiff resistance in town meeting; and when it was finally built by private subscription in 1869, he gave the dedicatory address. Forty-three of the young men he had grown up with had died; he listed each one, how and where he died, and in the process gave support to a surprising medical statistic—that the Vermont soldiers, universally admired for their healthy good looks and marching ability, were more susceptible to disease than soldiers from any other state, dying of measles, mumps, and other ailments, often in the first weeks of enlistment. Of the Peacham "boys," eleven had been killed in battle or died of their wounds; seven had died in prison; and twenty-two had "died of disease," with three more described simply as "died in hospital."

Isaac concluded his listing: "Forty-three in all. Sixteen lie in yonder cemetary, one in Danville and one in his native Canada. The others are scattered from the Potomac to the Rio Grande and all fill *honorable graves.*"

This large toll from a small town was only the most dramatic of many changes that the stay-at-homes among Roxana's children saw as the century moved along; for they lived with change that was nearly as great, though not so noticeable, as that met by families who moved away.

It can be almost as traumatic an experience to be left behind as to leave. The town of Peacham lost a third of its population between 1840, when Martha moved west, and 1888, when Ella came back from Minnesota. Some Vermont towns died entirely during that period. Peacham did not; but it lost much of its lifeblood.

Though the railroad, which first came up the Connecticut River valley in the early 1850s, took more and more families away westward, it also opened up the Peacham area to commerce with the towns and cities of southern New England. When Roxana first moved to the Watts farm, household life was almost entirely self-sustaining; the farm provided wool for her weaving; meat, eggs, milk, butter, and vegetables for her cooking; tallow for her candles and lye and fats to make soap for her washing. By 1860 her daughter Alice was buying cloth to sew—and, once, even a dress from a peddler; and though Father Watts kept stubbornly to his tallow candles, Alice and Isaac and Ella were reading by kerosene lamps. In turn, increased trade developed southward; by the mid-1870s Isaac and Alice and Charles Choate were counting on a good income from shipping choice butter to the Boston market. A letter of 1878 also mentioned the faint beginning of an important modern Vermont industry: "Peacham is pretty well filled up with summer visitors and old residents back on a visit."

As the century moved along, labor-saving machinery, which would greatly ease the burden of both housekeeping and farming, began to enter their lives. In 1869, Lyman bought a sewing machine for his pregnant wife; by 1872 Alice was using one too. By 1878 Isaac's wife was rejoicing in a new washing machine that was "like the old one only different and washes much faster." Only people who had done all this heavy and tedious work by hand could appreciate the new liberty that the machine gave them. Isaac, too, welcomed machines into his life—the thresher when it came each year, and the new mower which replaced a broken one. On one day in August 1867, the new and the old came together: "Finished mowing with the machine but have about 1½ acres to mow by hand. Shall be pretty glad to see the last of it."

Religion and the church stayed closer to the lives of those who stayed at home than to those who left; but it too changed its power and its place as the century went along. The old evangelical style expressed itself chiefly in Isaac and Alice as guilt at not measuring up to the old standards of personal redemption; in Dustan, as dignified resistance to its theological demands; and in Lyman, as despair at not being able to recapture the old power to bring souls to Christ. But the three youngest Wattses "united with the church," supported its place in their community, and contributed strength and energy to the new directions of social change—temperance and abolition. Temperance in Peacham was no longer a crusade, but a way of life by their time, as the result of a remarkable process of religious and social pressure that had made Peacham by 1852 essentially a prohibition town, a position to which each of Roxana's children subscribed. Freedom and the Union cause claimed their enthusiasm, as Alice's work for raising money for supplies for the Union Army and records of war service of Lyman, Dustan, and Isaac will show.

The movement toward freeing another group that felt constriction rather than enslavement—women—began to move with glacial slowness during the century, and Roxana's two youngest daughters moved with it as far as the countertide of their own lives would let them. Alice and Ella went away briefly, Alice in the hope of an education that would free her, Ella as a working woman with a position that she valued; but each came back, forced by circumstance and duty to take up the life that she had hoped to leave. They lost the campaign, but unlike their older sisters in the West, they had identified the goal.

No less than their siblings who had moved away, all of Roxana's stay-at-home children lived with change, adjusted to it, and grew from it. The stories that follow lie hidden under those gravestones in Peacham Cemetery.

Returned from California

Many Vermonters who went west eventually returned to their native state. Two of Roxana's sons, Dustan and Augustus, went to California, stayed long enough to be considered emigrés, but in the end came back in a "reverse migration" that often occurred but received little notice in diaries or letters.

Both brothers returned to Vermont with no disgrace. They had not borrowed large sums of money for their ventures. They had not left family in Vermont who relied on their financial success. They were young unmarried men with a skilled trade.

For many New Englanders, California symbolized independence and economic opportunity. Neither Dustan nor Augustus realized this California dream, and both returned to Vermont to their family and their wheelwright trade.

Dustan S. Walbridge (1832–1864)

Wheelwright, Gold Rush Miner, Soldier

ROXANA'S FIFTH child and first son, Dustan Walbridge, strikes the modern reader of the Walbridge-Watts papers as the quintessential Yankee—handy, resourceful, inventive, practical, ready to turn his hand to anything, and possessed of a keen, inquiring mind that made the most of whatever events and ideas came his way.

Only four years old when his father died, Dustan was too young to help his mother maintain the family farm in Wolcott. Instead he came with four of his siblings to the Watts farm on East Hill in 1840 when his mother married Lyman Watts. He found two stepbrothers waiting for him at the farm: Lyman, almost his twin, and Charles, three years younger and only a few months older than his own younger brother, Augustus. By the time he was fourteen, he had another brother and two new sisters.

As Dustan grew up, he attended Peacham Academy intermittently between the ages of fourteen and eighteen. He learned the carriage-making business, and by 1850 Roxana wrote that he was "in Marshfield at his trade making waggons and sleighs and we think he is going to be a first rate work man." Throughout his life, the census and other official documents listed him as "wheelwright" or "carriage maker."

Soon, however, the California gold mines drew the eighteen-year-old west, and he spent a year or so trying to "make his pile" in a claim. Two months after her arrival in San Francisco, Chastina commented on Dustan's situation in a letter to Peacham: "We were waiting this time to have Dustin come down [from the mines] . . . But he did not come & he has since written us that he thought it doubtful whether he came down at present. . . . [There is] a shop close by where we board, where they repair old waggons & make some . . . milk waggons, some for two horses & some for one . . . This is all the shop there is at the mission & there a[re] lots of milk men all around, so they have a great deal to do where the[y] run once &

twice a day every day into town. Dustin does not wish to come down until his claim that he has is proved He says it is a back claim & it will be nearly six months before he can work it. He believes it to be good & hates to leave it untried." But the project came to nothing, and later in 1853 Dustan was in San Francisco, boarding with Chastina and Alfred while he followed his wheelwright's trade, earning $4.50 a day, hoping to put together enough money to start a business back in Vermont. Chastina wrote Roxana that Dustan bragged that "he can make the nicest waggon bodies of any one in the city. What they make principally are those big Job & Furniture waggons, big as lumber waggons at home but not exactly in the same style— They are Elegant things of their kind—I suppose Dust is a very nice work-man—The men who employ him put the utmost confidence in him, & merely tell, what they want done & he does it after his o[w]n fashion."

From San Francisco came the first of Dustan's highly individual letters—articulate, observant, thoughtful, and spelled by a system all his own. "I hope John [Way, married to his sister Sarah] wont go west," he wrote to Roxana in late 1854, "for I want him to take charge of our Blacksmith department in *Walbridge & Co's Cariage Factory.*" And he added, "*fiddle-stick* to go out there [west] where they have to chace their young ones downe with dogs every Saturday to wash them and put on a cleane shirt—nonsence!"

In the same letter he tells a tall story of the kind popular at the time, and later a stock in trade with Mark Twain: "Nothing new going on here now a days—the last excitement in the mines is about the *soap mine* they have found up at Table Mountain, the whole inside of the mountain is cleare soap—each man that has a clame just boors a squair auger hole in the mountain at the foot untill he gets in to the soap—then the pressure at the top causes it to be forced out, in a squair bar—which has only to be clipped off this right length—packed and marked and it is ready for the market—*fact.*"

Turning his observant eye to San Francisco, Dustan wrote to his brother Lyman: "Large brick buildings are taking the place of the low wooden shanteys on every side. Granite and freestone as material for building are used quite extensively, our market cant be beet, in quantity quality or variety of its productions. Fruit stands at nearly every corner of the streets, loaded with fruits of all kinds that you could ask, mellons, peaches pears and grapes, of the finest quality raised in this state apples is the only fruit that is inferior to the fruit in any part of the atlantic states, they sell here at 25 cts pr pound."

And for political life in 1853: "*Leckshun* is just over, and although full returns have not been received from the various *presincts* we are quite certain that *our side* [Alfred Rix was running for justice of the peace] has beete. It is the fashion here for every candidate for office to do his own electioneering and besides going around and verry modestly setting fourth their good qualities and capabilities for the particular office that they are seeking, and asking your vote, they are expected to stand *treat* for at least a weake before election—they also get out large *posters* and stick up to let the people know who is *the* man to vote for and now on any of the principle streets you look and as far as the eye can reach you can see these same *posters* entirely covering every place that they could possibly be stuck on." His pen sketch reproduced here is of a city block entirely covered with posters.

On the Fourth of July in 1856 Dustan described the activities in San Francisco to his thirteen-year-old brother Isaac back in Peacham: "Today is the *glorious fourth,* and as I have been around and seen all the *sights* as long as their is any satisfaction in seeing them. I have returned, and after taking off my coat and tight shoes and putting on some easy slippers and seating myself in an easy chaire, in my nice little room.—I think—I know that I would not change places with any of the *bould soldiers* that are parading today, for what is their better then easey slippers and easey chairs for one when he is tired. well after seating myself, I thought of nothing better to do than writing home, although I have nothing particular to write. . . . The selabration which is *passing* off, today is no *great shakes,* although their is three verry fine companies out besides the fire department, and a fire company from Stockton they all had fine uniforms, and good music and certainly made a verry fine appearance and I suppose it was not their fault if they did not succeed in awakening 'glorious enthusiasm' in my heart. it *did* wake me up to such a sence of my duty which I owed to my country that I came home and fired my *colts* at a mark several times . . . then assisted Julian in firing some Chinese crackers.—I then became perfectly cool again and went about my business as though nothing had happened.—but give me your regular old country *floodwood* trainings for developing patriotism where a man can fire big guns and then the *sham fight* which comes verry near a *real* fight,—their is some fun in such trainings—some life some *snap and go off* (although that cant be said of some of their guns)."

The "pile" that he hoped to make for a fair start in the carriage business never materialized, for with each newly arrived steamer, the number of skilled wheelwrights increased, keeping wages low. In the end what took him home was the assignment of escorting his six-year-old nephew, Julian, home to live with his grandmother Roxana.

In October 1857, Dustan journeyed with his brother Augustus out to visit Sarah and John Way in Minnesota. He had already joked with John about the opportunities there: "It seemes *you* think you have at last found

Dustan Walbridge's drawing of political signs for San Francisco election, 1853. Included in a letter from Dustan to his brother Lyman, September 13, 1853. Courtesy Lynn A. Bonfield.

the Eden of the western world, and it seemes you found it none to soon for by your account of the emegration, if it continues long their will have to be a great many turned *out* of Eden, for the *want* of an *apple* or some thing else to *eate*—but if you have fairly *squat* in the *midst of the garden, you* may be allowed to remain—especially as those big *angels with fiery swords* that used to stand guard on the *other* side of the *Jordan* are rather scarce now a days." He and Augustus worked as carpenters for a year. However, rural Minnesota in the 1850s had little to offer them. The 1860 census lists five wagon makers in Monticello, an ample number for a town with fewer than one thousand people, so the Walbridge brothers returned to Vermont and soon began a business in St. Johnsbury.

In 1860 Dustan married a young woman from Peacham Corner, Abbie T. Hardy: he was twenty-eight; she, eighteen. One of his inimitable letters, to Clara in California, described his new situation: "I can hardly realize it now—when they ask me how my *wife* and *baby* are getting along it seems as though there was some *mistake* that they dont mean me—but if I study on it awhile I see just how it is—Yes—I am maried and got a *baby* it is funny but is so—was married the eighth (a year ago) of last Oct.—and in ten months I made 26 buggies, and my wife had a fine healthy baby—not bad working was it—but the bother of it is—in these hard times I dont know what to do with either the buggies or the baby. our baby is a girl—I wanted a boy but Abbie went in so strong for a girl that I had to give up to her this time. We call her Nellie Florence Abbie claims the privilege of naming all the girls and I am to name all the boys . . . We now live at St Johnsbury—have been living hire about six weeks, just commencing housekeeping—what a jobb it is—what an everlasting running and getting things and then the milkbills and the wood bills and meat flour potatoes and what not have to be got. then what a nice bonnet Mrs. Higgins has got for *only* four dollars and what nice delain you can get at Mrs. Johnstons for 25 cts pr yd, and such a pretty little hood for baby only a dollar—all such things are new and interesting to an old fellow like me that has lived so long in single blessedness—and makes a thoughtful man *like myself* more thoughtful of the ways the *money* is come to meate all these new expences but *not a bit sorry* he *done it* for although there are some little vexations attending all these things with cares and duties multiplied it gives a man something to live for, and if he has a wife that is not extravagant and tryes to do the best she can as mine does—and a little one to look up with its little innocent face and talk . . . baby talk to you when you come home from work, I think it *pays*—there is but one consideration that makes me in the least regret taking such responsibilities upon me, and that is a *War* concideration. It makes me feel *mean* to think that *my Country* calls for men in her hour of need and I an able bodied man am here *not* ready for her call. I feele as though I *ought* to go,—but Abbie cant bair to hire me mention a thing about going she has a *little one* and her folks think I ought not to think of going."

His patriotism made him unable to hold out for long, however. On August 6, 1862, he enlisted as a private in Company A, 11th Regiment Vermont Infantry—later 1st Regiment, Vermont Heavy Artillery—which was assigned to one of the defensive forts surrounding Washington, first Fort Totten and then Fort Slocum. His description from Army enlistment records reads as follows:

Age_____29_____years; height____5____feet____8____inches.
Complexion_____Light_____
Eyes_____Grey_____; hair_____Brown_____
Where born_____Wolcott, Vt._____
Occupation_____Carriage Maker._____

Dustan described to Clara the scene of soldiers leaving camp in Brattleboro for the forts near Washington, D.C.: "We came here most of the way by rail.—were greeted on Every side with cheers, and waving of flags & handkerchiefs, many of the places in *New England*—the little girls would want to be *boosted* up to the car windows to give the *soldiers* an apple or shake hands with them.—" Now that he was away from home, the letters began again, and they are so full of keen observation and forthright comment that it is hard to select individual passages. In this same letter to Clara in San Francisco he also described the early days in Washington: "We had a pretty hard time for a day or two—pretty hard marching for green hands—and not enough to eat,—on account of so many soldiers arriving there at this time,—averaging about 8000 pr day—but are now getting enough to eat,—and plenty of hard work to give us an apetite for our *hard bread* & *Salt Horse* . . . There are 10 forts in sight of our camp—and the dome of the capitol building is also in sight . . . It is hard for a free spirit to be subject to the petty tyranny of officers sudenly raised to posicions of power, as a soldier is subject to but it is something that does not fall to the lot of every generation to take part in such a contest as this—I meditated a long while before I concluded to enlist but I have never been sorry for it yet."

He wrote to Sarah in March 1863, "I enlisted as a *private* and have not been *promoted* to anything of any account. I am *not* sorry that I enlisted, and still think as I did . . . in regard to this war—we must *whip* them or we mite as well *clime a tree* and stay there. we can do it to." He went on to address a subject close to Sarah and John. Up along the Minnesota River, near enough to be of concern to the new settlers in what would later be Northfield, tensions between settlers and the resident Sioux Indians had begun to erupt in incidents that were to lead into the Sioux Indian wars later that summer. It was an uneasy time for the Ways; and Dustan, reacting out of family loyalty and ignorance of the years of official deception and fraud that had shaped Sioux anger, wrote, "And then when the war is over I will come out theire [to Minnesota] and help fight Indians . . . That Indian trouble up theire is a bad business—although I think there is no cause for fear now, they are looking out for them and it is easy enough to wipe out the whole race if they set about it." In this he was echoing the popular thinking of his time about a situation that has had to wait many years for the national conscience—guided and ruled as it has been by Americans of European descent—to see differently.

In October of that year Roxana died. Dustan felt the loss keenly. "Our Mother is gone," he wrote to Clara, "and for *us* our *old home* is gone—as is also all hope of ever meeting together again, around the old fireside, with *hir,* who has always caired more to see *us* happy, and prosperous than for hir own ease and comfort . . . hirs has been a life of care and sorrow and anxiety, and if she has found rest we ought not to wish hir back."

Thoughts of death stayed with him through this letter: "I remember well the idea that I used to have, and of stating it to you and others, that I should be killed in battle but I can see why it was so—I had thought of dying in different ways—and theire was no way that seemed to me to be as glorious as to fall, in the vigor of manhood fighting valiantly for the right . . . I am as liable as every soldier is to meet such a fate . . . but I hope and believe that . . . we may yet spend many happy days where we can see each other and where our little ones can visit back and forth, as we used to go cousining."

Thoughts of death may also have led him to examine and formulate his own religious beliefs. In a long letter, courteous but firm to his brother Lyman, by then a student at divinity school, he wrote: "You tell me to study the Bible—viewing it in a certain light, in the light that you view it in—is that quite fair—Should we sirch for *truth* by first forming an opinion and then try and make everything conform to that opinion or should we first divest ourselves of all prejudice in every way . . . and weigh calmly all the facts, keeping them always as *simple* and *clear* as possible."

He went on to outline his views on prayer, which apart from the thinking of a few, Abraham Lincoln among them, would have been nearly heretical among his peers: "I do not know as prayers are answered but I know it does no harm to try and lift the mind to the great author of our being and I do often when I am thinking of these things and of the affairs of my Country, try and free my mind from all selfish thoughts, and fixing it upon the great Maker of the Universe asking, if such things are granted to guide me to the *truth* in all things and give me more knowledge and a clearer sight to the *right* way."

His thoughts on women and marriage were independently arrived at and based on observation: "I think now that a girl ought never to get *married* before they are twenty Abbie makes a kind affectionate Wife, and for one so young, a careful Mother. She tryes to [do] the best she can, and we think everything of each other, but she is not such a one as *Chastina* was, so conciderate about *everything*, and so *correct* in hir views. Abbie tryes to be economical but she dont understand *how* to be, verry well, she was never brought up to it."

He developed in a letter to Alice this hint that his own marriage was unequal in respects other than age: "Abbie has done everything for me that she knew how and the best she could she has been a faithfull wife I think and as such I am bound to do all I can to make hir happy—but I thought if she had been brought up under different influences she would be better fitted for bringing up our little girl and when I went away I was anxious that she should be with Mother as much as possible—and hoped the influence of our home would do hir good for she is one that is confiding and easily influenced by those she trusts, and I wished such influence to be always for good. . . . When Mother died then you and Ella were all the ones that were left of *My* folks that Abbie could sympathise with. I know she felt Mothers loss, severly, and I hoped that you would all three of you be to each other as sisters. I know your tastes are different from hirs—but all that have lost dear friends, and feele lonely, have common ties for sympathy."

He had no such reservations about his daughter, Nellie. "Our little *Nellie* is *awful* smart," he wrote to Clara in San Francisco. "She runs all around, and talks anything almost, and can *sing* in fine style, besides playing the Piano, a remarkable Child *I* think, takes after hir Father—I should like to see the little scamp—I am missing a great deele of comfort, that I should take with hir. You know I always liked little children. how much I used to think of Eddie—when I was theire. when he used to hang to me, when I left for work at noon, and I presume I should think as much of my own."

As Dustan looked around him at the war, his opinions of its conduct, and of military life in general, sometimes came smoking up off the page: "All the men that are not detailed for guard or other duty are regularly sent to work, they do not have to work verry hard—in fact they dont *do* but a verry little, because everything is conducted on the Celebrated principle discovered by Damnphool, they detail *Carpenters* that never was inside a carpenters shop and give him a few old tools not fit to use and set him at it, give him 40 cts pr day extra, and let good carpenters shovel and pick."

Another satire on army incompetence went to John Way: "You are terrible on ducks—it wouldnt do to have you down here—you dont make *serimony* enough about it to put a military touch on it *you* ought to have *reported* to some Superior officer that you had discovered Ducks in force at such a place, he would have sent a detachment to make a *reconnoissence*, and if they reported Ducks he would look in his books and find that the way to capture *ducks* was to lay salt on their tails, and would have sent a requisition to the War department for 500 bbls of Salt that is the way we do things here to make it *still* more military the man that furnished the *Salt* would have to mark about $5,00 pr bbl on it—"

He expressed his dismay at the military result of this bureaucracy: "I suppose you get the news theire pretty regular—about the *war* and have learned of more *Splendid retreats,* &c of the *Union* Army. I suppose by this time our Army can *retreat,* pretty scientific, but it tires them so that they must rest for a few months after they get where they are *safe*. One cant help but be a little savage about the way all our *big Victories* turn out." Just the week before, he felt that the war "may take [a] shape that none of us dream of, and the end, none of us can tell when or what, but I think the end whatever it is will result in making mankind at large more free—"

Farming in Maryland where he camped earned some comments, too: "It is rather a pleasant Country about here—Any quantity of Apple & Peach Orchards—it is quite hilly, mostly verry poor land . . . The *natives* . . . Are in all improvements about farming &c. about fifty years behind the times. they build a chimney, and see if it will *draw,* and if it will *draw* well—they build a house beside it."

Meanwhile he made his way in the army. He was soon promoted to corporal and his general "handiness" evidently made itself apparent, for he was often withdrawn from general duty and put on special tasks. "I am at present making a Topographical map of the country around our Fort within the range of our guns—have been at it about a month, have three men to work with me—the *Instruments* I use are of my own make—out of pine boards and strips of brass but I will get a good map."

In July and August 1863 he was, to quote the army records, "Absent on det.[ailed] serv.[ice] in Vt. to conduct recruits to this Regt." It meant a visit home, which does not figure in the family letters but was described later by a friend: "I shall always remember him now as he looked last summer when he was home. He was a very good looking soldier and appeared to feel well . . . He was all taken up with Nelly his little girl. He left her a baby and when he came back she run around and could sing like a bird."

Back in Washington, he was promoted, early in 1864, to sergeant major, and less than a month later, transferred from Fort Totten to Fort Slocum and commissioned a second lieutenant. In March he began arranging for Abbie and Nellie to visit him, but in April telegraphed her not to come, because the troops were moving out of the forts and into action at last. The telegram came too late; Abbie had already started on the journey. Since the order to move troops was delayed, they had their visit and all went well.

The marching orders finally came, moving both Dustan and Isaac into action. On June 2 Isaac wrote in his diary: "Marched a short distance and threw up intrenchments this afternoon. This place is called Cold Harbor, I believe. We shall probably see fighting enough to suit anyone."

Cold Harbor was a wide place in the road, so insignificant that at first no one in the Union Army was entirely sure of its name—Cold Harbor, Coal Harbor, Cool Arbor—but it was to gain fame as a fatal spot, full of dread, the one battleground that no veteran ever expressed a desire to revisit. The third of the great battles that began General Grant's aggressive campaign to end the war quickly, it was incredibly bloody and disastrous even for an army used to disaster. Grant said of it afterward, "I regret this assault more than any I have ever ordered," and it created in the army and in the nation a mood of caution and dogged endurance that was to characterize the rest of the war.

Dustan was one of the casualties of this grisly battle. "The fight was pretty warm ahead of us," Isaac wrote on June 3. "Brother Dustan was wounded in the arm, though I don't know how badly." It was worse than he could imagine. Dustan's right arm, the arm with which he earned his living, had to be amputated; and with only one surgeon in the field hospital for all the officers of the 6th Corps, the operation could not have been anything but hasty and brutal, one among many done by that exhausted doctor. Then followed transportation in a jolting wagon over rough roads

Dustan Walbridge in Civil War uniform, ca. 1864. Photograph copied by A. C. Harlow, Montpelier, Vermont. Courtesy Choate Farm Collection.

to an embarkation point, and from there by steamer to Douglas Hospital in Washington. Alice wrote to Sarah that Dustan "had good accommodations . . . after he reached W. but he was four days reaching there after his arm was taken off and that was very hard."

Sophia Way, in Peacham, wrote the rest of the story from her vantage point on East Hill, to Sarah, out in Minnesota: "I hardly know how to

Gravestone of Dustan Walbridge, Peacham Cemetery. Photograph, 1994, John Somers.

write the sad news we are all familiar with here. I suppose you are some-what prepared for it by hearing that Dustin was wounded and you probably feared as others do that to be wounded in the army of the Potomac is certain death. It has proved so in his case Poor Dustan died last Sunday morning at Washington and was buried today in Peacham with Masonic Honors there was a very large Funeral Our folks all went but me and the baby. I went out at the Corner of the Orchard to see the procession It was a very long one.

"When the news first came that he was wounded he was reported as doing well and that probably he would be home in a short time twenty or thirty days perhaps, and that there was no *need* for his wife to come but Abby said she could not live twenty or thirty days and she should go, and she did go, altho some opposed it much. She arrived there Tuesday and found she *was* needed very much He was very glad to see her and knew her until the last moment and the last words he called her name.

"They say the Erysipelas got into his arm and the marrow of the bones turned to jelly . . . Now Sarah I know just how you feel and I know it is *very hard* . . . How your Mother would have felt this summer if she had lived."

It is no surprise that the funeral procession was a very long one. And Dustan's gravestone is one of the most beautiful in the Peacham cemetery, speaking eloquently of his family's pride in him and of their sorrow at los-ing him.

D. Augustus Walbridge (1835–1881)

A Case of Mental Illness

IN 1878, in a letter to his sister Ella, Isaac Watts wrote of their brother Daniel Augustus Walbridge, "I think he is more of an enigma than ever." He was an enigma then, and he remains one now. No good record of his life exists and the random references to him in letters and diaries all seem to carry an edgy tone, a mixture of bewilderment, apprehension, and solicitude, with a hint of irritation thrown in.

No known photograph of him survives. He apparently kept no diaries. Only a few letters remain of those he wrote during his forty-six years. An initial mystery is why he was always called Augustus, never Daniel as one might expect with a child born posthumously and named after his father. Who was this empty center of family unrest?

One fragment of Augustus's letters is an intimate note written to his ten-year-younger sister Alice in 1859 from Lyndon, where he was living as an apprentice. It suggests a division in the depths of his personality: "They told me . . . that you like your new quarters very much [in school at Castleton]; which I do not at all wonder at from one of your age who has always lived in dry old Peacham. A person living *there* cannot become acquainted with more than twenty persons in a long life time! and perhaps those will not *all* be *agreeable* acquaintances. I think it does one good to 'go around' some even if they don't go far! (but generally the further the better). I do not mean to say that I don't love *home;* for certainly it is the dearest place on earth. But one cannot see hear nor learn anything at home; therefore it is a good idea to go out once in a while."

Born in October 1835, Augustus was four and a half when the Walbridge and Watts households merged, the youngest child of the combined families, but barely gaining that title from his new brother Charles, who was only six months older. It is tempting to imagine the subtle and perhaps not always so subtle jockeying for position taking place in those first months.

Clearly Augustus was bright and well grown. When he was seven Chastina wrote to Martha, "I wish you could see Aug he is one of the best boys to learn that there is, always at the head of his class he studdies Geography & Grammar this summer have always heard it remarked by the teachers that he has been to that they 'should like to have a whole school of such boys [as] A.' "

Another note began to sound very soon, however. There was an incident when Augustus was eight, of which Roxana wrote, "Augustus met with quite an accident last spring they were all a Chopping wood at the door and Charles let his axe fly out of his hand and it struck Augustus on the knee and cut the knee almost through it hung together by verry little on one edge the Doctor dressed it and put his leg in a box and he had to lie in that situation about three week but it done well and he has got so that he does not go much lame."

Here are two events—being merged with another family and having a severe injury—that would be hard for a child to handle in any case, and that might permanently affect a certain type of child.

Roxana continued to write good news of him, "Augustus is large of his age is a good schollar and a verry steady boy." Chastina called him, more ominously, a "sober boy." By the time he was sixteen, family concern began to surface, and Chastina wrote in her diary on June 28, 1852, "Augustus is unwell & somewhat nervous I should think. Mother talks of going to Dunham with him to see the Doctor." The two of them left a few days later to go to Canada and see Roxana's brother, "the Doctor," who has already figured in the earlier story of David Brown's death. The results of this visit are unknown.

It was not a good time or place to be "unwell & somewhat nervous." Very little was known about mental illness this side of its violent stages, and the treatments for those were often fully as violent as the illness itself at its worst. In Vermont by this time the Brattleboro Retreat, or "Insane Hospital" as Chastina called it, had been open for nearly twenty years, advocating humane treatment of the "poor insane" rather than the "blood-letting, strong purges, and various shock treatments" common elsewhere. Roxana most surely had known of the retreat, for a nephew of Lyman's, Alvah Watts, had been sent there in 1851 after acting first "crazy" and then "deranged & raving," having attempted "to cut his mother's throat" with a butchering knife. In any case, Augustus was not ill enough to be institutionalized, and he was far luckier than most in having a family whose loving attention followed and cherished him all his low-key, depressed life to its dramatic end.

In the spring of 1853 Augustus made his own attempt to deal with his ailments by invoking the great faith that New Englanders had traditionally maintained in the healing power inherent in being close to salt water. Roxana wrote to Hubbell and Augusta Gregory, "Augustus . . . is gone to sea not as a Sailor but on a fishing vessel. he went on purpose for his health as he is naturally verry bilious and he was in hopes it would help him I don't know what he will do when he comes back but Dustan wants him to learn a trade so if he ever comes back they can work together he taught school last winter with good success."

Dustan—his own Walbridge brother, three years older—was a strong influence in his life, and as long as Dustan was alive, Augustus seems to have done fairly well. Apprenticed to Mr. Miller, a local carriage maker, he fulfilled Dustan's wish that he learn a trade.

When he was nineteen he had another accident, and Roxana wrote on July 5, 1854: "Augustus did not get so that he could work until about the 10th of June he lost all the bone from the first joint to the end and it is a great *bungling* looking thing now yet it is better than none." He appears to have been accident prone. Recovering, he carried on, leaving his apprenticeship at twenty-one as was the custom, and setting up in business. As Roxana wrote: "Augustus has got so that he is a good work man he has sent 9 Buggies out to Cal to Dustan [in San Francisco] they have not arived there yet but Dustan has sent him a draft of $500 the price he paid Miller They cost him 125 each boxed ready for shipping he is in hopes to make something on them but cant tell yet."

In 1855 Dustan had written to his brother-in-law John Way: "I have always calculated to go home so to get theire by the time Augustus get his trade liarnt, so that we mite go together into business—or on a *tramp* as we call it when journeymen go from place to place to work to pick up new ideas." He was delayed by lack of funds, but in 1857 he came back to Vermont, and he and Augustus went journeying, as he had planned, out to John and Sarah Way in Minnesota. They spent a year in Northfield helping to build the schoolhouse while they investigated possible opportunities for carriage makers. In the end, forced by the economic depression of the times to give up, they came home and set up in the wheelwright trade in St. Johnsbury, but with limited success and much discouragement.

In 1861 Augustus took his own advice to Alice and set out for California ("the further the better"). Dustan, with his usual sense of responsibility for Augustus's welfare, wrote to "Sister Clara" in San Francisco: "I suppose that Augustus starts soon for Cal.—perhaps you will see him before you get this . . . Our folks [Mother and Father] thought it was not a verry good notion but I thought it was the best thing that he could do.—there is nothing doing on our trade hire now and I dont know when there will be again.—he is not one that is good for *knocking around* and finding jobbs, is not a *money katcher* and if out of work is rather apt to be gloomy, have the *blues* &c.—and for such times has not quite enough energy and goahead about him—the same as it was with me.—You know these are bad faults, but I dont know as he can help them. I hope Russel [Clara's husband] or someone will get him a steady jobb . . . and then if he does get out of jobbs and dont seeme to take the right course to help himself to one, dont be afraid to give him some advice in the matter he will take it all in good part.—he is as still as ever never says much and does not *show* his apprecia- tion of kindness as much as some but has as fine feelings as anyone.—"

By the end of the year Augustus was working in Mountain View, which he described in a letter to his family in Peacham as "the healthiest place in Calif.—a farming country." He added: "I am working in a small shop where they mostly do repairing. I am my own boss and the only wood worker in the shop which is pleasanter than being dogged around by Old Casebolt." In 1862 Dustan, his mainstay and mentor, enlisted in the army; Augustus never served in the Civil War, although because of his age he was eligible for military service. California, where he lived during those years, had no draft.

Along with their constant concern for him, family members occasion- ally felt free to express irritation with this difficult man, and even Dustan was no exception. Out in California Augustus began to hold some opin- ions that did not sit well in the East. Something he wrote drew from Dustan an exasperated comment in a letter to Alice written from camp near Wash- ington: "I am glad if Augustus has come down from his *high horse* a little. I have not written to him yet, but when I do shall endeavor to make him comprehend that *Uncle Samuel* still owns that little patch called California and that some things can be done as well as others."

By the time the war was over the two most important people in Au- gustus's life were gone. His mother had died in the fall of 1862, and in late June 1864 Dustan died in a Washington hospital of wounds received at Cold Harbor. A letter from Clara described how these events affected him: "Augustus has been here several weeks, is out of employment now. I dont know what he will do next. Shouldn't be surprised if he went back to the States. He seems more gloomy than usual, some days he scarcley goes out all day. He feels Dustan's death severely, but sometimes I think he might be more cheerful, but suppose he cannot change his nature."

With Clara as his emotional support, Augustus stayed on in California. Julian Rix, his nephew, mentioned him as still there in 1869; but by 1876 he was back in Peacham, living at the homestead on East Hill with his brother Isaac, his sister Ella, and Isaac's daughter, Meroe. That year Isaac's diary noted Augustus and Ella going off for a month's visit to Baltimore and Philadelphia where they toured the Centennial Exposition, a mammoth, six-month-long celebration of the country's hundredth birthday and its reunion after the divisions of the Civil War. Ella and Augustus were among the eight million people who visited it, and its many marvels were easily worth the weeks that they allotted to it. Alexander Graham Bell's newly invented telephone was on show, as well as an early typewriting machine. The arm and hand of the not-yet-completed Statue of Liberty held up its torch. Artworks and exotic plants from all over the world showed what beauty and strangeness the globe had to offer. One exhibit especially may have caught the attention of these two visitors from Vermont: the stump of an oak, nearly two feet in diameter, felled entirely by the intense rifle fire of the battle at Spotsylvania, the first fighting that Dustan and Isaac experienced. Even in the pursuit of pleasure, however, Augustus met with misfortune. Isaac wrote to Ella from Peacham: "How are you enjoying the show? Has Augustus found his valise, and how does he stand it?"

Isaac's family changed, but Augustus continued to be part of it, with Isaac's second wife, Ellen, Meroe, and Ella. In 1878 Ella was visiting the Minnesota family, and Augustus occupied her room while she was gone. Ellen's sprightly letters to Ella, full of family news and town gossip, have in them a few glancing references to Augustus, whose name she misspells consistently. "Agustus is the same as ever," she wrote in April. "I have no idea that he intends to marry. Marietta had not taken a school the last time I saw her." The juxtaposition of those last two sentences was not accidental, as later events will show. Marietta Clark Hurd was a young Peacham widow who could "take a school" if she was single, but would be unlikely to do so if she were to marry.

In October Ellen wrote to Ella, "Agustus is still here and is better than he was awhile ago." At about the same time Isaac wrote: "[Augustus] was real sick for a few days. I think he is more of an enigma than ever. Most everybody claims to believe that he is going to be married but I dont believe that there is any foundation for the report other than a desire for gossip." And in a December letter: "Ellen says she dont see the least symptoms of matrimony in Augustus and that he stands around more than usual."

Whatever Augustus's plans were or were not, everything changed at the farm on East Hill when Isaac died in March 1881. Isaac's widow Ellen must have been in an emotional turmoil as she decided what she and her daughter Helen, one and a half years old, would do.

Augustus was in turmoil too. On September 9 he finally married Marietta, who—to judge from Ellen's earlier speculations—had been waiting four years for him to make up his mind. A week after the wedding, the *St. Johnsbury Caledonian* took up the external aspects of the story:

September 16, 1881: Mrs. Ellen Watts sold her farm last week to Augustus Walbridge. Stock, grain and everything except household furniture was included in the sale. After having owned it for a day or two, however, Mr. Walbridge concluded that he did not care to own the farm. Consequently the farm was sold back to Mrs. Watts, who was nothing loth.

A letter from Augustus to Clara written a week after this news item described the inner state that had led to this outer confusion: "Your kind letter was duly received and I will answer immediately as you wish. I am very sorry circumstances are such that I cannot come to Cal. I have lately married the lady whose name you have heard connected with mine with the intention of buying the old farm. I bargained for it and backed out again thinking it was too hard for me. There seems to be nothing for me to do here & I have no energy to go into any kind of business So that I feel *very bad* not knowing which way to turn. My wife & Ella think I had better have the farm. But it is getting run out and I feel that I should make a failure if I undertook [it]. So that I am driven almost to distraction to know what to do. I wish your letter had come before these events happened. I would have gone to you & yet I dont see as I can now.

"My wife is smart & well and much too good for me, for I am so torn to pieces in my mind *and body* that I dont know as I can treat her well as I ought for I feel that I made a great misstake in marrying at all. That disease that I have had so long has Completely unstrung me and made me very cowardly about undertaking anything difficult I dont know what I *shall do* I am so stirred up that I cant think of anything to write I am very sorry I cannot come to you."

The *Caledonian* reported a further farm transaction:

October 7th, 1881: Augustus Walbridge has re-purchased the Watts' farm.

On this same day, sister Alice's husband, Charles Choate, on his West Barnet farm, wrote in his diary: "Augustus and Ella down and they are in a lamentable condition."

And on November 11, 1881, The *Caledonian* reported the sad, defeated ending:

Last Tuesday Augustus Walbridge committed suicide by hanging. He was found suspended from a beam in his horse barn, about four o'clock, by the hired man. For some time his health has been very poor and he [was] subject to long fits of melancholy. He was no doubt temporarily insane. Those left to mourn his untimely death have the sympathy of the entire community.

Charles Choate's diary described the day, "Alice David and I attended Augustus funeral. . . . It has been a cold raw day."

After only two months of marriage, Marietta was left a widow for the second time. Ellen and baby Helen were adjusting to life at the Corner where they had moved. Ella had returned from Minnesota to help after her brother Isaac's death and now had to deal with this second death. Alice and Charles, still mourning their two-year-old son, who had died that May, and working long days on their own farm with their three other children, were the most stable ones in the family, and everyone gravitated to them. Charles's diary entries listed the family's comings and goings. On November 14, "I went to East part in afternoon Ella came home with me." On the nineteenth, "Marietta down in the afternoon." On the thirtieth, "Brought Ellen and her baby down in the morning." Life went on; the chores were done as reported in Charles's diary—"milking," "spreading manure," "getting Grist from the mill," "moving hay," "churning and Stamping the Butter," "hauling Straw and corn fodder"—but the main concern of the family was supporting one another through this year of tragic deaths—of Isaac in March, baby Nelson in May, and Augustus in November.

Suicide was not new to the Peacham community. Almost forty years earlier, John Mattocks, Peacham's most notable citizen, having served three terms in Congress before becoming governor of Vermont in 1843, suffered the loss of his nineteen-year-old son, George, a Harvard law student, who, according to the *Caledonian* on January 29, 1844, "was found in his room . . . with his throat cut from ear to ear, and dead. . . . A razor was found in the room which it is supposed he used for the purposes." The headline read: "Melancholy Death." Chastina called it "a most shocking affair" in a letter written at the time. Governor Mattocks felt so strongly the shame and stigma of suicide in his family that he immediately retired from public life.

The effect of Augustus's suicide on the Walbridge-Watts family is unknown. Marietta remained in Peacham and, seven years later, married a local lawyer. After Augustus died, there was no further mention of him in the family letters or diaries—only a poignant hand-written note someone added to the envelope of his letter to Clara: "Uncle Gus' last letter."

Lifelong Vermonters

By 1860 four of every ten Vermonters had left their native state in search of a better life, most going out west. Those who stayed at home missed the excitement of a move, the anticipation of success, and the adventure of something new.

Lyman and Isaac, each guided more by a sense of responsibility than by personal ambition, traveled temporarily in order to study, to serve in the Civil War, or to visit relatives, but they made their permanent homes in Vermont.

Though the number of Vermont farms did not decrease during the westward movement, the decrease in population resulted in a shortage of farm help, and farmers had to increase the wages of good hands when they were lucky enough to hire them. Charles Choate, Alice's husband, spent days at the beginning of hay season traveling from village to village and farm to farm trying to locate help. Farmers who remained in Vermont had a hard time making a successful living.

Few professions existed in northern Vermont during this time, but one that did was the ministry. Lyman, who had preached off and on in the villages around Peacham during his schooling, sought the pastorship of several churches and finally settled in Barnet, just southeast of Peacham. He had other opportunities—he could have stayed in Massachusetts where he served as an assistant pastor for several years or gone west as his mentor David Merrill had to make a name for himself before being invited back home—but Lyman chose to establish his reputation in his home area.

Some children who remained in Vermont became leaders in their communities. Both Isaac and Lyman held town positions—selectman and school superintendent—through the years; Isaac also became a state legislator. Following in their father's footsteps, they gave freely of their time and accepted civic duties as a matter of course.

Although it was adventurous to move away, Lyman and Isaac preferred the comforts of home and the security of familiarity. They married women they had known from childhood. And these women may have expressed more strongly than Martha and Sarah their desire to remain close to their families. Isaac's first wife, Lizzie Way, had been raised on a farm just north of the Watts farm, and as a young mother, she relied on her family's help after her daughter was born. Lyman's wife, Sarah Chamberlain, came from one of the most wealthy and respected families in Peacham, which must have brought her some status. She too was close to her family and with her sisters had helped nurse their only brother before his death. For whatever variety of reasons, Lyman and Isaac chose to make their homes close to their birthplace, combining family responsibility and community leadership.

Lyman Sargeant Watts (1832–1872)

A Village Pastor

To a degree unimaginable today, ministers held positions of power in New England communities of the eighteenth and early nineteenth centuries. They were expected and entitled to speak firmly and even aggressively to their congregations about public behavior, individual lifestyles, and, most important, the soul's relation to God and the need for acceptance of God's will. Perhaps the closest equivalent of the authority of ministers then is the respect and influence of the medical profession today.

As the nineteenth century moved past its midmark, however, various forces began to impinge on the power of the clergy. Rapid industrial and technical development, a relative increase in comfort and ease of living, the opening of the frontier westward, even the recently established mental hospitals and the part they played in dealing with the casualties of the Millerite religious hysteria had all brought about a change in the direction of religious attention. Gradually and almost imperceptibly the major concern in pulpit and pew alike had begun to shift from the next world to this one, from making souls ready for the next world to making life in the here and now all that it could be. The temperance and abolitionist movements claimed more and more of the churches' attention as the power of ministers to regulate individual thought and behavior began its long decline.

All these changes had hardly begun to make themselves apparent in the hill towns of northern Vermont when young Lyman Watts, Roxana's elder stepson, felt called to the ministry. In May 1851, at the age of eighteen, he "made a profession of religion," as his obituary puts it, "dating his conversion about six months after the death of the Rev. David Merrill, his pastor." This marked a true and permanent conversion which influenced the course of his entire life and pervaded his personality and character.

For a serious, thoughtful, intellectually inclined youth, David Merrill would have been a compelling role model. Born and educated in Peacham like Lyman, he had completed his education at Dartmouth and Andover Theological Seminary and made a name for himself in New England and the Midwest as an intellectual and effective preacher. His famous "Ox Sermon," an early and at the time revolutionary suggestion that the producer of liquor was as guilty as the drinker, was published by the Urbana, Ohio, Temperance Society and had a circulation of approximately three million in the United States and abroad. His preaching style was purely intellectual; as one report has it, he "always read his sermons, rarely looking at his audience. When asked why he made no gestures, he replied 'when I have nothing to say, then I may need them.' "

The young Lyman listened and learned and went his way determined to become a minister. Almost before he began the long process, when he was twenty a siege of ill-health interrupted it. He dealt with his sickness in the time-honored fashion of spending the next six months on or near the sea.

He turned the time to good account, however, as he reported in December of that year, 1852, to his old friend Ashbel Martin, who had gone to California like so many other Peachamites: "You will recollect that my health was rather poor when I wrote to you last & not getting any better I started the 1st of July for the salt water I went out a fishing & was gone 2 weeks just long enough to find out how good it felt to be *sea-sick* When I returned to Boston I received an offer to come to Maine selling books. . . . So I have been engaged in that business the past summer. . . . I have walked all the time & send my trunk & books by stage. . . . I am now teaching school at $18.00 per month I am very pleasantly situated have a small school & not very hard though I have 3 or 4 who would be ugly if they dared to The schools here are very short Mine lasts only 6 weeks but I have 2 so that it makes 3 months."

Even he was not entirely immune to the California fever. The letter continued: "I wish I was with you in California & if I was at home think I should go Chastina is going this winter & I should like to go with her but I am engaged now & was before I heard she was going."

This same letter both raises and answers the question of how much his stepmother Roxana meant to him: "I can feel for you now better than I could if I had remained at home True I am not so far away but I hear often yet I am alike deprived of their counsel & advice. . . . A mothers counsel & advice True I have never had my own mother to go to as you have (& you know not how great a blessing that is) yet I feel that I have a mother & more since I left home than ever before." It would seem that Roxana's letter writing included Lyman as well as her absent daughters; and abroad or at home they would certainly have shared in religious interests and conversations.

He was away from home for most of the time that followed during the thirteen years that it took him to become a minister. Frederick Wells's *History of Barnet* explains why Lyman's education was so prolonged: "Both

Lyman S. Watts, ca. 1864. Photograph taken by Warren, Post Office Block, Cambridgeport, Massachusetts. Courtesy Choate Farm Collection.

before and during his college course he taught many terms in various schools, east and west." He taught in Ohio during the winter of 1855 and again in 1858, when he was already enrolled as a student at Middlebury College.

A fragmentary diary, kept at Middlebury in 1857, concerns itself very little with all this effort—beyond a brief report of a school-teaching session during the winter vacation—but very much with the state of his soul and its relation to Christ, indicating his major ministerial goals and the general direction that his ministry would take throughout.

January 21: Commence this diary especially to promote growth in grace. I commence with the desire that I may be honest with myself and God at all times. Nothing special today. Thoughts wandered while reading and praying. . . .

March 26: This has been a good day to my soul. Though how ill prepared I am for the society of heaven. . . . Had conversation with a professor, Mr. F. who has got into the dark but is anxious to have again the smiles of the Savior. I longed to point him to Christ but how feebly did I do it. shall my mouth ever be closed? . . .

May 27: . . . I have spent a vacation two weeks at home and what barrenness during that time and what sins did I commit. surely the Lord is merciful in sparing me. May I not be at ease in Zion. . . .

June 10: This day attended the Installation of Revd. Mr. Hyde. . . . Was more than ever impressed with the sacredness of the office. What a holy man should a minister be! Could such a worldly sinful wretch be one? . . .

June 20: Went out with Mr. [illegible] to converse with different families on the subject of religion. We visited 10 families. I often questioned my motives but prayed that I might go with the right spirit. I fee[l] as though I was abundantly blessed myself, and hope it had an influence upon others. . . .

July 11: Visited in Cornwall with Mr. W. Often questioned my motive did not feel as a dying mortal conversing with dying men about their souls should. I hope the visit was not without some benefit to me and others.

He was at that point just short of twenty-five years old. Two years later, after several more interruptions for terms of school teaching, he graduated from Middlebury, Phi Beta Kappa, salutatorian of his class, excelling in mathematics.

Two years of teaching followed, the first at Castleton Seminary, where his younger sister Alice attended as a student. Lyman himself had brought about this great event in Alice's life by persuading his father that it would cost no more than sending her to Peacham Academy and offering to pay her travel costs out of his own skimpy purse. The young ladies at Castleton liked him and wrote a flowery letter of appreciation accompanied by a book "as an offering sacred to the shrine of *Friendship*" when he left to go back home and become principal of Peacham Academy, his old school.

He held this post for one year, and in the fall of 1861, at the age of twenty-nine, was at last financially able to enter the theological seminary at Andover, Massachusetts.

The seminary catalog for 1864, the year Lyman graduated, is instructive. No time was allowed for other work: "Experience has proved that the labor of *teaching,* and of other similar avocations, during term-time, is an evil. . . . Even the vacations should not be unnecessarily spent in exhausting pursuits." Financial burdens were eased as much as possible, however.

No expense is incurred for instruction, and none by undergraduates for rooms in the public buildings, except three dollars a year for the care of rooms and beds, and for repair of buildings. Each student pays also three dollars a year for the use of the Library, and five dollars a year for the care, warming, and lighting of lecture rooms and the chapel, for the ringing of the bell, and for other incidental expenses. . . . To those whose pecuniary necessities require it, about a dollar a week is given from the funds of the Seminary. . . . The Trustees have appropriated a productive tract of land, for the gratuitous use of those students who may choose to cultivate it. The exercise in the garden or the field is not only serviceable to their health, but it also yields to them a pecuniary profit.

The intellectual and spiritual formation of the seminary's students covered three intensive years. In the first year they studied the Bible and learned Hebrew; in those days it could be assumed that a college graduate already knew Greek. In the second year they studied theology, dealing with such matters as the existence of God, the immortality of the soul, total depravity, regeneration, sanctification, judgment, "with frequent examinations of the Class, on Ethical and Theological topics." In the third year they learned how to preach, and studied "Sacred and Secular History." At the very end of the second term of that year, almost as an afterthought, they were given a short course in "Pastoral Theology: Religious, Intellectual, and Social Character of the Clergyman; Pastoral Visiting; Catechizing."

Such a course of training, long on theory and talk, short on the practice of human relations, could produce as its end result young men bursting with an assurance amounting to fanaticism. Lyman was no exception. While he was still in seminary he was moved to write an earnest letter to his brother Dustan whose contents can be inferred from the reply: "Dear Brother, I received a letter from you, I think at least a month ago, and should have answered before this, but I really did not know *how* to answer it for, to have answered it, or rather written another without saying anything about the subject of Religion would have implied that letters on that subject were distasteful to me which would have belied my feelings. For I was glad to get just such a letter from you, and you may be assured that I shall never be *displeased* with anything of the kind, and to have answered it in *my* way of thinking would have been to commence a contriversy with you upon religion, which I did not and I presume you would not desire, but I will just notice a few things which did not seem plain to me. I think it is true as you say that there is a natural longing for something beyond this life, but is this an honest reason for a belief that that longing will be grati-fied. . . . you say there is a natural feeling of *guilt* in man and an expectation of punishment, but no idea of forgiveness. I think that is not borne out by facts. I never hird of a nation of people that had any ideas of future punish-ment, but also had a belief of rewards. . . . You say man alone is not capable of conceiving or evincing an idea of *love* such as is presented in the person of Christ. will you for a moment divest yourself of that reverential feeling with which you have been educated to regard the verry name of Christ, and look at it as though [you] had hird the story for the first time, accept as true that he was a God, but encumbered with our mortal body. . . . Suppose he felt all the pangs that a mortal will feele in like trials, is there not many *men* that have layed down their lives for the good of others. . . . But I am not writing to convince you that you are in eror—for I have no wish to and if I had should not expect to, but only write that you may see the things that come up before me to make me think different from you."

This patient and tactful response to what must have seemed an imperti-nent and arrogant letter—though undoubtedly one that Lyman felt himself constrained by the Holy Spirit to write—showed how far Dustan's travels and independent habits of thought had moved him from the religion of his childhood. Writing to "Sister Ella" two days later, Dustan allowed himself to poke a little fun at Lyman, who was spending his six-week seminary vacation preaching in Calais, Vermont: "It seems Lyman has mad another of his flying visits to Peacham, and is as full of business as ever—going to straighten out the *Calais* folks. I wish he could do all the good that is in his heart to do."

Dustan knew how much Lyman got in his own way, but Lyman did not. Armed with the shield of his faith and the belt of his truth and the breast-plate of his righteousness, he continued on his path, finished his seminary course and on graduation in 1864 was appointed pastor of the Congrega-tional church and superintendent of schools (a common combination of positions in that era) in Dracut, Massachusetts, where he had worked as a student pastor.

The following spring, on a short leave of absence from his parish, Rev. L. S. Watts was appointed by the office of the U.S. Christian Commission (set up by the YMCA to promote the spiritual and temporal welfare of the men of the army and navy) as a delegate to the Union Army for a four-week period. The list of necessary qualifications is in itself a character sketch: "can command audience in the open air, of rank and file . . . a knowledge of the world, experience in business, and ability in affairs . . . adapted to interest and benefit others in social meetings and personal inter-course . . . piety and patriotism, good common sense and energy." He reported for work on May 26, in Washington, where the troops were stationed waiting discharge; was assigned to the 20th Corps and—by good luck—to his younger brother Isaac's 6th Corps, and left on June 27 when his term expired. Isaac, fretting impatiently in camp, saw Lyman nearly every day during the last half of his stay, listening to his sermons and going to his prayer meetings. Lyman was tired and ill when the month was done; of all the "necessary qualities" he was shortest on energy.

In 1867 he came home, or close to it, as pastor of the Congregational Church and superintendent of schools in Barnet, seven miles from Pea-cham. Established as he was, he could now marry. He chose a young Peacham woman, Sarah Chamberlain, daughter of the proper and pros-perous Deacon E. A. Chamberlain and one of four intellectually inclined and well-educated sisters. Sarah herself was Lyman's intellectual equal, hav-ing been valedictorian in her class at Lasell Seminary and having taught in several private schools and seminaries. More than that, as Lyman's sister Alice commented in a letter west: "She is real good." Her obituary in the *Caledonian,* printed just one month short of the third anniversary of her wedding, spoke of her as "more than usually energetic, prudent and influ-ential as a pastor's wife"—a fit helpmate indeed.

Not long after the wedding "Brother Charles" and his wife Lodoska came from Illinois for a visit. The Watts part of the family was together again, and they celebrated the occasion as Isaac reported in his diary: "We all went to Barnet today to get some pictures taken at the artist's. Stopped with Lyman to dinner and got home at dark."

The photograph shows them all: Father Lyman, his five children, and the wives of his two eldest, Lyman and Charles; formally dressed and posed, four seated, four standing, all gazing steadily at the camera, all in black, the

Watts Family, Barnet, Vermont, 1867. Front row, left to right: Alice Watts, Lyman Watts (father), Isaac N. Watts, Ella Watts. Back row: Sarah Chamberlain Watts, Lyman Watts (son), Charles Watts, Lodoska Spencer Watts. Courtesy Choate Farm Collection.

women wearing white standup collars, the men in vests and white shirts. Isaac's coat is on crooked and Charles's vest has a button undone; otherwise they are perfection. Son Lyman and his wife stand at the back, Sarah leaning a little forward like the figurehead on the prow of a ship, her expression intense and determined, mouth set: a handsome, strong, tall woman. Lyman stands beside her, not much taller than she, his head slightly tilted; his expression is firm, a little grim, patient, and above all, conscientious. He wears a beard, of course.

This was the man who came to Barnet, his training complete, his character formed, his ways set. A good man. Not everyone in Barnet was up to appreciating him, however. A young man who grew up in Peacham Corner wrote of Lyman, "He hasn't got a heart as large as a match." And indeed he had been trained to a rigid and pressing style of ministry, as demanding upon others as it was upon himself.

No one could have said that he was not hardworking. Anyone familiar with a minister's responsibilities today will wonder how the daily round could have been accomplished over a century ago, with no telephone, no automobiles, not even very passable roads. But Lyman managed. He made pastoral calls around Barnet on foot. Longer trips he made in a carriage, or riding with someone's team, or in "the cars"—the railroad—or, in extreme cases, riding the freight. As for the lack of a telephone, the post office was then a speedy twenty-four-hour resource and there was the stage as well to send messages and parcels by. He wrote of one day when Alice, recently married and living in West Barnet, was sick: "Alice wrote to me this morn. Went to Druggist & got what she wanted & sent it back by stage"—all just about as quickly as it can be done now. If visitors were coming by train, however, it might be necessary for him to "go to the Depot" three or four days in succession before they finally turned up. And it was an all-weather life, in rain and snow, heat and cold, with very little protection for the traveler in any of it.

What kind of minister was he? Wells's *History of Barnet* describes him as "a very spiritual man"; a friend and fellow minister spoke of "his almost extreme conscientiousness." In combining these two qualities he was almost guaranteeing himself a life of despair; for he was swimming against the tide of the century's increasing worldliness, all the while blaming himself for his failures, which he attributed to his own shortcomings as a vessel of the Holy Spirit. But he carried on.

On January 1, 1869, Lyman began to keep a diary which, though he could not have known it at the time, would record at once the outward progression of an extremely hard year and the inward process that would turn this high-minded, right-thinking, hard-driving, and hard-driven man into a human being at last.

The diary starts off at a brisk pace, with a prayer meeting every night through January, a month chosen by the churches of the area to be a period of spiritual renewal, with all the religious emotion that such occasions call forth. Lyman noted the crescendo as the month went on: "I believe 28 rose for prayer tonight. . . . Some over 60 rose for prayer & a large number took part. . . . Was more feeling, I think, than usual—Hope God is leading some to him self. . . . Meeting in eve fully attended 64 came forward. . . . Considerable feeling, tho Christians seemed backward." And he recorded the decrescendo on January 31: "Had good attention, but not those manifest signs of the Spir[itual]. presence we have had before. . . . Some over 50 came forward. Had a good meeting but I fear some are going back. O for the power of the H. [Holy] Spirit." On February 3 he struck a more personal note: "Feel very tired & somewhat discouraged—Hope God will not leave us yet. There are so many souls to be saved or lost."

In January also, wanting to spread the word into Norrisville (now East Barnet) where two factories had sprung up to take advantage of abundant water power, one making bobbins and the other textiles, he made frequent visits to a different type of congregation. "Went into Factory into lower room [for a] few minutes & then in[to] weave room. Had long talk with Sarah Gilmore. Hope she gave herself to Christ." On the twentieth, "went to Worth's Mill. . . . In P.M. went into Factory," seeing a long list of people in each place. Here a definite class line emerges. Mr. Worth and Mr. Norris, the owners, and their managers all receive titles; the workers are usually mentioned by first or last names only, depending on whether they were women or men, but never "Miss" or "Mr."

It was a busy month, but the rest of the year was not much quieter. There was visiting to do every day, as well as a meeting or two. Sarah helped with the Sunday school when she could, but it still took a good deal of Lyman's time, with its frequent concerts and exhibitions and the responsibility of choosing its curriculum and its library (he worried that some of the books suggested were too much like novels). There were regular prayer meetings every Wednesday or Thursday night; a young men's prayer meeting occasionally on Fridays; a Sunday school teachers' meeting every Saturday night. There were baptisms, often emergency calls for babies about to die; weddings, often with only a few hours notice; and many funerals, for a population larger than that of Barnet today. Once, knowing how busy he would be in the intervening days, he began writing the sermon for an old woman's funeral an hour or two before she died. There were meetings with his fellow ministers, either informally or at the Caledonia County Ministerial Association (where he preached the opening sermon and was chosen moderator) to which he went in June, before the statewide General Convention, held in Brandon that year, to which he and his carpet bag also went.

Above all, there were Sundays, fifty-two of them a year, each one including church in the morning, a concert, an exhibition or a meeting in the afternoon, a trip to Norrisville for prayer and preaching and a prayer meeting in the evening in Barnet. And the sermons! Even today, when sermons are shorter and less rigorously intellectual and scholarly, many ministers find their peace of mind destroyed by the demand to be publicly inspiring once a week on schedule. Each week Lyman faced his challenge, and the diary showed how much he agonized over it. First he had to produce a full-dress, written-out sermon, covering many pages (he speaks in one entry of having written only eleven pages of his text so far). Then came what he called an "Extempore" sermon, delivered from careful notes, for the afternoon meeting and, probably, Norrisville. He thought about these sermons all week, chose a subject as soon as one came clear, read and studied and

wrote when he could, and was happy if he got it done by Saturday afternoon. Occasionally he found himself desperately writing until the bell rang
for morning service. (Fortunately he lived across from the church.) These
were backbreaking duties, accepted without question by ministers of the
period, and Lyman expected of himself not only that he would do them,
but that he would do them well every week. The entry for a Saturday in
July showed the tension he felt: "Rose at quarter before 5 this morn & went
into the study where I stayed till almost 6 o'clock P.M. except time for
breakfast & dinner. Finished my sermon, but it has been hard work to write
& is [a] poor sermon."

It was a demanding life, and one that Lyman's conscientiousness did
nothing to ease. Little joy was expressed in the diary, or peace, or pleasure in
life. Many times he mentioned "pleasant" weather; sometimes he spoke of
a "pleasant" time at home or visiting on East Hill; but mostly the diary was
concerned with meeting requirements, either external or self-imposed.

As superintendent of schools, he examined prospective teachers and
visited the one-room schoolhouses scattered over the area. He kept his East
Hill family constantly in mind and ran countless errands for them. He
helped Sarah with the housework, particularly the Monday wash, and
bought a washing machine to help the task along. He planted and tended a
garden to provide vegetables for the household and sometimes worked in it
until it was too dark to see. More and more frequently the diary entries
closed with the words, "Am very tired tonight." Simply keeping things
going had become a desperate struggle.

The year did not improve as it went on. Sarah was increasingly unwell
during the early summer; the cause became apparent in the entry for
August 5: "Sarah did not sleep any all night. At 7 o'clock I went for Mrs.
Potts. At 8 called the Dr. who said she wd hardly be sick today. At 11 went
for Mrs. Clement. Dr came about 12. Sarah suffered severely till a quarter
before 2, when God gave us a little girl. . . . All are quite comfortable
tonight. . . . Good pr[ayer] meeting this eve." Sarah was slow to recover
and for a time she was seriously ill and in great pain with a breast abscess.
The baby, named Jennie Chamberlain Watts, was often "worrisome." Lyman's sleep, his work, and his all-important sermons suffered while he took
care of both patients, with an occasional neighbor acting as night nurse to
give him a rest.

The last part of the year was full of fatigue and a numb acceptance out of
which emerged a curious kind of simplicity, in which he did his work as
well as he could, letting it go at that—not evaluating and not worrying. On

December 21 he had what must have been a harrowing experience, shattering all his expectations of himself; but his comment on it was brief, preceded by a characteristic summary of an errand run for the family: "This morn went with Ella to sch[ool] in Warden Dis[trict]. . . . Then drive to Danville to [Caledonia County Ministerial] Assn. Was chosen Moderator & took charge of the Greek Lesson. . . . Preached to about 80 in eve. Had good atten[tion] but Assn. criticised severely, tho no more than I deserved." No anguish, no self-blame; just the fact and the acceptance of it. Fatigue had brought him a certain kind of peace.

He seems also to have come to a new level of humanity and faith. On December 15, one of the factories burned down, "a hard fire and a sad one for us." At a prayer meeting the next night, "having references mainly to the recent fire," he read Psalm 46 and the last verses of Habakkuk, choosing out of all the Bible two of its most beautiful evocations of trust in a God of the afflicted:

> God is our refuge and strength,
> a very present help in trouble . . .
> There is a river,
> the streams whereof shall make glad the city of God.

And from Habakkuk:

> Although the fig tree shall not blossom,
>   neither shall fruit be in the vines;
> the labour of the olive shall fail,
>   and the fields shall yield no meat;
> the flock shall be cut off from the fold,
>   and there shall be no herd in the stalls:
> Yet will I rejoice in the Lord,
>   I will joy in the God of my salvation.

There is little more to tell. Sarah recovered and lived well into the next year, when she died suddenly and unexpectedly after a short illness. Lyman, as his obituary two years later says, "never recovered from the death of his wife." Another factor was at work as well: tuberculosis, the plague that was to kill each of the Watts brothers in turn. He went into a slow, long decline, resigned his pastorate in 1871, and spent the following winter in Florida at Haynes Landing on the St. Johns River in search of warm weather to help him regain his health. But the winds were cold and he did not improve. Coming back to Peacham, he died on June 3, 1872, two months short of his fortieth birthday.

The entries in his 1869 diary for December 29 and 30 told of two trips to the depot to see several families off for settlement in other parts of the country. "They left in good spirits. A large number were there to see them start. It is sad to see so many going away."

It is sad to see Lyman and Sarah going away, not able to enjoy the fruits of all their hard labor at home and in the parish, not able to relax into the peace and human gentleness that might have come to them with experience, not able to see their daughter grow up. Above all, it is sad to see Lyman kept by his own temperament and his physical frailty from doing all the good that was in his heart to do.

But if his choice of texts for the service after the mill fire offers any kind of clue as to the direction of his spiritual growth, perhaps after all those weary years of serving the harsh God of his own conscience, he at last came to feel what he described in his Middlebury diary as "the smiles of the Savior."

Isaac Newton Watts (1842–1881)

Soldier, Farmer, Citizen

IN FARM families it often happens that a son is elected almost from birth to be the one who stays at home. In the Watts family, the life of its youngest son, Isaac, was from the beginning subordinated to the needs of the farm. "Does Isaac make a good teamster?" his older brother Lyman wrote when Isaac was ten. "I should think he would get tired. I guess he wished the whole hill somewhere else if he drove to plow the whole. I should think he did very well." Other family letters speak casually of his being taken out of school to do the spring plowing. His training had begun.

When he was thirteen, an age at which his younger sister Alice was already turning out well-phrased sentences as additions to her mother's letters west, he wrote a badly blotted, inarticulate, almost-illiterate letter to his little nephew and niece in "Minesota Teritory." "how do you like out west is it cold there . . . how do you like the wolves & Indinions do they come to your house much . . . one of my calves will almost handle me you must not let the wolves catch you bub I cant [think] of any mor so goodbye"

His mother filled out the sheet, writing to her daughter Sarah. "Isaac has tried to think of something to write to the children but he says he cant think of anything when he begins [to] write he is just the same good honest boy as ever he and Alice have got almost through the Arithmetic . . . Alice says she will write a whole letter next time we send you one."

A clear picture emerges. Good honest boy that he was, willing to do what was expected of him, he was already several years behind in academic skills, working with Alice, two and a half years younger—hardly able to write or even collect any thoughts to put on paper.

In his quiet way, however, he gradually developed ideas of his own and increased his writing skills. When he was a little over seventeen, his mother wrote in one of her letters west: "have decided to have Isaac name Newton and will have it changed on town books." From then on he was Isaac Newton Watts, forsaking Isaac Watts the hymn writer and joining Isaac Newton the scientist. The next winter he wrote for the winter term at Peacham Academy a paper, "Science and Progress," which he esteemed highly enough to keep all his life. Later, when he was a new soldier in the Union Army, stationed near Washington, he went to town one day and wrote home, "The Patent Office and Smithsonian Institute are the greatest sights that are to be seen." His choice of the Smithsonian is clear enough, given his interests; but the Patent Office? Was it his dream to be one of those ingenious Yankee inventors who changed life in many ways during the nineteenth century?

He had a right to dream. As his obituary says: "In his youth he was a promising scholar, and fitted for college at the Peacham Academy, under the instruction of Prof. C. O. Thompson . . . who gave him high commendation." A whole lifetime of intellectual pursuits waited for him out in the world—if he had only been able to get clear of the farm.

Isaac Watts was born on August 16, 1842, into the large family of combined Walbridges and Wattses, two parents and eight children. His looks were a novelty to the dark-haired, dark-eyed Walbridge children; as Chastina wrote to Martha: "he is a little white head light skin and light blue eyes. but he has got *spunk* enough, I can tell you."

As he grew up, Isaac went quietly about his business, doing the necessary farm work under his father's direction and getting his education when he could, walking the two miles to Peacham Corner on weekdays for school and on Sundays to church.

He clearly loved his family. In letters and diaries he referred to Roxana as "my dear mother" and this wording does not seem to be a mere formality coming from him. His Watts brothers were "Brother Charles" and "Brother Lyman," as was "Brother Dustan" of the Walbridges. Augustus, however, was simply "Augustus"; and when he came to live at the farm, Julian was "Rix." "Father" stood a little in the distance, a figure of sometimes irrational authority. The six sisters were all addressed impartially as "Dear Sister." "Sunday evening at home" figured nostalgically in his war diaries, as did his mother, who died soon after he turned twenty.

Before he was eighteen, the Civil War began, taking away many of the Peacham "boys," Isaac's brother Dustan among them. The obituary tells Isaac's official story for that period: "When ready for college, in 1863, in the darkest days of the war, he was among the men drafted for service in the Union Army. Contrary to the wishes of his father, who offered to pay his commutation and aid him also in his college course, provided he would consent to carry out this cherished purpose of his life, young Watts . . . with rare conscientiousness refused the offer. Keenly sensitive also, and unwilling that the stigma of a 'drafted man' should be attached to his name, before the official requisition of the draft could reach him, he hurried to the rendezvous at Brattleboro and there enlisted as a volunteer."

Family letters, however, tell a different story. In May 1863, Dustan wrote from Fort Totten in Washington to his "Dear Sister [Ella]: Does Father have any one to help him this summer except Isaac . . . I hird that Isaac had some notion of Enlisting but that Father would not here of it—I do not blame Father for not wanting him to go, as he seems to be all the one left him to see to things—but I dont envy the man that *hangs back* these times." When Isaac turned twenty-one in August of 1863 and became subject to the draft, he was able finally to go against his father's wishes.

Mustered in service on October 9, 1863, he was assigned to Battery M, 1st Regiment, Vermont Heavy Artillery, based at Fort Slocum, one of the defensive forts ringing Washington, only a few miles from the fort where Dustan was stationed.

"Abe's pet lambs," these troops were called, assigned as they were to the safe job of guarding Washington. Still, settling into camp had its hardships: "I[t] blew all the morning pretty hard and just before noon commenced blowing a perfect hurricane. . . . Quite a number of the tents blew down and though ours did not we expected every minute when it would and thought we would be on the safe side and move into the barracks. They are pretty much done except the bunks, which cannot be made yet for want of lumber . . . I don't know but I can sleep just as sound and rest as well on the floor with a blanket under me as I used to at home on a good bed. There is nothing like getting used to a thing."

In the same letter he asked for a box from home: "I want my boots, a couple of pocket hdkfs. and a towel. . . . My clothes have been good, but will rip a little as every thing else that is sewn with machines. I want about 15 lbs. of butter and 8 or 10 of sugar. . . . If you have or can get some cheese without too much trouble, put in two or three pounds . . . a hank of linen thread and a little ball of yarn. I want my razor strop put in, a quire of paper and bunch of envelopes."

Describing Christmas Day, he wrote: "We had great times here . . . running races, catching a greased pig, climbing a greased pole, and wheeling a wheel-barrow at a mark blindfolded. It was quite an affair. The race and wheelbarrow match were won by our Co. prize three dollars. The pig

Isaac N. Watts, ca. 1863, in Civil War uniform. Courtesy Special Collections, Bailey/Howe Library, University of Vermont.

was given to the man that caught him and ten dollars for climbing the pole but no one could do it. They closed up with an oyster supper in the evening, but I could not go to it."

In January 1864, he began to write in the first of the little pocket diaries that he kept throughout the war and for a few years afterward. It recorded days of drilling, artillery practice, and a kind of Sunday that he never got used to: "Sunday in the army is a far different thing than what we have at home. In fact it is no Sun. at all." Three months later: "Sun. again and about as quiet a one as I have spent lately, though some of our boys have been pretty drunk. It is strange what men will do with themselves."

His place in the scheme of army things was modest, but he was carrying it well. Dustan wrote to Alice: "I have not seen Isaac for a few days but understand he is well he stands it first rate, and takes to Soldiering as well as the best. he did not get any office—but he will be one that improves from acquaintance and their is always a chance he is a little to modest like his Brother it wants *brass* in the Army."

Dustan was commissioned a second lieutenant in February; Isaac was made corporal in March; and in April came a charming domestic interlude when Dustan's wife, Abbie, and small daughter, Nellie, came for a visit. "Abbie got here all safe last Friday, though she was pretty tired. She and Nellie look pretty natural, I can tell you, and a good deal like home. I took supper there Sun. night, the first time I have eaten at a regularly set table since I came from home. Nellie was pretty shy of me for a while but came around sociable as need be before I had been there long."

In May Battery M and the regiment were assigned to the 6th Army Corps. From then on Isaac saw active service in some of the most famous battles of the war, beginning with Spotsylvania and Cold Harbor. For him, as for the rest of the troops, it was march, find food, make shelter, march, march. They ate "Mrs. Lincoln's cookies"—hardtack—and whatever else they could scavenge; lived in tents and kept warm, or cool, the best way they could; and marched endlessly, so much of it forward and back, to and fro, that they decided the generals had no idea what they were doing. Isaac wrote to Alice on August 1: "Sat night we started back the same road we came on marched all night and nearly all day yesterday, getting back nearly to Frederick City. It was an awful hot day and very hard to march. I can't see the use in marching back and forth and not see a reb in a dogs age."

Dustan was wounded in the battle of Cold Harbor and died in a hospital in Washington two weeks later. "I can hardly make myself believe it . . . it is hard, very hard," Isaac wrote. In a letter a week later he continued the same theme. "You will all feel pretty lonesome now I suppose, since Dustans death but I hardly think you will miss him more than I do. . . . I should like to have been at home last Sun. and gone to the funeral. I cant make it seem even now that he is dead. When near his Co. I have frequently looked around for him before I would think, that he was not there and never would be again. I have heard many of his men speak of him and I don't think there was one among them but liked him well, better than any of the others by a good deal. Perhaps they would talk so to me when they did'nt think it, but I think not."

Isaac seems never to have had any idea of the interest that the Vermont Brigade began to excite as the war went on. He tended to report only marching and more marching; and his diary shows no knowledge at all of a dramatic episode in the brigade's career. When the 6th Corps was sent to the defense of Washington on July 12, 1864, they arrived too late for President Lincoln, who had come down to the dock especially to welcome them. Upon learning that only officers would be in the first steamer to arrive, Lincoln said with disappointment, "I do not care to see any major generals. I came to see the Vermont Brigade."

In August, the 6th Corps, including the Vermont Brigade, was transferred west to campaign in the Shenandoah Valley. "We . . . marched through Md. by Frederick Jefferson &c to Harpers Ferry, Where we crossed the river and are again camped on the sacred soil of Old Virginia. . . . It has been a pretty tough march as the roads are all turnpikes and filled with little stones so that it came pretty hard on those having thin shoes. . . . We were in Leesburg and I spent my time mostly in picking blackberries, getting and stewing apples and keeping cool as possible. There are plenty of berries if there is time to get them and orchards all along the road."

The soldiers knew how to take care of themselves by that time: "Last night I made a raid on a corn field and the result was [we] have had some roast corn though it is hardly large enough to be good yet. We stopped two days last week close to a grist mill and near a number of good farm houses. The boys lived pretty well. They could buy meat, bread, pies and milk, get plenty of . . . meal at the mill and taking it all around we lived high. The best thing I had was some corn meal pudding that I made myself."

They had also toughened up during the months in the field. "I'm pretty sure I could go [to Peacham] looking as I do now and not be known. I am tanned black, have got a zouave cut on my hair and have not shaved since starting on the campaign."

Then came the battles of Winchester in September and a month later, Cedar Creek, a decisive battle of the war, and one in which the Vermont Brigade distinguished itself. Isaac described it to Alice: "Yesterday morning our pickets were attacked about 5 o'clock and by daylight the rebels had worked their way around in rear of the 8th and 19th Corps capturing arty. and about every thing else that there was to be had completely routing both Corps and leaving it for the 6th to check their sucess or give them a complete victory. We went out on the doubl quick and fought them, falling back in the mean time about three miles. Our lines were then formed so we mad a permanent stand. . . . Gen. Sheridan rode in just then and his presence was as good as a reinforcement of ten thousand. As he rode along he said never mind we'll give it to them yet before night. . . . At 4½ o'clock P.M. We charged and after a hard contest to get them started, in which many fell on both sides, we didn't give them a chance to stop till they were across the Creek and then the Cav. followed them up taking prisoners and cannon by the wholesale. . . . During the day I fired about eighty rounds at them and others accordingly. So you can imagine it was pretty warm work."

Three weeks later they passed over the same ground on their way to winter quarters, and he wrote: "Yesterday we passed back over the old battle field. It didn't look much as it did three weeks before. All that showed marks of a battle was occasionally a cluster of graves, a few dead horses scattered around and houses that were in range perforated with bullets till they looked some like a pepper box." Of the winter quarters he wrote: "We have got a cozy little tent and a *pretty big fire place* which keeps everything warm and nice and is really pleasant to sit by in the evening. When we first came here it was a fine oak woods and any quantity of fences near. The fence has all gone and nearly all the trees are laid low. Whenever an army stops for any length of time it leaves traces that will take years to outgrow."

In November he reported on the presidential election just past, in which soldiers in the field were for the first time allowed to vote: "We had a very quiet election last Tues. I voted for 'Abe' of course and our reg. gave him 220 majority. Some of the old regiments went for McLellan but in the Brig. Lincoln had about 450 majority. I think that is pretty well considering how many there are that are not voters. McLellan men were, as a general thing, rather inclined to the rufscuff of the lot and I guess it is so throughout the country."

Being in winter camp gave Isaac time to think over the recent past and philosophize a bit. "It seems a little singular," he wrote from Strasburg, "that some will be where bullets fly like hailstones and escape while others are hit about every time they come under fire." He knew what he was talking about; a few weeks later Alice in Peacham reported to Augusta in Michigan, "A bullet went through the top of [Isaac's] hat at Winchester and at Strasburg he fired 80 rounds of ammunition." In November the 6th Corps, and with it the Vermont Brigade, was transferred east to another winter camp, in preparation for the spring drive on Richmond. From Petersburg Isaac wrote, "I don't know the number in our Co. that have been with us all the time but guess it is not over fifteen out of over 130 that started last May."

In the same letter he reported a strange incident: "A short time ago a rebel officer started to relieve his pickets and by mistake got outside his own lines and into ours. His men wore blue coats and neither side discovered the mistake for sometime. The reb. saw it first, stopped made apologies to our officers in charge, explained matters and marched his men back to his own lines without any fighting by either party."

Such casualness did not survive the coming of spring. In March the sharp campaign began that took Petersburg and Richmond and brought about the surrender at Appomattox, after which the 6th Corps was sent on a forced march after the fleeing Confederates: "Made about 23 miles. . . . Made one mile in 13 minutes. . . . about 20 miles today. . . . About 110 miles since Sun. morning."

It is unclear how Isaac first heard of Abraham Lincoln's death, but on April 19 he wrote his father: "I suppose according to all accounts the President must be dead. That is the hardest thing that has happened to the North for the last century, as I look at it. I am a little afraid of Johnson, but perhaps he is all right and will settle this business up all right."

In June, Isaac found himself back in the Washington forts, detailed first as ordinance sergeant and then, a month before discharge, made first sergeant.

While he was waiting impatiently to be discharged, he wrote a letter to his sister Alice that had great importance for them both. He had just seen "Brother Lyman" in the city. "Lyman told me you wanted to go to Hadley [Mount Holyoke Seminary]. I think you can go without any trouble. I suppose Father will not want you to but don't think he will make any great objection. If it will make any difference about it by my coming home, I think you can go without doubt. I have mad up my mind to be home in the fall and think I shall. I should go on and make my calculations for going and that will help it along as much as anything."

What has happened? Had he given up his own dreams? Was he giving his sister the chance he wished he had had? His obituary offers an explanation: "Returning home, the two years interruption of his studies, with the consideration of the age and circumstances of his father, led him to abandon finally the idea of a collegiate course, and he at length settled permanently upon the homestead."

Mustered out of the army on September 2, 1865, he arrived home the next day. "Everything is the same. I should hardly think I had been gone a week instead of over two years." A week later he wrote, "Was taken sick last Sun. morning and have been an invalid ever since. . . . Have had an intermittent fever and no very pleasant job either." After that, except for one minor entry, the diary (which he had kept meticulously every day during his wartime service) was silent until December 31: "Farewell to 1865. . . . To me it has been an eventful year. A year ago I was a soldier and must hold myself in readiness to do whatever told. Now, though free from that, I am not yet my own *boss,* exactly, and dont suppose I ever will be. I have to come around on time every day. Well a fellow must work and it is good for me."

His diary entries were regular though laconic in 1866. They show a young man, plagued with "intermittent fever"—probably malaria—doing hard physical work without the strength or health to enjoy it, but grasping at all the small enjoyments that came along—sleighing on moonlight nights, going to singing school, playing croquet, sitting up late at his courting in Barnet and hoping it was going well, going to church and reproaching himself for his wandering mind, sometimes even falling asleep during the sermon after a late night out. An entry for July 18, 1867, carried an echo of the former student: "As it was cloudy this morning I harnessed up and started for Hanover to attend Commencement exercises there. Had a pleasant ride, interesting exercises and got into the world outside of Peacham."

The year's work was incessant. In March and April, tapping the maple trees, boiling the sap, sugaring off—465 pounds recorded in 1866—and sawing and splitting wood. In May, plowing and harrowing; sowing wheat and oats; planting potatoes, beans and corn; and working for three days on the public road. In June, hoeing, shearing sheep, and "drawing muck"—spreading manure. In July and early August, haying—54 wagon loads in 1866—and cutting oats and wheat. In September, cutting corn, picking apples, marketing sheep and lambs. In October and November, husking corn, plowing, "picking" and "drawing" stone. All this was in addition to the daily chores, which probably took three or four hours, depending on how many cows they had. And there were extra projects, like cutting and boring logs for waterpipes and laying a new waterline. Or helping to build a new small barn. It was hard work and he was not suited to it. Late in May of 1868 he wrote in his diary, "Hope I shall be able to see over the work some time so I shall not feel compelled to work every day." And a few days later, "This is one of the days when I get the blues and wish I were out of this hard work."

In the slack times during the winter he taught at one or another of the one-room schools roundabout, but he was a poor disciplinarian, constantly defeated by erupting noise. On January 22, 1867, he wrote in his diary, "Teaching will make a fellow feel severe sometimes, if he is ever so good-natured." And six days later, "School is pretty noisy and part don't care for anything else while some try hard to learn. Such I like to teach at any time."

Courtship occupied some of his evenings. He went to Barnet, usually on Wednesday evenings, and sat up late with Julia McPhee, who had been one of his occasional correspondents during the war years. He was a persistent suitor, but things did not go well, as his diary records after one visit: "As I did not go to bed till after 2 A.M., I have not felt very keen. . . . If I only knew what someone would do about something I should like it." Occasionally he felt hopeful. In a long reminiscent soliloquy, he summed up the past, the present, and his future hope: "This has been an anniversary day to me for several reasons. Three years ago, how many of my comrades in arms saw for the last time the 'Good old flag.' Captured that day, they languished and died in rebel prisons, a few of the many coming home again. That day too I first heard of Brother Dustan's death. . . . This is also the natal day of one that is very dear to me and I hope may sometime be my own better half. . . . Altogether I think I shall always remember this 23rd day of June on all occasions while reason lasts, as a great day in my life."

Julia would not say yes, but she could not bring herself to say no, or if she did, Isaac did not want to hear it. The courtship dragged along. After one inconclusive October evening in 1867 at her house, he made up his mind to leave the situation to itself for a while and go west for the winter, visiting his sister Sarah and her family in Minnesota, and then his brother Charles in Illinois, where he worked in Charles's law office and discovered how little he liked indoor work. He watched the mails for Julia's letters, which arrived about once a month, and went home in March to resume his courtship. But there was no life in it. On Christmas Day in 1868 he "took supper" at her house, and received his final answer. On New Year's night he wrote in his diary: "Have spent the eve. in writing on various matters, closing it just before midnight by writing to an old and dear friend (Julia McPhee) but one that can be nothing to me in the future. So ends the old year. All thy joys and sorrows are over."

After that last sad entry, he did not keep a diary until 1876. In the seven-year interval disaster had struck the family several times. Brother Lyman and his wife, Sarah, had died, leaving a baby daughter. Brother Charles had died out in Illinois in February 1875, leaving his family in financial distress. Father Lyman had died in the fall of that same year. Isaac himself was a widower with a five-year-old daughter, Meroe. In 1870 he had married Lizzie Way from just up the road on East Hill, who appeared often on the outskirts of events in the earlier diaries. She had died in 1874.

Isaac was a great anniversary rememberer and often these entries give a fuller picture than his on-the-spot ones. One of his anniversary diary entries told how he had come to feel about his wife: "Just six years ago, that Lizzie and I were married. . . . Six years ago, the day was beautiful. Just the kind for a happy wedding day. Today is windy, blustering and disagreeable every way. A perfect contrast to that happy time. So it is with me to a great extent. My plans changed, many of my hopes blighted and my life so different from what it was and what I hoped it should be. . . . O! Lizzie! I do miss you."

Death stood close at hand for the people of those days. Roxana had miraculously raised all eleven of her children and stepchildren to adult-hood, but eight of them were to die before they were forty-one. Lyman, Charles, and Lizzie had all died of tuberculosis, a great plague of that era.

Isaac himself was not well. "Should like to feel better if I could" is a refrain through the diary. He had spells of "ague"—chills and fever—and a constant cough with bleeding spells that put him to bed for a few days and led the doctor to prescribe some of the cruel medicines of the time. But he kept moving. The diary records his plans to take over the farm, buying out his father's other heirs, his Watts sisters and the families of his dead brothers. On his thirty-fourth birthday he spent "most all day getting deeds &c for this place. The first time in my life I ever owned Real Estate." The Peacham Grand List for 1876 assessed the East Hill farm of 125 acres at $2,025, the summer pasture on Macks Mountain Road of 45 acres at $81, two horses at $188, eight cattle at $215, thirty-two sheep at $112, and one hog at $10. The Watts farm was an average-sized farm in Peacham. Most important, it was owned by the family with no debt, although after his father's death, Isaac was in debt over the next few years and slow to pay his sisters their inheritance.

Peacham Grand List for Lyman Watts's Farm, 1830–1880

Year	Acres/Value	House/Value	Oxen	Horse	Colts	Cattle	Sheep	Hogs	Debts	Value of Personal Property
1830[1]	60/$441	1/$125	2	1	1	11	20			
1840[2]	60/$420	1/$285	2	2	1	10	40			
1850	145/$2,400			3		12	20	3	$250	$274
1860	171/$2,425			2		22	28	2		$1,300
1866[3]	170/$2,400			2		15	52	1		$1,545
1870	170/$2,400			2		14	26	1		$1,215
1875[4]	170/$2,106			2		10	32	1		$1,741
1876[5]	170/$2,106			2/$188		8/$215	32/$112	1/$10	$700	$1,482
1880[6]	170/$1,837			4		11	28	2		

Source: Peacham Town Records

[1]Year Lyman purchased farm
[2]Date of marriage of Lyman and Roxana
[3]Four years after Roxana's death and first year Isaac home from the Civil War
[4]Year before Lyman's death
[5]Listed as Lyman Watts Estate
[6]Year before Isaac's death

Isaac N. Watts, ca. 1877. Courtesy Peacham Historical Association.

Life was more leisurely now that he was working for himself and could choose his own times and methods of managing the farm. He farmed out the maple sugaring on shares, and used hired help regularly. Other responsibilities began to come his way. He was a town auditor and selectman, did jury duty, was elected town representative to the state legislature, and in the fall of 1878 he went to Montpelier for the legislative session.

In 1877 he married again, another Peachamite, Ellen Boynton. The diaries ended, but there were letters—lively letters, six from Isaac, seven from Ellen—to Ella in Northfield, Minnesota, in 1877 and 1878. They were remodeling the house: "As you may suppose we have had a very dirty

Ellen Boynton Watts, ca. 1877. Courtesy Mary C. Morrison.

mess of it . . . we saw something new to do at every turn and it was only by biting the thing off short that we have got so near done as we have," Isaac wrote. Six months later: "Ellen wants me to say we have a new washing machine. It is like the old one only different and washes much faster." Ellen was slowly and carefully getting on good terms with Meroe. Except for Isaac's persistent cough and slowly ebbing energy, the whole picture is one of happiness and peace.

One of the letters in the collection is from Isaac to Ellen, written from the Representatives' Hall on official State of Vermont stationery: "My Dear Wife how I wish you were here with me this pleasant week. Several members have their wives here now, and I wish you were. Make all your plans to come and before it gets too late so the days will be short. . . . Kiss Meroe for me and keep one for yourself from Your Dear Husband Isaac N. Watts."

To be a Dear Husband is rare at any time, and rarer still in the emotionally frost-bitten Vermont of his era; but that is what he was. Unlike his father, he loved, respected, and enjoyed the women in his life, his mother, his sisters, each of his wives in turn, and his daughters.

When he died of tuberculosis in March 1881, he left the guardianship of his second daughter, Helen, to "my beloved wife," an unusual action for his time, when fathers generally left their children to the guardianship of some other male. He asked that Meroe stay in her stepmother's care, a request that was disregarded when Meroe's grandmother Way and her aunt Mary Jane took charge of her upbringing.

Isaac died at thirty-nine, a competent farmer and a respected citizen of his community and state. He died too young, like most of Roxana's children, but he had made a good life out of the necessities that hedged him in.

SUBJECT TO FAMILY CLAIM

YOUNG VERMONT women had fewer choices than did men in the years right before and after the Civil War. Men left the family farm and went off to school, to teach, to establish a profession, or to be a soldier. It was common practice and almost expected in a large family that the boys—all but the one designated to continue the farm—would seek their fortune elsewhere. Some girls also left home as teachers and missionaries, and a few sought an advanced education. But the difference was that men could make their new home their permanent home, and women—particularly unmarried women—were subject to what social worker Jane Addams later called "family claim." They were expected to return home if and when the need for them arose. This is what happened to Roxana's two youngest daughters.

Both Alice and Ella were at Roxana's bedside when she died in 1862, and the next day the older girl, Alice, was expected to fill her mother's shoes on the farm. Girls much younger than Alice accepted this duty when necessary.

When Alice went off to Mount Holyoke in 1865, she followed the lead of five other Peacham girls, the first having gone in 1853. Of those five, none became farm wives. Two went on to teach school outside of Vermont; four married—three married professional men and although the fourth's husband's occupation is not known, the graduate died in San Francisco, so she was certainly not a farm wife. The unmarried one, Jane Chamberlain, taught school in New Jersey, Indiana, Wisconsin, and New York, and also spent ten years as a missionary in Turkey. Alice had good reason to believe that her future after Mount Holyoke would lead her away from the Watts farm. But family duty called and she returned to Peacham after only one year away at school to keep house for her father and brother.

Ella, too, had dreams which easily might have taken her away from the Watts farm. As a young woman, she began traveling, visiting her brother

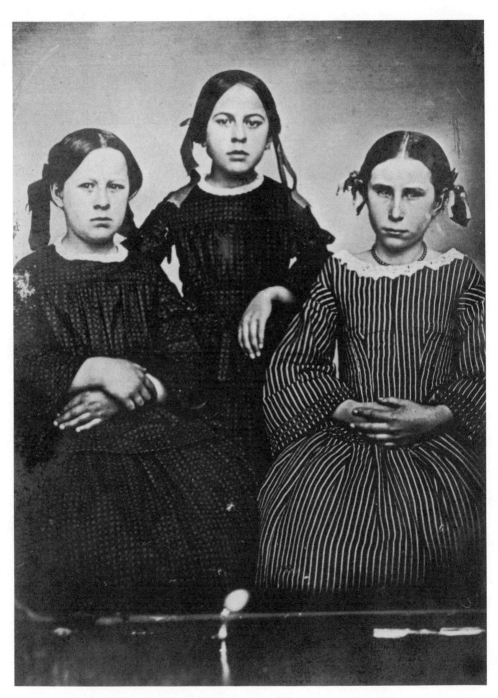

Alice and Ella Watts and Lizzie Way, 1856. Courtesy Choate Farm Collection.

Lyman at Lowell, her sister at South Hadley, and friends in Boston. When Alice returned to the farm after her brief exposure to higher education, Ella headed west to stay with her sister Sarah. There in Minnesota she took on jobs she was familiar with—sewing and taking care of the sick and elderly. Eventually she found a job in one of the new institutions established in the second half of the nineteenth century which paid women good wages as well as room and board. She settled at the Minnesota School for the Deaf into what might have become a permanent position, if she had not been recalled to raise her brother Isaac's orphaned daughter. Later, she married her sister's widower and helped run a farm that had its ups and downs and never-ending work.

Alice and Ella tried but were unable to escape the hardscrabble existence of Vermont farm life. Responsibility stated itself as "manifest duty" or "God's will" and brought them back from the ventures they had made into the outside world. In their diaries and letters, neither expressed regrets. Like Roxana, they were proud of their contributions to the farm, content with their church and community, and satisfied with their young ones. The descendants of these children are still active in Vermont life.

Alice Watts Choate (1845–1882)

From Student to Farm Wife

ALICE WATTS exemplifies the early aspirations of American women for formal higher education. She did not achieve her goal, but her failed attempt shows all the more clearly the obstacles that stood in the way of women of her time.

It was taken for granted that women could be summoned at any time to attend to whatever need might arise at home. It was taken for granted that when they married they would abandon any career they might have. Most important, it was taken for granted that they were not serious enough or intelligent enough for the arduous task of higher learning.

Only the most rigorous dedication to a definite professional objective could overcome this cotton-wool resistance. Some women managed to become doctors; some women became excellent professional teachers. But Alice did not have this kind of dedication. She only wanted what middle-class women of today can have as a matter of course—a general liberal education.

She was a bright, promising child, more aggressive than was considered suitable for a girl. Her older sister Chastina wrote, "Alice, three & a half years old, goes to school to Tina, as she calls me. she spells everything she hears & sees almost and is a real little rogue. I have to scold at her becaus she likes to play with the boys."

Her older brother Lyman, the intellectual of the family, also became interested in her development. When she was fourteen, he set in motion a plan to enroll her at the school where he would be teaching. "I have just written to Alice," he wrote to his father, "& must also send you a few lines to answer your questions. . . . The tuition & board would be a little more at Castleton than at Peacham but I will pay all that it will cost there more than it would to send her to Peacham if you hired her board there, so that it will cost you no more to send her to Castleton than to Peacham except her travelling expenses & I would rather pay that than to not have her go. I have forgotten what the fare is to Rutland but think it is about $5.00."

This was in August of 1859. A neat little wallet-sized book bound in leather ("Daily Miniature Diary for 1860. New York: Published Annually for the Trade") recorded the closing days of Alice's term at Castleton.

January 1 began with good thoughts: "At Castleton. Many friends, warm and true, I doubt not, have wished me 'Happy New Year'—and may I so conduct myself, that I shall not regret the actions of my life in 1860. Attended church this afternoon for the first time in five weeks. Have commenced reading the Bible again, and may this little book keep strict account of my progress. . . . I expect to find much pleasure in writing upon its *now* unspoiled pages. May it not be a record of sorrow or shame, but of pleasure, happiness, and improvement."

But on January 2: "My little book can receive the record of no very magnanimous deeds performed to day. I have recited in Algebra and French, after trying hard to get excused from the latter. . . . I intend to go into my Latin class tomorrow; but may not."

And on January 3: "Have spent the most unhappy day that I have known in Castleton. Mother wrote me to come home. Sadness was caused more by the suddenness of the request than any other reason; have written home to beg a few 'days of grace' and I sincerely hope they may not want me."

She had settled quickly and happily into the emotional closeness that was accepted among young women at that time. Lena ("dear girl") was her roommate and dearest friend, who gave her for her fifteenth birthday, January 6, two presents: "A little oak leaf candlestick, saying playfully, 'to light your path next year,' " and on the day itself "a useful as well as a valuable gift and a comical little toy—a whip—which has chastised me many times to day." Modern eyebrows rise at this, but the gift was given and taken lightly, and made, whether intentionally or not, a perceptive comment on Alice's tendency to castigate herself. The diary is peppered with cruel phrases. "What a brute I am!" "Am and have been cross and wilful all day." "Oh! I am so wicked." "I make a fool of myself every day." "I cannot endure myself."

She was happy at Castleton. But Lena was leaving. "She goes Monday," the entry for January 13 recorded. "Dear girl, how sad it will be then, for me especially." On January 16: "As Lena said last eve: I must write in my diary 'she's gone'; Poor, dear girl! . . . I once thought it would be impossible to love any one as I do her. Have been the happiest with her that I ever was. . . . It is all *gas* to talk of 'the frailty of school-girl attachments' for I know it to be false."

She loved the people at Castleton, one in particular; but her attitude toward school life ("the same dull routine") and her studies was less enthusiastic. "Girls are all busy and fearful of examination days, which are close at hand. I was absent from class so much during my sickness that I expect to fail, and shall be disappointed if I do not. Worked the dreaded *31st* in Algebra on the board to day." Her diary the next day, the nineteenth: "Have had some dispute with my brother [Lyman] to night concerning my late hours. Told him I *must* study, and he as persistently said *I should not.* Have not decided whether to *do right* or go to studying." In any event, she did neither, for the entry continued: "Walked with the girls to night down to the depot. . . . Examination has not yet excited any dread or fears in my mind, but some of the girls are nearly crazy."

In spite of her offhand attitude and her period of sickness, she did not fail any of her subjects, though algebra was on the edge and she missed two questions in the French examination. After being obliged to copy her final English composition because it contained so many errors, she had the honor of reading it in public.

Her religious life did not fare so well under this casual treatment. "Mrs K—, Cassie Adams, and Lyman talked with me concerning my religious feelings. Oh! if I were only half as faithful for myself as others are for me, I would be a Christian very soon."

She left for home on January 25, having managed to stay nearly the full term. "I hated to come and leave the girls very much, but *the one* is gone and so I did'nt care so much. Almost failed in Algebra this morn—yet not quite." The diary entry is a good statement in brief of her hierarchy of values at the time.

The diary gradually peters out as the year goes on, but not before it has given a picture of life at home seen through fifteen-year-old eyes.

She went to singing school at the Hollow, "conducted on the do-re-mi-fa-sol principle." She bought two dresses in two days, one from a peddler. She heard from Lena, writing from Covington, Georgia, almost home on her long journey south. And on February 4: "Guess it is not decided to let me go back to C— with Lyman, but stay at home. No one knows how much I love the dear place. Perhaps if my parents did, their decision would be different. That $70 paid for my bills will cause me more unpleasant thoughts than any other. . . . If I could be rich, for two years only. Vain, fruitless, foolish wish!"

Her health was bothersome. She had many headaches and caught a bad cold, which turned into a persistent cough. "Got a $1.00 bottle of 'Weeks Magic Compound' for my cold," and the next day, "have begun to take

Alice Watts, ca. 1860. Photograph taken by Gage's Portrait Gallery, St. Johnsbury, Vermont. Courtesy Choate Farm Collection.

some Homeopathic medicine for my cough which is no better." A few days later, "my cold is much better thanks to Homeopathy doctrine." She sewed on two dresses "considerable; so much that my finger is pretty well pricked" and got an infection which plagued her for a week or more.

On February 16 she wrote a description of life at home: "Scolding and fretting from Mother; impatience from me; remonstrance on Lyman's part and an insight into 'how we got our education' by Father are the regular exercises of the day. . . . It has snowed all day, and is blowing hard now. Rooms are secured at Blanchard's for *our accommodation* this spring, unless the folks scold so much there is no going anywhere, which is a very probable result."

The rooms at Blanchard's were for her and a friend to live in during the week while they studied at Peacham Academy for the spring term, going home on weekends. Anyone who has ever walked or even driven the mile downhill and mile uphill between East Hill and Peacham Corner will understand why this arrangement was necessary. Isaac and Julian, it seems, were expected to walk the distance daily, but the girls in the family were not required to do the same.

At the academy Alice studied Latin, French, and philosophy, and was a member of the literary society, for which she "dreamed up," wrote, and read several compositions. She continued the same kind of desperate struggle as at Castleton to get her lessons done in the face of seeing friends, writing letters, riding in the moonlight, and other social pleasures. School life was less intense than at Castleton because of the weekend breaks and because it was less fascinating and absorbing. But she enjoyed it. On April 27 she wrote, as if surprised at herself, "one week more, and the term closes. Shall be sorry after all."

A week later she wrote, "Came home this morning at 11 o'clock. It has been very lonesome and I know what is my destiny for the summer—to work and bear scolding."

Two things weighed on her that she may not have been consciously aware of. Several years later, shortly before he was killed, her older brother Dustan tried to explain and apologize for one of them. "Before Mother died," he wrote, "from what I had seen of things at home I had thought that you considered Mother hard on you and sometimes I thought not without reason. You know she used to hold hir *first children* up as models, and make comparisons—until I thought you had about as soon see old Nick himself as to here anything about hir *first Children* I knew it was wrong and did not like it any better than you—and had more than once resolved to talk with hir, but I couldnt do it, she was always so kind and self sacrificing to me—but I knew you took it hard." A strong believer in "contentment"—acceptance of one's lot in life—as a virtue and one of God's gifts, Roxana would have found it hard to be patient with a discontented girl.

The other weight on Alice was her older brother Lyman. As a dedicated Christian, working his way toward the ministry, he had no idea how heavy-handed his religion was, especially to a girl too disorganized to meet his expectations, too honest to pretend to feel what she did not feel, and too sensitive to disregard his religious urgencies. Her constantly lost campaign to read five chapters daily of the Bible was surely initiated by him; the self-castigations in her diary often follow a letter from him or a talk with him. "Lyman has just been preaching to me concerning religion. I am terribly wicked and never expect to be any better. No, I *expect* to, truly; but there seems no prospect." Even when he talked to her about more everyday things, his effect on her was catastrophic. "Lyman talked over old times with me and I cryed so that my eyes ache."

The 1860 diary continues. She worked hard, baking, cleaning, washing, ironing, sewing—learning the difficult art of housekeeping under the critical eyes of her mother and grandmother. She tried to read her scheduled Bible chapters, but was often far behind, as a cryptic "-26" or "-29" at the bottom of the diary page would show. In the fall she went back to school, studying geometry among other subjects.

She found happiness where she could, in letters from friends, a pleasant day, an early-spring taste of maple sugar, a horseback ride on a clear evening, or the wild flowers as they came into bloom. Above all she loved the moon; her diary faithfully records its visits, "perfectly splendid" as they were. In July she wrote, "Clear sweet moonlight bathes everything in a flood of mellow azure light So calm and refreshing."

She recorded storms too. "There is a thunder shower—a conflict of elements—without, but a more desperate one within my breast." The language is familiar. It might be Emily Brontë's in far-off Yorkshire. Though there is no record of Alice reading *Wuthering Heights* (1847), she had just been reading Charlotte Brontë's *Shirley* (1849) and had learned how to make a cry from the heart, even if only to her diary.

For the next five years she was at home, attending the academy irregularly, here a term and there a term. She strove unsuccessfully for "contentment" while life swirled around the quiet household, as the Civil War began and the Peacham "boys" enlisted one by one and went away.

In 1862 her grandmother and mother died nine weeks apart. By that time Alice had come to a better appreciation of her mother and could write: "Mother's death has made a vacancy in the whole family nothing else could, and no one can ever fill." One of her mother's family activities, the letter writing, she picked up quickly and easily, since she had been sharing it for several years. She wrote to the Western sisters and brothers, especially Martha's daughter, Augusta; she wrote Dustan and Isaac in the Army of the Potomac. She took her place as the center of "Home."

"I am 'boss and all hands' at home in the housekeeping line," she wrote to Augusta. "It came pretty hard to see to every thing at first but I am getting accustomed to it so I shall get on bravely I don't know how I shall make it taking care of the butter next summer but must do the best I can. We shall have six cows I expect."

There were breaks in the routine. It is good to read about one of them especially. In December 1864, she wrote Augusta: "I had a nice visit last summer from my old friend Lena who used to be at Castleton with me— She was in Louisiana two years after the War commenced and had hard work to get away She came up the Miss. on a Transport to Cairo—I had a nice time while she was here."

Active on the home scene during the Civil War, Alice tried to "*knit* two hours" a day—Dustan thanked her for the "footings"—and joined the women who "meet to sew for soldiers" once a week. In order to raise money for the sewing projects in 1863, the young people put on "an old folks concert and tableaux at the Academy" on Christmas night. From admission fees, they collected forty-six dollars. In 1862 Alice wrote of "pretty high" prices including calico and tea, and in 1864 of wages up to two dollars a day for hired hands during haying in July. The most shattering experience for those at home was the return of wounded soldiers and of the bodies of those who died. In her diary of 1863, Alice recorded the fate of her cousins and neighbors: "In February Asa Sargeant came home blinded in one eye from disease." The next month "John Hand remains brot home," and Elijah Sargeant died at Fairfax Station, Virginia. In April "John Cassady died." At the end of the year Alice totaled the deaths "in town"—thirty-four died, eight of them soldiers. Then she added on the last page of her diary: "This year more mortality in town than since 1811." It was a hard time and a lonely one. As Isaac wrote to Clara in California: "It is hard for the girls—and makes rather a lonesome home for them, but as you said 'nearly all N.E. homes are lonesome now.' "

Alice had made herself capable and competent for her job at home; but she was not happy in it and longed for another try at the academic life. She wrote to Dustan about it, and he replied: "I know you are not happy their, and probably could not bring yourself to be contented or to think that household duties was your Sphere of usefulness—and as one *thinks* so is he—I think that it is best for you to go to School untill you have a good education and then—that is far enough to look ahead, probably your design would be to teach perhaps you would do as your schoolmate that has just visited you did, but at any rate you never would be satisfied unless you finish your *Education,* so that is the way to do it, I know you will have the chance if you are only *patient.*"

Taking heart from this encouragement she attended the spring term at the academy. The war ended. Ella grew skilled enough to take over the work, Isaac came home from the army, and in the fall of 1865, Alice went off to Mount Holyoke Seminary at South Hadley, Massachusetts. She chose well. Mount Holyoke Seminary had been founded in 1837 by Mary Lyon, one of the pioneers in improving and enlarging women's education. In her planning Mary Lyon had resisted the heavy pressure of the time to center her curriculum on domestic training, on the one hand, or, on the other, on the "accomplishments" of embroidery, china painting and other charming skills designed to grace elegant homes. Some measure of the frustration that drove her reveals itself in the story that when the cornerstone of the first building of her seminary was laid, she stooped down and wrote on it, "The Lord hath remembered our low estate." From the beginning Mount Holyoke was an institution of learning, with fees purposely set low enough to attract middle-class young women in search of knowledge, many of whom came intending to become teachers and missionaries. In the interests of economy the curriculum required that its students do some housework; every Wednesday was a day of recreation. Otherwise, it focused on a demanding course of study that included Latin, mathematics, science, history, English, and, of course, Bible and religion. The religious atmosphere was pervasive and on frequent occasions revivalistic, which was surely a factor in the willingness of traditional New England families to let their daughters enroll.

Alice's year there was the same as that at Castleton: it contained a great deal of involvement with people and only an average involvement with studies. There was a teacher, Miss Reed, much loved by the group to which Alice belonged; there were the friends of her "section," who valued her cheerful and gentle ways; there was a special friend, Julia, even dearer than Lena had been at Castleton. Last of all came her studies, which weighed on her mind, and which she found demanding: "I never had two such hard

lessons to learn as I had to day and I must study like any thing for tomorrow. . . . I've been writing a composition about Cardinal Wolsey, and it has
'most killed me."

She kept a diary intermittently during the first half of 1866, which documented a growing realization that she would never be a serious scholar.
One entry stated it plainly: "Lessons went hard though I had learned them.
I am quite discouraged about ever doing any thing or making any body, and
shall just go home next year more contented I hope to do what seems to be
manifest duty. Why can't I do better?"

When the academic year ended, she came home to that manifest duty. A
letter written to her by a friend who visited the Watts farm that fall painted
a picture of Alice's situation and how she was reacting to it: "You were the
only Christian in the house, & with many doubts in your heart; housekeeping cares were heavy for you & perhaps a little distasteful, at least for the
time when you were longing to be in school for the year. Your father's ideas
and your own with regard to the way in which household duties ought to
be done did not always agree, & you missed the sympathy & expression of
affection on his part which fathers often give to daughters. You were
worried about Rix too, & wanted to see your sister happier. . . . *I* should
feel all these things as burdens, & I could imagine many ways in which your
patience might be tried—many days in which you longed for congenial
school-friends & school-life, & when life had a kind of dreary, barren look,
& prayer failed to make all things new."

She had periods away from home when she taught in the district school
and at Peacham Academy, but they only clarified her views on her situation, both inner and outer, and in February 1868, she wrote to Augusta:
"Father froze his feet this winter and has been so lame he could hardly walk.
He and I have been alone all winter [Isaac was in the West; Ella teaching at
Danville]. . . . I do not go out much only to church and to singing school,
which I attend *regularly* with cousin Asa Sargeant two nights a week. . . . I
was *twenty three* last month. I don't regard a life of *single blessedness* as the
happiest by any means, but I have lived so thus far because I am needed at
home and because the chances I have had to accept another home, have
never pleased me."

An offer that pleased her came within a few months, as an entry in Isaac's
diary for November 19, 1868, described: "Alice's wedding day and a very
fine one too. Snow enough for sleighing and not very cold. Spent the day in
preparation for the event and all had enough to do nearly all day. The
ceremony was performed at 7½ o'clock P.M. and was a very pleasant affair.

A few of us went to W. Barnet with them. So I have lost a Sister and gained a Brother."

The "Brother" was Charles A. Choate, a young man who had recently come back from travels in the West and begun farming on a place which his father had helped him to buy, southeast of Peacham on the road to Barnet. Alice came to a simple farmhouse, a bit larger than the one she had left, white, with a low porch along its front. Like the house her mother had come to on East Hill, it was just a few feet from the road, the only differ-ence being that where once Alice had lived on a hill, now she lived in a valley.

Alice wrote Augusta two months after the wedding "from my new home and in my new name. I was married Nov. 19th to Charles Choate, whom I have always known, more or less. His parents live in Peacham. He came home from Cal. and Idaho where he had been for five years, some-thing more than a year ago. He has a good farm here, a nice house and everything pleasant and comfortable. It is some more than three miles from here to Father's. We go to Peacham to church. He is nearly seven years older than I, about two or three inches taller, has dark hair, blue eyes, and no whiskers. He has been all over the U.S. a great deal, and is not well contented to settle down in old Vermont and turn farmer. I presume he will not stay here a great while. He wants to go back to Cal. but his parents are very unwilling. He came very near dying of sunstroke last July, and his head has troubled him a great deal since then. I had rather go to Cal. than West, but rather live in good New England than go to either place."

Alice's first child was born within a few days of the wedding's nine-month anniversary. A note found in her papers at the Choate Farm, crudely written in an unknown hand and carefully preserved, showed the extent to which motherhood was a sisterhood of shared, intimate knowledge: "Things my nurse was very careful about First—(that I should 'make water' within a few hours of baby's birth and often afterwards, gave me camphor sling, and kept a cloth wet with hot camphor & water on my bowels) (2nd) was very careful that my breasts should not get hard and painful drawing out the milk with a breast pump—and rubbing them over with butter, rubbing it in well and wiping off, not washing—She has been very careful to have me moisten the nipple & breast and wet the baby's mouth before allowing her to nurse. She has been very careful that my limbs should be kept warm. and has been careful that my Swathe should be pinned up once or twice every day &c. I have a great overplus of milk & have to be careful about drinking very much."

Inheriting her mother's fertility, Alice was to bear seven children in the first twelve years of marriage. At the time of her 1872 diary, however, she had only two, David and young Charles, called "Chub." Both had many colds and sore throats, and she often wrote of them as "worrisome." One diary entry noted, "It takes so much of the day to tend the babies that there is little time to read or write or think collectedly."

Besides baby tending there was plenty of farm work to do at the Choate farm. Spinning and weaving at home were things of the past; the Lowell

Alice Watts Choate and Charles Choate with David and Chub, ca. 1873. Tintype, courtesy Choate Farm Collection.

mills where her sister Sarah had worked as a young woman had taken care of that. Clothes were mostly still made at home. Alice had a sewing machine, and someone came in to sew for her once or twice a year. Although life was easier than it had been for her mother, anyone who reads the seven diaries from her married years can still be awed by what she was called upon to do: weekly washing and ironing, hanging the clothes out to dry, rain or shine, freezing or not; baking pies and bread; helping to process meat on slaughtering days—salting beef, curing hams, rendering lard, making sausage and mincemeat, and even candles from the sheep tallow; tending chickens, raising chicks (she mentioned setting a hen on "eggs from Massachusetts") and preparing the eggs for market, a regular source of small income; taking care of the milk from their cows, churning, filling "tubs" of butter to sell; cooking daily for Charles and the hired hands, and for the threshers when they came; berry picking, making jams and jellies and preserves. Some strange occupations emerge. "I have been pounding up crockery & bones for the hens to-night"; "I have been grating carrots, which is the meanest work I do any time of year"; "I whitewashed the buttery."

These farm diaries follow a curious pattern that makes them seem strangely impersonal, since Alice mentioned everything that both she and Charles did, often without specifying who did what. Finally the reader comes to understand that Charles's activities were always detailed first, with hers briefly mentioned at the end.

Charles was busy too, first of all with the yearly routine of a subsistence farm, already described in Isaac's story, but also with what appear to be specialties, entered into in high hopes. The first of these was sheep; the diaries from 1872 through the first half of 1875 are full of lambing, sheep pasturing, "picking ticks," the constant building of pens in the barn area— and no profit, unless the cash-flow records at the end of each diary are incomplete. There was a settling-up of accounts with Father Choate in January of each year. In 1872 Alice wrote "Chas went up to the Corner and looked over accounts with his Father. Came out minus as usual." And in 1873: "Chas . . . looked over accounts with his Father. Came out $50.00 better than usual."

A picture of Charles begins to emerge from the diary entries. He worked hard but never got ahead of either the work or his debts. It is difficult at this distance to assess the farming practices of that time and decide how much of his days' endless activity was productive work and how much was fruitless running around. He was away from the farm to see someone about something nearly every day, and sometimes several times a day, while some years it took four hired men to keep up with the work at home.

He had many "sick headaches"—probably migraines—which would come on after a session with his father on finances, a long day of uninterrupted work on the farm, or some great unhappiness like the death of his brother Schuyler in 1875. In February 1874, a failed arrangement to buy another farm put him to bed for two weeks with headaches and facial neuralgia.

He was sociable and liked to go off in the evenings up to Peacham Corner or to West Barnet. In one diary entry Alice spoke of him as "up to village so as to kill time." In another: "Charles has spent his usual number of hours at the store." She knew him well: "Charles has gone up to see Trussel about sheep pasture to night. Presume he will be sick abed tomorrow."

With all that, however, the picture is clear that he was a good man, who worked hard according to his lights and did his best as he saw it.

Alice occasionally read a magazine, and once in a great while mentioned reading a book. On November 15, 1873, she wrote "I finished Middlemarch to-day." It would be interesting to know what she made of this story about an intellectual woman in a deadening marriage; but she says only: "Have spend a good deal of time over it this week—more than was profitable."

The sheep enterprise failed; the sheep were sold off: "The last call for them I hope." When Father Watts died in 1875, Alice inherited a little money, which eased their situation somewhat. The diary for 1875 also recorded a difficult pregnancy and birth chiefly through the absence of entries and by comments like one on March 13, 1876, "I did the washing for first time since last June." The new baby was never really well. On May 21, 1876, Mother C., Mary, Ella, and Aunt Margaret all came to the house. "They put a lot of mullein leaves on baby." On the 24: "I held baby two hours in forenoon and he slept in my arms . . . he died bright a little past five o'clock." And on June 18: "I . . . went up to babys grave for the first time. I cant realize it at all"—the phrase by which she expressed great grief, as at the death of her "Brother Charles" the year before. There is no diary for 1877, during which a baby girl was born and died within six months, so frail that they never named her.

Butter became the chief money-making product for the Choate farm. Alice, who had learned buttermaking from her mother, churned twice a week. If she was not able, Charles or one of the hired hands did it. When railroads increased their trips along the Connecticut River after the Civil

Alice Watts Choate (pregnant) and Charles Choate with David and Chub in front of Choate farmhouse, West Barnet, Vermont, ca. 1880. Courtesy Choate Farm Collection.

War, opportunities arose for shipping farm products to more, and more distant, markets. Alice and Charles, who at first had packed their butter in tubs and sold it to nearby stores, now began to make more elegant "stamped" butter for the Boston market, signaling the evolution in agriculture from self-sufficiency and local marketing to a farming style keyed to new urban centers. Examples of the wooden boxes used to transport the butter (they were returned empty to be filled again) can be seen at most Vermont historical societies, along with a wide selection of butter molds made by local carvers. Once the butter was divided into blocks, it was stamped—purely for decoration—with an imprint on the surface of the butter, often an agricultural motif such as an ear of corn, roses, or a sheaf of wheat. This new enterprise evidently did well, for the 1878 diary recorded ever-increasing poundage, and a less harried lifestyle, with time for visiting and even a party or two. Two entries struck a new note: August 31: "All hands went to St. J. [St. Johnsbury] to the Circus." September 17: "Went to the Fair at St. J. . . . Spent several pounds of butter & more too." Records at the end of the diary showed an income of $518.94 from the butter, apparently a satisfactory cash crop for the time.

With that, Alice's voice is silent, for her diaries cease and no letters have survived. Life moved quickly by in the next four years. A boy was born in 1879 and died before he was two. A daughter, Elsie, was born late in 1880, and a son, Isaac Watts, in the fall of 1882. Alice died a month later, at the age of thirty-seven. Both babies lived.

There are two ways to look at Alice's life. One is through her mother's eyes. Roxana would surely have been well pleased with the way this sullen, passionate, rebellious daughter had learned to live productively and lovingly within the circumstances given her, accepting what life gave her and turning it to all the good she could.

The other way is through modern eyes, looking on as one would watch a ship slowly sinking. There was no way for her to express her vague aspirations enough to clarify them, no way to bring out what she felt so strongly to be in her. In a sense Alice Watts died many years before Alice Choate did.

Lucy Ella Watts Choate (1847–1915)

The Care Giver

SOMETIMES ONE child in a family will grow up and grow old carrying the weight of all the family experience, individual and collective. In the Walbridge–Watts family, Ella was that child. Alert and impressionable, she watched the joys and sorrows, aspirations and failures, illnesses and deaths of her parents and most of her older siblings. As she grew she learned more than one child need know about all that could go wrong with human hopes and human lives, and how cruelly—and how early—death could claim them all.

Hers was a life governed by memory. In 1889, when she came home to Peacham to take charge of her orphaned niece Helen, Isaac's daughter, she remembered her own childhood and tried to bring up the child in a firm, cautionary style far different from Ellen Watts's cheerful ways. Mindful of all the deaths from tuberculosis in the family, she instructed the adolescent Helen to save her small inheritance for her burial, because tuberculosis "ran in families" and she was doomed. When Helen, defying this piece of wisdom, wanted to use the money to go to college in 1897, Ella remembered her sister Alice's abortive attempts at higher education, and advised Helen that there would be no point in it because academic learning would be useless for a farmer's wife.

When, in 1891, Ella married her sister Alice's widower, Charles Choate, and took over the West Barnet farm as he grew ill, she ran it in the fashion that she remembered from the days of her father; and, honoring the importance of getting in the hay, she almost ruined Helen's wedding plans in 1902. As Stephen Chase, Helen's fiancé, reported it: "We decided to be married as soon as possible but Aunt Ella and 'Chub' insisted that we wait until after haying. We were equally adamant and finally prevailed when we threatened to elope and stop on the way for a justice of the peace wedding. Such a move would be a disgrace to the family and provide neighborhood scandal, so Aunt Ella, herself, set the day of June 26th in the week before haying was to commence."

Four years later in 1906, while on a Minnesota visit, Ella wrote to thank Helen for a Christmas gift and the letter quickly turned into a litany of remembrance: "Meroe [sent] . . . the enlarged [photograph] of your father such as she had sent you—I think that was taken when he was 20, before he went in the army, and think the Choate boys look some like it. . . . I think your baby's picture is very nice indeed and since that came I have wanted to see him more than ever—you were not quite as old as he is there when your father died, and if he had curly hair as you had then he would look much as you did when you were baptized two days before he died."

The letter goes on to mention Sarah's and John Way's dimming eyesight (her own was still excellent) and an illness of "Sister Clara" out in California. Names of the younger generation pepper the pages: Meroe, Isaac's oldest child; David, Chub, Elsie, and Isaac, Alice's children; Nellie, Dustan's daughter. A paragraph stands out, full of a fascination with disaster that grew out of the many deaths in her own experience: "Mr. Sargeant of North Dakota was here today—he and his wife had been down in Southern Minnesota where her sister lived—she had two daughters and someone from the U. was in love with one of them and because she would not marry him he went there one night and shot both daughters and the mother and then killed himself—the daughters both died but the mother lived but is very bad off—it is a terrible affair—I had read of it but it seemed worse as he told of . . . it—I felt thankful you were married and settled, Perhaps you will think it strange that I thought of that but I did."

Her constant dwelling on the family's past could take on an aspect of clutching possessiveness. Customarily (in the Peacham cemetery at least) the husband of several wives is buried at one side of the plot, with his first wife beside him and subsequent wife or wives lined up on the far side of the first wife; yet when Charles Choate died in 1902, Ella left a space between him and Alice for herself.

From an early age she knew her worth: she could be useful. When she was only sixteen, Dustan enlisted her help in settling a coolness that had developed between him and Alice over Alice's not keeping in close touch with his wife, Abbie. Ella was at Alice's right hand during the first years after Roxana died. And when, freed by Isaac's return from the war, Alice went away to Mount Holyoke Seminary, Ella, at eighteen, acted as housekeeper on the Watts farm. Later she took care of her father as he aged and died and of Augustus as his condition worsened and he returned home. She

Ella Watts, ca. 1867. Tintype, courtesy Roberta Choate Gaudette.

went to stay and help at the Choate farm at the death of each of Alice's three infants. She was at hand during Isaac's last illness and when Augustus hanged himself in the barn.

Being useful could be psychologically costly, however. At about the time of her nineteenth birthday when she was keeping house for her father, she broke under the strain of all that was expected of her and had to leave the farm for an extended visit to Lyman in Lowell. Alice wrote her an anxious mixture of frivolous and religious exhortation: "Go on the street and see the pretty things. Don't send your hat back, unless you can get a better one. . . . Please do try to take pleasure in all this which comes to you . . . I'm sure I don't know what to say to you Lyman can tell you better than I, and God will tell you better than either of us can. . . . You must give up this idea of yours that you have sinned past God's pardon for I know it is not so." Lyman for his part wrote anxiously to his father suggesting that Ella be allowed to stay away from the farm awhile longer.

She recovered, and went home again, this time to share the housekeeping with Alice until Alice married, two years later, at which time she carried on alone during the period before Isaac married Lizzie Way, and again after Lizzie's death in 1874.

From time to time she went visiting—to the Centennial in Philadelphia, to friends in Massachusetts, to Sarah and John Way in Minnesota. One such visit, in 1878, presented a lively sense of her as a person in her own right, through the affectionate series of letters that Ellen, Isaac's second wife, wrote to her from the Watts farm. Full of gossip, housekeeping, sewing and gardening news, they offer a delightful picture of an easy and happy relationship between these two sisters-in-law.

"We have had a nice winter so far [Ellen wrote in January] . . . and until about a week ago I have washed dishes in the backroom so you must know the weather has been mild. We have the soapstone stove in the sittingroom and I have put the old rag carpet down. I put a large piece of oil cloth around the stove and another strip by the kitchen door. I think you would be surprised to see how well it all looks. Last week I made and put down my carpet and fixed one of the rag carpets and put it down in your bed room which Agustus occupies now. . . . I commenced a letter to you . . . [but] was so busy sewing I did not find time to finish it. I have made a pair of shirts for Ike and two night dresses (*that trail*) for Meroe besides fixing her shims and skirts and making her hood which she thinks is pretty nice. I lined it with blue and pinked the edges.

"We were speaking of you the other day (Meroe and I) and I said, what if

Aunt Ella should get married out west? Oh yes, says Meroe, by and by perhaps I should have a little *cousin*. . . . She talks about the Osgood family [an imaginary family] more than ever and I believe Mrs. O. has had *several children* since you went away. . . . Please remember me to all the friends there and also remember that when you are tired of staying there or anywhere else we shall be happy to welcome you *home*."

In April, Ellen wrote that Alice and Charles "are balling their butter this Spring and it looks very nice indeed. We are using ten pound boxes which are horrid things to pack for they are square instead of round. I told Isaac the other day that you ought to be here you liked new fangled notions so well."

Later the same month: "My dear Ella I am very glad that you are having such a nice time, it must be very pleasant to be comparatively free from care after being as confined as you were here, and I hope nothing will happen to prevent your carrying out your plans. . . . I have quite a number of house plants. Your sensitive plant is no bigger than it was when you left and I dont think it is so large but it 'still lives' and is a curiosity."

In July: "I have a nice flower bed out between the kitchen door and the shed. I took up your pinks and pansies and they are in full bloom. I wintered over your geranium and several others. They are all budded and the bed will look nicely in a little while. I have gone into house plants quite extensively. I have eleven different geraniums, two kinds of fuchsia (both in bloom) besides the plants flowering simple English ivy etc. I wish you were coming home this fall I think you would like the changes that have been made. . . . Your beds are both upstairs and the room is hardly ever used."

She reported more flower news in August: "My flower bed is lovely now for all my geraniums are in bloom. I have a beautiful double white petunia that Lodoska gave me, and a red and white one that Mrs. Way gave me. Those pinks and pansies that were up in the garden have been very full of blossoms, especially the pansies."

The last letter of the series contains a mysterious reference: "Has anyone written you that Mrs. John [Elwell?] had a baby? Just see where you might have been."

These artless and charming comments reveal several elements in the lives of country women of the time. One is the outlet for creativity that plants and flower gardens provided for farm women. They grew greenery indoors in winter to a point where whole windows might be filled with standing plants; in summer they grew plots of bright flowers and heavy curtains of green vines to shade their porches.

The other is the importance of being married. At the time when Ellen wrote these letters, Ella Watts was thirty-one—considered an old maid. Neither woman had given up hope for her yet, evidently, but, lightly as Ellen handled it, the topic lay heavy between them. Unless she had independent means, an unmarried woman might live her life as an unpaid servant and a private joke among children of the family.

What Ella's plans, mentioned in one letter, might have been, were never clear. In any case, they did not materialize, for Ella returned east, back to the farm, to help out during Isaac's last illness; to see Ellen and little Helen and Meroe through the trauma of leaving the farm; and to endure the horror of Augustus's final mental illness and suicide in the fall of 1881.

She was in Minnesota again, visiting the Ways the next summer when the news of Alice's death came, but for once she did not come home to help, writing instead letters of exhortation to Alice's older boys to be "such good boys and men that she would be proud of you always. . . . Your home will never again be as it has been. I dont know but think perhaps Aunt Mary and Aunt Elsie [Charles's sisters] will have the little ones but you must not forget them if they do go away—the poor little things never will remember their mother . . . I am all of your mother's folks that you know much about and I hope you will not forget me for I shall not forget you."

It was to Ella that Charles confided his feelings about Alice and her death, addressing her as "Sister Ella": "It is useless to say Alice's death has been a hard stroke to me how hard I don't think any one knows and I can not fully realize yet that she is never coming back again and if I had not been obliged to keep going and doing I don't know what would have become of me."

Ella stayed in Minnesota, teaching, sewing, and taking care of ill friends. In 1887, she began work at the Minnesota School for the Deaf at Faribault as assistant matron, the title given housemothers, a job well suited to her lifelong training and experience as a care giver, and one that she loved. As an independent working woman she reclaimed the full name of Lucy Ella, which she had been given as a baby, and she was listed as "Miss Lucy E. Watts" in the roster of the school for the deaf for 1887 and 1888. The catalog described her: "Miss Watts has had experience in this work only since coming to this school, but she has already commanded the confidence and esteem of both pupils and officers. She is both efficient and faithful."

In early April 1889, however, a letter came to her that she could not ignore, calling as it did on old friendship and shared trust, and speaking out

Meroe Watts's twenty-first birthday, August 10, 1892, at West Barnet, Vermont. Back row: Horace Ewell, Chub Choate, Meroe Watts, Ben Way, Charles A. Choate, Isaac Choate; front row: Helen Watts, Ida Boynton Ewell, Lodoska Spencer Watts, Lucy Ella Watts Choate, Elsie A. Choate, Elsie Choate Merrill. Photo "taken by Cousin Jenny Watts on Cousin Meroe Watts 21st birthday from papa's piazza at W. Barnet August 10th 1892" (identification by Elsie Choate). Courtesy Choate Farm Collection. Barnet was the location of the second largest croquet factory in the United States.

of desperate need. It came from her niece Helen, nine-year-old daughter of Isaac and Ellen Watts:

Dear Aunt Ella

Mama passed away today at about twelve oclock. She gave me to you. Meroe will write a note to you.

From your loving and affectionate Neice,

Helen L. Watts

Helen's older half-sister, Meroe, completed the urgent message:

Helen's mother expressed the wish that you would come and live in this house and take care of Helen. . . . She seemed to think you could come and thought it would be the best way to leave her little girl. . . . It seems very hard to have Helen left

without a mother or father for I know how much she needs them. . . . I dont
know what you will think of this but hope you will come.

From what I have heard I do not think she had a thought but what you would
have it arranged so you could live with Helen and would rather have her here so as
to be near me for one reason.

Charles Choate, at the time of his marriages. The first photograph, ca. 1868, taken by Chase, St.
Johnsbury, Vermont, courtesy Choate Farm Collection; the later one, ca. 1891, taken by John A.
Whipple, Boston, courtesy Roberta Choate Gaudette.

Much as Ella loved her work and little as she wanted to leave it, she could not refuse this plea. Following the example of her mother, she prayed earnestly and after a long struggle came to feel that it was God's will and her duty to go home and take care of Helen in the little house that Ellen had bought at Peacham Corner. Ella sent her resignation to Superintendent

J. L. Noyes who replied, enclosing her final compensation, with these words: "I am sorry to think this is the last payment to be made to you. I have enjoyed your society and your work while here. I would gladly continue the same if it were in accordance with your mind and wishes. Any time you know of a good capable young woman like yourself who would like a position here please write me in regard to her. I am frequently in need of such . . . I shall always remember you with pleasure."

Life with Helen cannot have been easy or rewarding. Helen was not ready to accept a substitute, particularly one whose style of governance, well intentioned as it was, was so much more somber than her mother's cheerful ways. Photographs of a gathering at the Choate farm in 1892 show Helen at almost thirteen, defiantly lost and forlorn, standing as far as possible from her aunt Ella, who sits like a large rock on the other side of the group.

When Ella Watts came back to Peacham, Charles Choate had been a widower for seven years, living with his two older sons and a succession of housekeepers at his farm in West Barnet. He had had to turn his two babies over to the care of other people: little Elsie was sent to her aunt Elsie Merrill, his sister, at Peacham Corner, and Isaac was boarded out to a family in Peacham Hollow, below the Corner. Charles visited them regularly and occasionally brought them home to stay with him for a day or two; but it was not easy to hold his family together under such circumstances. He began to seek out Ella Watts.

Charles's diary records a few events in the courtship of this middle-aged pair. In the fall of 1889, he wrote: "Took up some vegetables for the folks & some to Ella" and later, "Gave Hellen birthday 1.00." The 1890 and 1891 diaries mention increasing visits—Charles to the Corner and Ella to the farm. In June 1891 he "went up to the mountain pasture forenoon Ella went with me home at noon," and another day: "I have done House work most of day Ella came down on the Stage and helped me some and I carried her home afternoon." He does not note the decision to marry, and the diary entry for the day of their wedding, August 20, 1891, is blank—perhaps because he had no farming entries to make.

By October, Ella, Helen and nine-year-old Isaac had settled in at the farm, with frequent visits from almost eleven-year-old Elsie. The diary recorded Charles's pleasure at putting together a lavish Christmas for them all: December 21: "I went to St. Johnsbury . . . done a good many errand & bought a great amount of Christmas good[s] Some $8.00 worth Home about dark barely enough snow for sleighing." And on December 24:

Choate Family, probably taken shortly after the wedding of Charles A. Choate and Lucy Ella
Watts, 1891. Elsie Choate, David Choate, Charles Choate, Isaac Choate, Lucy Ella Watts
Choate, Chub Choate, and Helen Watts. Courtesy Choate Farm Collection.

"Chubby [his son Charles] went up to Peacham and got Teat [his sister
Elsie] and Eltie [his pet name for little Elsie] and they staid overnight. . . .
Children hung Stockings at night and me and we had quite a merry time."

Ella ruled the household from the first, refurbishing, redecorating, and
rearranging a house in great need of attention, and restructuring the family
life as she picked up again the work of stewardship that she had done for
many years at the Watts farm. Charles aged, and he began to have heart
trouble. In the summer of 1900, he went for a rest to an old vacation spot of
his in Maine, where he and his sister had once had good times. On August
19, a day short of her ninth wedding anniversary, Ella wrote him to report
on the family—"the children will start for Minnesota tomorrow"; on the
house—"Chub took another load of lumber to McIndoes to have matched
and the ceiling is nearly all done now. . . . they expect to cement the cellar
next Wednesday"; on the farm—"they got the oats all in last Friday." And
she added: "I hope that this week it will be more quiet at home so you will
feel that you can stay here but you must do as you think best. . . . I hope to

Charles Choate with Old Grover at Choate Farm, West Barnet, Vermont, ca. 1890. Courtesy Choate Farm Collection.

hear from you tomorrow night and I do hope you will get better so you can come home and stay for I miss you ever so much."

Charles went from Maine to Brightlook Hospital in St. Johnsbury, but recovered enough to spend the last months of 1900 at the farm, the high point of which was a triumphant trip to the agricultural fair in Burlington, where he and Chub submitted a pound of butter that won every possible prize—a piece of excitement that landed him in Brightlook Hospital again. Ella, in bed with the "grip" that had also felled the rest of the family, wrote him the news of the farm and the household, adding, "Don't worry about us and get home as soon as it is wise."

It never became wise; the doctors advised him not to return to the farm, for he fretted about the place and the work endlessly, and got no rest there. He went to Peacham, to be cared for by the two Elsies, his sister and his daughter, in what his daughter later reported as a time of cherishing, sorrow, and strange happiness, with the beauty that such dying times some-

Lucy Ella Watts Choate in old age. Courtesy Choate Farm Collection.

times offer. Ella, meanwhile, remained on the outskirts of this intimacy, as she stayed at home to keep an eye on the farm.

When Charles died of congestive heart failure in April 1902 and Chub married in August 1903, Ella moved back to the little house in Peacham, from which she made occasional visits to Minnesota. Except for her sister Clara, she outlived all her siblings, most of them by many years. She died in 1915, at sixty-eight, at the home of her niece Meroe, in Laconia, New Hampshire.

In leaving her job and losing the identity she had established in Minnesota, she lost the new name that she wanted to be called; "Ella" and "Aunt Ella" she remained for the rest of her life. In the early days of their marriage, Charles made a serious effort to call her Lucy. He succeeded most of the time in his diary, but there were lapses even there and doubtless many more in his daily speech. But she had the final say: her tombstone reads "Lucy E. Watts."

The younger generation of Choates and Wattses gave her dutiful respect, but they seem not to have cared much for her. Today's Choates remember her as "not quite the thing." Helen's future husband, coming as a suitor to the farm, remembered her as "a large, forceful, slightly bear[d]ed lady [who] looked somewhat critically at me." Helen herself never came to terms with the stormy feelings that she had endured during adolescence. To them all, Aunt Ella was a force to be reckoned with but not loved.

Family memories have not been kind to Lucy Ella Watts Choate. But turning to the photographs and looking first into the expectant, searching gaze of the child who sits with her sister Alice and their friend Lizzie, and then into the face of the woman who came to rule the Choate farm, heavy-jawed and grim, a modern reader can see her as a woman for whom love had come to be defined as the burden of duty and service, never as happiness or tenderness.

Epilogue: Peacham Today

PEACHAM CORNER, where the blacktop of the Danville-Groton Road crosses the dirt road going west to Cabot and east to East Peacham, was in mid-nineteenth century the busy center of village life with four stores, blacksmith and millinery shops, hotel, the offices of a doctor and a lawyer, barber shop, and library. The town, then with a population of close to fourteen hundred, spread in all directions from the Corner: east to the old cemetery, the Hollow, and up to East Hill and the Watts farm which is now hidden from the roadside view by evergreens and shrubbery; north over the hill, past farms and houses, to the village of Danville, seven miles away, whose main street is the busy east-west road from Montpelier to St. Johnsbury; west to the Civil War monument and Macks Mountain Road to Cabot; and south to the residential cluster once known as Water Street but now called South Peacham with a general store, the only reminder of businesses that once lined that intersection.

Today at Peacham Corner, the only store caters more to the tourist trade than the general store did in former years. The store now features a bed and breakfast where visitors from all over the world come, especially during fall foliage season. Sharing a porch with the store is the Peacham Corner Art Guild, where local craftspeople have an outlet for their "Made in Vermont" products. Across the road is Peacham Library, organized in 1810 and now part of the Vermont Northeast Regional Library.

Climbing west up the dirt road from the Corner one comes almost immediately to the Congregational church attended by Roxana and all the Walbridge-Watts children. It had been moved down from the hilltop in 1844 when the center of town shifted east to the Corner. Celebrating its bicentennial in 1994, the church looked much as it always did except for modern window boxes filled with geraniums in summer.

On the south side of the road across from the Peacham church is a

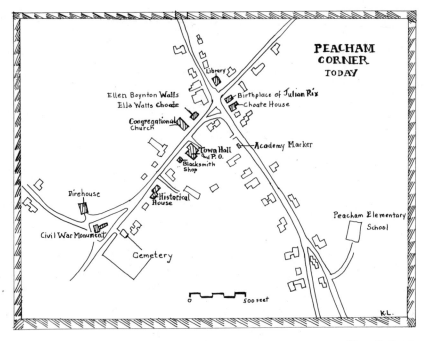

Karen R. Lewis

building currently used by the town clerk and postmaster, posts now held by either sex. Formerly the Methodist church built in 1833, this structure was purchased in 1930 by a summer resident who donated it to the Community Association of Peacham for "social purposes." The building was altered extensively for use as a gymnasium for Peacham Academy and by the town residents for roller skating, dances, and badminton. After the academy closed in 1971 and Peacham School, a private high school which took over the academy's buildings, closed in 1979, the "gym" sat empty for over a decade. It opened again in 1990 after major renovations with the town offices and post office on the first floor and the town hall on the second. Thus for the first time since 1844 the church basement was not used for town meetings.

Just north of the town offices are the remains of a blacksmith shop used for equipment storage by one of the few farmers still dairying in Peacham. A half-dozen dairy farms continue in Peacham and different kinds of farming are on the increase—tree farms, vegetable and flower farming, and sheep herding. New ways of using the land and keeping the hills cleared are suggested every year. Maple syrup, fresh eggs, wool yarn, and pure honey survive as cash crops in Peacham, and several houses have signs advertising these products on the road near their driveway.

Continuing to climb the hill on the south side one comes to the second district schoolhouse built at the Corner at the turn of the nineteenth century. (The authors do not know the location of the first school.) Once the third district school, now the firehouse, was erected near the top of the hill, a series of people owned the earlier school, among them Ernest Bogart who used it in the 1940s while writing a history of Peacham. Today owned by the Peacham Historical Association, the building is used for its annual meetings and visited by tourists who are in the area for the fall foliage and by school children throughout the year. They are fascinated by the telephone operator's switchboard from the first half of the twentieth century and a reproduction of the old-fashioned general store. The students come mainly from the Peacham elementary school, a building erected in 1969 at the south end of the village which has seventy-three pupils enrolled in 1993–94. After sixth grade, children are sent to high schools in neighboring communities, with their tuition paid through Peacham taxes.

Surrounding Peacham Corner are old white clapboard houses with green shutters. There are about thirty of these traditional houses at the Corner—and two brick houses, both parsonages long out of use for that purpose. In general appearance, Peacham is a New England village laid out much as it was two centuries ago. Over the years, shops, factories, and mills came and went. Many barns, too, have burned or been removed. Today automobiles fill the roads, instead of horses and wagons. In the summer months the whir of bicycle wheels can be heard as tourists and even some locals bike through Vermont, a part of the modern-day quest for physical fitness that past generations achieved less consciously through hard physical work.

In 1994 Peacham had 647 residents. Many are retirees—former professors, ministers, artists, musicians, business people—active in the social life of the area. There are also summer residents, adding another one hundred or so people in the months of July and August. Younger residents commute to jobs in the far cities of St. Johnsbury, Montpelier, and Burlington. A few work in construction or at logging in the woods, a baker and a dressmaker ply old-fashioned trades, and others, using the technological advances available at the end of the twentieth century, work from home offices.

All live in a town with no street signs or house numbers where most new visitors stop at the store or the library to ask directions to their destination. No descendant of Roxana Brown Walbridge Watts now lives in Peacham.

NOTES

When the writer or receiver of a letter is located in Peacham, Vermont, no location is given.

Diary entries where the date is given in the text are not endnoted.

Frequently used personal names and collection names are abbreviated:

ABBREVIATIONS - NAMES

AG	Augusta Gregory
AGM	Augusta Gregory Mills
ASR	Alfred S. Rix
AW	Alice Watts
AWC	Alice Watts Choate
CAC	Charles A. Choate
CW	Charles Watts
ChW	Chastina Walbridge
ChWR	Chastina Walbridge Rix
ClW	Clara Walbridge
ClWR	Clara Walbridge Rogers
DAW	D. Augustus Walbridge
DSW	Dustan S. Walbridge
EAC	Elsie A. Choate
EAR	Edward A. Rix
EBW	Ellen Boynton Watts
HSG	Hubbell Seth Gregory
INW	Isaac Newton Watts
JSW	John S. Way
JWR	Julian Walbridge Rix
LAB	Lynn A. Bonfield
LEW	Lucy Ella Watts
LEWC	Lucy Ella Watts Choate

LW	Lyman Watts (father)
LSW	Lyman S. Watts (son)
MCM	Mary C. Morrison
MWG	Martha Walbridge Gregory
RBWW	Roxana Brown Walbridge Watts
RKR	Russell K. Rogers
SW	Sarah Walbridge
SWW	Sarah Walbridge Way

ABBREVIATIONS — COLLECTIONS AND LIBRARIES

CaHS	California Historical Society
CF Collection	Choate Farm Collection
ChWR Journal	Chastina Walbridge Rix Journal, Rix Family Papers, CaHS
EAR Collection	Edward A. Rix Collection, Bancroft Library, University of California, Berkeley
INW Family Papers	Isaac Newton Watts Family Papers, VTU
JB Collection	Jack Barillo Collection
JWT Collection	John W. Turner Collection
LAB Collection	Lynn A. Bonfield Collection
MCM Collection	Mary C. Morrison Collection
MHS	Minnesota Historical Society
PC Collection	Paul Choate Collection
PHA	Peacham Historical Association
RCG Collection	Roberta Choate Gaudette Collection
R Family Papers	Rix Family Papers, CaHS
RGT Collection	Roberta Garry Trunzo Collection
R Journal	Rix Journal, Rix Family Papers, CaHS
VtHS	Vermont Historical Society
VTU	University of Vermont, Bailey/Howe Library, Special Collections
WC Collection	Watts-Choate Collection, VtHS
WG Family Papers	Walbridge-Gregory Family Papers, CaHS

ROXANA

information on the Browns' migration St. Johnsbury (VT) Caledonian, 8/8/1862, obituary for Olive Brown. The Battle of Bunker Hill during the Revolution reduced Charlestown to ashes. It never returned to its previous status as the second greatest New England port. The authors want to thank Harley P. Holden for loaning us Justin Winsor, ed., *The Memorial History of Boston,* which includes a chapter on Charlestown by Henry H. Edes, "Charlestown in the Colonial Period."

Peacham in 1800 Bogart, pp. 57, 222.

Peacham Academy Ibid., pp. 108, 120–23. For a history of the Caledonia County Grammar School, see its *100th Anniversary . . . Report.* No school catalogs exist from the years when the Brown children would have attended.

Peacham Congregational Church Bogart, p. 159; see [Peacham Congregational Church] *Anniversary Exercises of the Congregational Church* for a history of the church.

ideas debated There is no mention of women's suffrage or women's rights in any of the family diaries or letters.

town documents Peacham Town Records, Grand List, 1800.

young girl Bogart, pp. 291–92. The girl, Nancy Durrell, changed homes annually until 1812 and was probably considered a hired hand. She was apparently an industrious girl, for by 1812 her master was paid only thirty-nine cents a week, her own good work earning the rest of her keep. For a lengthy description of the process of bidding off the town poor in Rhode Island, see Ferraro, pp. 249–65.

town records for Roxana Peacham Town Records, Grand List (1840), pp. 322–23; Watts and Choate, pp. 296–97, 304. Families listed by Watts and Choate are under the name of the male head of the household and although Daniel never lived in Peacham, Roxana and the Walbridge children are listed under his name.

married at nineteen Roxana was three years younger than the average New England bride of this time (Cott, pp. 13–14). Her husband, Daniel Walbridge (1796–1835), served as Wolcott town surveyor in 1820 and was elected selectman in 1821 and 1822. He purchased lot #77, one hundred acres (the town was originally set up in one-hundred-acre lots), on September 18, 1820, for $150. (notes by Wolcott town clerk on LAB's letter of inquiry, 11/13/1991, and Wolcott Land Records, 2: 234). Walbridge died of "a Billious complaint," RBWW to HSG/MWG, Leoni, MI, 4/16/1843, WG Family Papers.

close-knit Walbridge family Daniel was the oldest of eleven children born to Oliver and Elizabeth Smith Walbridge. Their first four children were born in Cabot, and around 1801, the family moved to Wolcott. Here Oliver built the first grist- and sawmill in the town, also the first two-story house. Daniel's parents and siblings remained close to Roxana, the children visiting their grandparents until their deaths and traveling to see their aunts and uncles in Vermont and up-state New York (Wallbridge, pp. 80–81).

gender order important Ulrich, *Midwife's Tale,* p. 221: "The particular mix of boys and girls in a family, and their order, also helped to shape a family's destiny."

sold the farm According to Wolcott town records, Roxana Walbridge was "guardian . . . of minor heirs of Daniel Walbridge," and as such she was given "license" in June 1839 by the probate office in Morrisville, VT, "to sell and convey the Real Estate of her said wards" (Wolcott Land Records, 2: 234). In July 1839, she sold the farm to Jonathan Eaton "for the Consideration of Three hundred dollars" (ibid., 4: 327–28); The Peacham Grand List of 1840, made before her remarriage, has Roxana with "2 cows at 3 years" and $500. We assume that the money is what was transferred to Lyman when he became guardian of the Walbridge children.

Roxana returned to her parents' household A common practice among widows with young children was to return to the home of their parents. See McFarland for the story of Sally Ward, widowed at twenty-five with six young children, who returned to her family in 1850 (p. 106).

evaluation of Olive Brown RBWW to HSG/MWG, Jackson, MI, 9/24/1843, WG Family Papers; ChW to HSG/MWG, Jackson, MI, 2/9/1844, ibid.

"[T]ell your Brothers wife" RBWW to HSG/MWG, Jackson, MI, 9/27/1844, ibid.

a woman's identity Premo describes the "discontinuity of widowhood" (p. 29). See Chambers-Schiller on the importance of marriage "from [which] flowed all else . . . a woman's social role, her status, any economic security she might have, and her identity in the family and community, in the church and body politic" (p. 15).

"I have a good home" RBWW to HSG/MWG, Jackson, MI, 8/3/1843, WG Family Papers.

property of Lyman Watts Peacham Town Records, Grand List (1840), pp. 322–23. Lyman's older brother, Thomas Watts (born ca. 1789), was the third largest land owner, with 155 acres. Lyman Watts served as state representative from Peacham from 1858 to 1859 (Bogart, p. 466). The family papers include some financial notes, covering 1825 to 1842, detailing trade as a system of barter with Lyman settling his bills with wheat, corn, oak, "good gin," and "good meat stock." On January 11, 1842, after marrying Roxana, he paid his bill of $7.57 to his tailor with five bushels of wheat worth $7.50 and seven cents in cash (Bogart, pp. 285–86).

Another financial transaction of Lyman Watts was uncovered in San Francisco in 1990. A handmade barrel-topped trunk had been passed from generation to generation as westward migration took Lyman's descendants first to Illinois and finally to California. Inscribed on the bottom in iron gall ink is "To Lyman Watts in consideration 4 bushel of apples, Peacham, 1829." The chest is covered in deer skin and decorated with leather initials "L.W." The authors are grateful to Mrs. J. Lyman Watts of San Francisco for contacting us and for donating this artifact to the Peacham Historical Association. See *St. Johnsbury (VT) Caledonian-Record*, 9/29/1990, for article and photograph of the chest with Watts descendants Charles A. Choate III and MCM.

family identification with remarriages Cott and Pleck describe one result of remarriage as the development of a complex family structure with stepchildren and half-sisters and half-brothers (p. 39).

"It seems to me" RBWW to HSG/MWG, Jackson, MI, 4/6/1845, WG Family Papers.

families were large Bogart, pp. 224, 241.

cape-style cottage Either one or two stories, this style house had a center entranceway and a center chimney with two rooms on either side (Hubka, pp. 32, 39–42). A kitchen ell was located to the east with a back entrance to the mud room from the dooryard. Beyond the mud room was a milk room, then a horse barn, and finally a large barn. The privy was probably on the far side of the mud room or in a shed off one of these unheated buildings. Most coming and going was through the dooryard with the front door used rarely. The children's refrain is used as the title of Hubka's book.

"plastered & painted" ChW to SW, Lowell, MA, 12/2/1847, LAB Collection.

David Brown's illness RBWW to HSG/MWG, Jackson, MI, 4/16 and 9/24/1843, 6/23/1844, WG Family Papers; ChW to HSG/MWG, Jackson, MI, 2/9/1844, ibid.

David died in six weeks RBWW to HSG/MWG, Jackson, MI, 9/27/1844, ibid.

"[L]ittle Isaac grows well" Ibid., 4/6 and 10/5/1845.

Diphtheria killed whole families AW to AGM, Grass Lake County, MI, 5/6/1862, ibid. Alice wrote: "Does the Diptheria a throat disease prevail in Mich? It has and does now in Vt. very fatally in a great many cases. There is one family of six all sick in town now. One little boy in town has died. In the towns about here a great many have died." From 1840 to 1860 consumption accounted for one-third of the deaths in Peacham, according to records kept at the time (Bogart, pp. 231–32).

"It has been verry sickly" RBWW to HSG/MWG, Jackson, MI, 4/16/1843, WG Family Papers.

agricultural fair RBWW to AG, unidentified place, 9/28/1856, ibid. Bogart writes that the People's Agricultural Society of Caledonia County was formed in 1855 as a rival of the Caledonia County Agricultural Society, dominated by St. Johnsbury (pp. 317–18). A poster from the 1858 fair, preserved in the Peacham Historical Association, lists all the towns Roxana mentioned with the addition of Cabot.

"Sally has done . . . spinning" RBWW to HSG/MWG, Jackson, MI, 8/3 and 9/24/1843, 9/27/1844, WG Family Papers; Stilwell, identifies "mother and daughter power" where nearly all home production was the work of women (p. 101).

"The Boys all grow" RBWW to HSG/MWG, Jackson, MI, 6/23/1844, WG Family Papers.

men tend the gardens Interview by LAB with Charles A. Choate III, 7/20/1987, West Barnet, VT. Bogart assigns the gardening to the Peacham women (p. 70).

Lyman handled commercial exchanges ChW to HSG/MWG, Jackson, MI, 2/9/1844, WG Family Papers. The exact quote is: "Father has gone down Country now with a load expect him to be gone about one week." For a colorful description of the head of the Hibbard family of Waterford, VT taking their farm production for sale in Portland, Maine, "after a heavy snow was on the ground and the sleighing [was] good," see Lee, pp. 2–3. The authors are grateful to Edward B. Lee, Jr., for allowing us to review his family collection at the Lee farm in Waterford, summer 1992.

"*Mr W[atts] values his farm at about 20 hundred*" RBWW to HSG/MWG, Jackson MI, 9/27/1844, WG Family Papers. This and other letters show Roxana's lack of understanding of numbers past one hundred.

maple sugar Bogart, pp. 70, 315, 356, 360. As early as 1776 there is a record of settlers making maple "shuger," and by 1849 the Vermont production was more than six million pounds. Caledonia County was one of the top four leading Vermont counties for sugar production and Peacham ranked high there; see also Fairbanks, p. 491.

"*Hazen road*" Bogart, pp. 47–48, 95.

"*Business has been verry brisk*" RBWW to HSG, State Center, WI, 4/22/1850, WG Family Papers; RBWW to JSW/SWW, Northfield, MN, 1/19/1856, LAB Collection. Roxana added, "It is selling at 2 dollars per bushel." Other sources for Watts farm production: ChW to HSG/MWG, Jackson, MI, 1/18/1846, WG Family Papers; AW to AG, unidentified place, 7/15/1855, ibid.; ChW to SW, Lowell, MA, 12/2/1847, LAB Collection.

joined . . . Church [Peacham Congregational Church], *Manual of the Congregational Church*, p. 19. See Cott for an account of the increase to a majority of women in congregations although the church hierarchy remained strictly male (pp. 126–29 and n. 2), "*[M]an can appoint*" comes from RBWW to HSG/MWG, Jackson, MI, 9/27/1844, WG Family Papers; RBWW is unknowingly quoting from *Don Quixote*.

individual interpretations of Scripture Doan, p. 121. For a comprehensive study of Millerism, see Doan, who focuses on the writings of forty-three men and women active in the movement.

"*You wished me to write*" RBWW to HSG/MWG, Jackson, MI, 4/16/1843, WG Family Papers.

"*[S]eek first the kingdom*" Ibid., 8/3/1843.

"*we send . . . 7 scholars*" RBWW to HSG, Rock Prairie, WI, 12/20/1846, ibid.

granddaughter . . . "can read" Ibid., 12/27/1850.

Roxana mentions 134 people We have borrowed this research concept of counting the people mentioned in RBWW's letters from Robertson and Robertson, p. 244. All but one of the letters we have of Roxana's were sent to her daughter Martha and Martha's husband and daughter, and they never lived in Peacham. Therefore most of the people Roxana wrote about to them are from Wolcott, showing how widespread Roxana's community was.

"*I can't make it seem . . . like winter*" ChWR, San Francisco, to "Dear Friends [Family]," 12/15/1853, 6/14/1854, EAR Collection.

"*the family are all a bed*" RBWW to HSG, Rock Prairie, WI, 12/20/1846, WG Family Papers.

"*[We] have each of [us]*": ChW to SW, Lowell, MA, 11/8/1847, LAB Collection.

"*The girls are very busy*": ASR to "Dear Friends [Family]," 12/15/1853, EAR Collection.

family exchanged ChWR, San Francisco, to "Dear little brother and sisters," 4/1853, EAR Collection; RBWW to HSG/MWG, Jackson, MI, 4/6/1845, WG Family Papers.

"*I am growing old*" RBWW to AG, unidentified city, MI, 2/18/1858, WG Family Papers; AW to AG, unidentified place, 2/22/1861, ibid; AW to AGM, Grass Lake County, MI, 5/6/1862, ibid.

description of Roxana's death AW to AGM, unidentified place, 11/30/1862, ibid.

"*wife of Lyman Watts*" *St. Johnsbury (VT) Caledonian,* 10/10/1862, obituary for RBWW.

Dustan on Roxana's death DSW, Fort Totten, Washington, DC, to SWW, Northfield, MN, 3/14/1863, JWT Collection; DSW, Fort Totten, Washington, DC, to DAW, unidentified city, CA, 5/17/1863, ibid.

MARTHA

"*found imposed upon them*" R Journal, biographical pages.

"*the difference of disposition*" Ibid.

Seth Hubbell Hubbell, pp. 14, 25.

"*remember Grandsir Hubbells*" RBWW to HSG/MWG, Jackson, MI, 9/24/1843, WG Family Papers.

Gregory family purchase Michigan land Peck, pp. 98, 107, 109–11. For the description of Jackson County written about a decade earlier, see the letter by Lucy Stow Morgan in Warner, pp. 218–21.

Gregory family in census U.S. Census, Leoni Town, County of Jackson, MI, 1840, p. 161.

"*receive that long looked for letter*" RBWW to HSG/MWG, Jackson, MI, 4/16/1843, WG Family Papers.

fire in Gregory farmhouse Ibid., 8/3/1843.

"*The Girls have already begun*" Ibid.

"*I received your last letter*" Ibid., 9/24/1843.

"*the sollem news of the Death*" Ibid., 9/27/1844.

"*verry sorry on our part*" Ibid., 4/6/1845.

"*We want to know whither*" ChW to HSG/MWG, Jackson, MI, 1/18/1846, ibid.

Hubbell wrote the news There are no letters from him but the responses Roxana wrote tell the story. The Cradit Cemetery in Jackson County lists three bodies buried in the same lot: Martha, "wife of H. S. Gregory," "William A.," and "Arlone," at whose birth Martha had died. This information was sent by the Jackson County (MI) Genealogical Society, letter to LAB, 4/24/1990. The death date for Martha Gregory was incorrect.

childbirth mortality Degler notes that in Massachusetts there were 141 deaths per thousand births in 1900, no lower than it had been in 1850 (pp. 72–73). See chapter on Alice for additional information on childbirth mortality.

"*It is with feelings of great commotion*" RBWW to HSG, Rock Prairie, WI, 12/20/1846, WG Family Papers.

"*Now Augusta dont feel*" RBWW to AG, unidentified city, MI, 2/18/1858, ibid.

"*I assure you that we were all glad*" ChW to HSG, Janesville, WI, 8/6/1847, ibid.

Chastina wished him "happiness" Ibid.

Chastina sent "best respects" Ibid., 9/12/1847.

Roxana was "verry sorry to hear" RBWW to HSG, unidentified place, 9/12/1847, ibid.

"*I am going to take the liberty*" Ibid., 1/29/1850.

Figures for divorce and separation Degler reports that "as late as 1867 the number of divorces granted that year in the whole country was under 10,000," a minuscule number (pp. 165–66). He does find a rising rate of separation. See also Riley for changes in Vermont divorce laws and practice (pp. 46, 62, 81).

"*reconciled and live together*" AW to SWW, Northfield, MN, 8/14/1862, JB Collection.

"*You wrote that you thought of selling*" RBWW to HSG, unidentified place, 9/12/1847, WG Family Papers.

"*was glad to hear that Augusta*" Ibid., 5/29/1853.

"*Elvira Sargeant*" AW to AG, unidentified place, 2/22/1861, ibid. Elvira Sargeant (1837–1865) married Aaron Wesson (1836–1862) on January 31, 1861 (Watts and Choate, pp. 268, 316).

E. A. Mills Butterfield, pp. 747–48.

"*I am glad that you have a kind husband*" AW to AGM, Mt. Sterling, WI, 2/17/1868, WG Family Papers.

Augusta's children Obituary for AGM, unidentified clipping 1903 given to the authors by Hazel Mills. HSG died in 1879; E. A. Mills lived until 1907.

"*I was very sorry to hear of your misfortunes*" ClWR, San Francisco, to AGM, Mt. Sterling, WI, 2/22/1863, WG Family Papers.

SARAH

"*Sally has done*" RBWW to HSG/MWG, Jackson, MI, 9/24/1843, WG Family Papers.

girls to be hired out Cott, pp. 28–30. The quote is from ChWR in R Journal, biographical section.

"*Sally lives at the hollow*" RBWW to HSG/MWG, Jackson, MI, 6/23/1844, WG Family Papers.

"*to work in the factory*" Ibid., 10/5/1845.

weave shop Peacham Town Records, Grand List, 1845.

"*the Billious fever*" RBWW to HSG/MWG, Jackson, MI, 10/5/1845, WG Family
    Papers. Bilious fever was "a severe gastrointestinal infection" according to Ul-
    rich (*Midwife's Tale,* p. 68).

"*I am a going back . . . to work*" SW to HSG/MWG, Jackson, MI, 10/5/1845, WG
    Family Papers.

changes in women's role There is little documentation on Olive's role other than a few
    notes in Roxana's and Chastina's letters, and those refer to her last years. It is
    known that Olive took care of her husband in his final sickness, although she
    required help at night. Nursing the sick was a woman's job and Olive provided
    this service as long as she was able; RBWW to HSG/MWG, Jackson, MI,
    9/24/1843, ibid. For Roxana's role, there are her letters which speak of spin-
    ning wool and making butter and cheese in amounts far greater than one family
    could use (ibid., 8/3/1843, 9/27/1844). In addition, a letter Chastina wrote
    makes it clear that produce was being sold from the farm "Father sold his butter
    at 17 cents at the house" (ChW to HSG/MWG, Jackson, MI, 1/18/1846,
    ibid.). In the patriarchal society of nineteenth-century New England, produce
    and even the farm and house were often referred to as "his." See Sarah Snell
    Bryant diaries, 1795–1847, Houghton Library, Harvard University, for another
    example of this. On the rare occasion when Roxana summarized her own
    activities, such as in the letter of September 27, 1844, it is clear that she was not
    speaking of her husband's work. When writing of the crops and farm animals,
    she did so in paragraphs identifying her husband's activities. For a fuller descrip-
    tion of the changes of women's role, see Cott, pp. 19–62.

mill girls For information on mill girls in Lowell and for descriptions of many
    aspects of their life and work that are referred to here and in subsequent para-
    graphs in this chapter, see Dublin, *Women,* esp. 24, 38, 42, 67, 80, 130, 134–35;
    Cott, pp. 36, 56, 60–63; Zonderman, p. 266; Weisberger, p. 85; and Robinson,
    pp. ix–xi. By the time Sarah became a Lowell factory girl, the influx of immi-
    grant Irish women had made the labor force secure for the mill owners who
    then began to push for higher yields by a constant speed-up of machinery.
    While Sarah was at Lowell, the Ten-Hour-Day campaign was fought, but there
    is no mention of this or any other workers' causes in the family papers.

old maid ChW to MWG, Jackson, MI, 6/23/1844, WG Family Papers.

"*Sister has don very well*" SW to HSG/MWG, in Jackson, MI, 10/5/1845, ibid.

domestic service Dublin, *Women,* p. 13.

"*has been to work*" RBWW to HSG, Rock Prairie, WI, 12/20/1846, WG Family
    Papers.

"*go off to work in a factory*" Ashbel Martin in White Rock, CA, to his sister,
    4/10/1854, Ashbel Martin Papers. Boys who went to California for gold were
    admired, but girls who went to Lowell for wages were looked at with disap-
    proval.

"*The boys would go*" ChW to SW, Lowell, MA, [spring]/11/1848, LAB Collection.

Albert Clement was the son of Roxana's sister, and Horace Brown was the son of her brother. Both families lived in Dunham, Lower Canada.

"early after your departure" Ibid., 10/18/1847.

"Miss Kittredge" Ibid.

Peacham girls at Lowell It is possible to make an educated guess as to the identity of these young women. The only good source for the names of women born around 1830 is Peacham Academy's catalogs but they are not helpful in this case because students at the academy usually became teachers rather than mill girls. Jane is probably a Pattridge who lived in the Hollow and was a close friend to the Walbridge-Watts family since their cousin, Alma Brown, married Jane's brother, Albert Parttridge, in 1843. Mary is probably a Gilfilan, for Lyman came home from visiting the Gilfilans one evening and told Chastina to write the Lowell girls that they were well, also Mary Gilfilan later married Mark Varnum and one of Chastina's letters told of a party at the Varnums after which she wrote, "Tell Mary that they have got their *other* room papered, curtained, & carpeted. And I dont know what it is for, unless some of the boys are going to increase their *personal property.*" Esther is probably a Harvey who is listed in the academy catalogs around the same time as Chastina. Chastina wrote to Sarah, "Tell Esther if I could see her I would give her a good shaking," as if Esther were a scholar gone awry. Letters from ChW to SW, Lowell, MA, 10/18, 11/8, and 12/2/1847, [spring]/11/1848, LAB Collection.

wedding preparations R Journal, 10/9, 9/22, and 10/12/1849.

"At six o'clock" Ibid., 10/16/1849. Timothy Cowles (1777–1859) is listed as a "Hatter" in Watts and Choate, p. 83.

John Way Watts and Choate, p. 309; Merrill, "What I Know about the Ways." The authors wish to thank Sue O'Brien for loaning her copy of this reminiscence.

"Mr Way Sallys man has gone to California" RBWW to HSG, State Center, WI, 4/22/1850, WG Family Papers.

pregnancy rates for brides Rothman, pp. 45, 51; Ulrich, *Midwife's Tale,* pp. 149, 156–58. ChWR indicated a disgrace attached to premarital sexual intercourse and unwed mothers; R Journal, 8/14/1849.

From personal reminiscences given to the authors in the 1980s by older Vermonters from the Peacham area, we know that premarital sex was definitely disapproved of in late nineteenth century, but in cases where the couple married and began to assume the responsibilities of the community, there probably was little consequence of the first child's being an early one. Interviews in Vermont with Mary Jane Choate, Carolyn Long, Thelma White, summer 1987.

painful breasts Dr. Asahel Farr practiced in Peacham from 1849 to 1857 (Bogart, p. 235). Ulrich in *Midwife's Tale,* pp. 196–97, describes the common problem of "painful breasts." See chapters on Clarissa, Lyman, and Alice for similar problems.

"the Californian was at home" R Journal, 8/24/1850.

"*of my safe arrival in San Francisco*" *and other quotes* JSW, San Francisco, to SWW, 2/21/1850, LAB Collection.

the Eliphant To forty-niners no expression characterized the California gold rush more than "I saw the Eliphant." A good explanation of this is given in Levy:

> The expression predated the gold rush, arising from a tale current when circus parades first featured elephants. A farmer, so the story went, hearing that a circus was in town, loaded his wagon with vegetables for the market there. . . . On the way to town he encountered the circus parade, led by an elephant. The farmer was thrilled. His horses, however, were terrified. Bolting, they overturned the wagon and ruined the vegetables. "I don't give a hang," the farmer said, "for I have seen the elephant."
>
> For gold rushers, the elephant symbolized both the high cost of their endeavor—the myriad possibilities for misfortune on the journey or in California—and, like the farmer's circus elephant, an exotic sight, an unequaled experience, the adventure of a lifetime. (xv–xvi)

"*The mails that come*" JSW, San Francisco, to SWW, 2/21/1850, LAB Collection.

"*about the Claim that we bot here*" Ibid., 6/21/1850.

"*Mr Way Sallys husband*" RBWW to HSG, unidentified place, 12/27/1850, WG Family Papers.

"*situated on Lamoille River*" R Journal, 7/13/1851.

"*Sally and her man live*" RBWW to HSG, unidentified place, 5/29/1853, WG Family Papers.

"*Australin fever*" ASR, San Francisco, to JSW, Hardwick, VT, 5/22/1853, LAB Collection.

"*John Way & John Martin*" AW to AG, unidentified place, 7/15/1855, WG Family Papers. See Bowen for the route taken by another settler, immigrant Theodore Bost, in April 1855 to Minnesota from Ashland, New York: stagecoach to the railroad, train to Chicago, steamboat to St. Paul (p. 26).

New England families moving west It is difficult to say which Peacham family moved to Northfield first, but it can be assumed that the first families wrote back to Vermont praising the cheapness of the land, the fertility of the soil, the healthiness of the climate, and the community plans for schools and churches (Stilwell, p. 223).

five other Peacham families Watts and Choate list John's mother and brother with family as living in Northfield (pp. 309–10). Among the Watts families, the Lambert Watts family, a nephew of Lyman's, moved to Northfield in 1858 (Letter, Margaret Watts Bevan, great-granddaughter of Lambert Watts, to LAB, 12/10/1983). See also Curtiss-Wedge for a biography of Lambert Watts (2:1479–80).

Isaac visited INW, Diary, 11/15–12/30/1867, INW Family Papers; INW, Northfield, MN, to AW, 12/15/1867, MHS. The authors wish to thank Kathy Marquis, reference associate at the Minnesota Historical Society, for locating this letter.

Minnesota census Stilwell, pp. 215–16.

"I got a letter" RBWW to AG, unidentified place, 7/21/56, WG Family Papers. See Bowen, for Theodore Bost's letters describing the 1855 drought; an explanation of the 160 acres which anyone could stake out, work, and then buy from the government for $200; and a description of his log cabin (pp. 35, 44, 49, 87).

hardships in Minnesota in mid-1850s Ibid., pp. 35, 141, 214–22, 269. The Northfield bank robbery by the James and Younger gangs occurred in 1876 (Curtiss-Wedge, 1:434–43).

Christmas SWW, Northfield, MN, to AW, 12/30/1863, JB Collection.

horse stud business ChWR, San Francisco, to SWW, Hardwick, VT, 1/30/1854, LAB Collection.

the Ways' house AW to AGM, Rawsonville, MI, 12/7/1864, WG Family Papers. Alice wrote, "John has been building a house this summer and Sarah has had to work very hard and has not written but once or twice all summer."

"old timers" in the community Northfield News, 8/20/1964. The broadside John Way used for advertising the stallion's service is still in the family archives according to John's great-great-grandson Chris Way.

After 1795 when the first Morgan arrived in Vermont, the art of breeding Morgan colts and fillies was popular. Stilwell wrote: "The best Vermont colts left the state at a price of a thousand dollars each. And with them went many of the fanciers of horseflesh to become famous breeders far afield" (Stilwell, p. 221; see also pp. 99, 173).

Isaac in Minnesota INW, Diary, 11/15–12/30/1867, INW Family Papers.

"went to examination at the college" Sarah's children, Martha and Edgar Way, were enrolled at Carleton Academy (later College) in its first year, 1867. Both were listed in the English course as opposed to the more rigorous Classical course. There were eighty-one students enrolled, sixty-three in the English course. Letter, Carleton College Archivist, Eric Hellemann, to LAB, 4/9/1990.

"pile of bus[iness]" INW, Northfield, MN, to AW, 12/15/1867, MHS.

the Ways move They moved to 708 St. Olaf Avenue. The Northfield News (3/31/1966), reported on the house sale after the death of the last Way to live there: "The house and considerable acreage, including [the] area across the street which is now Way Park, was purchased in 1882 by JSW who had come to this community from Vermont in 1855 and settled on virgin land 1½ miles south of town."

John Way as state legislator Toensing, p. 125.

Sarah and John died JSW died January 16, 1909; SWW died February 3, 1909. The cause of death for Sarah was "astric atrophy and anarmia, contributory, old age, complications," according to Dr. W. A. Hunt. The same physician attended John, whose cause of death was "Diabitic Coma, contributory, diabitus." Sarah was eighty-one, John, eighty-six. Records in Rice County Court House as found and quoted in letter, Dale E. Maul, Executive Director, Rice County Historical Society, to LAB, 3/11/1983.

three brief letters, All were additions to Roxana's letters to Martha, 4/29/1843, 4/6 and 10/5/1845, WG Family Papers.

"*She is improving fast*" INW, Northfield, MN, to AW, 12/15/1867, MHS.

"*She had a pleasant journey*" LEW, Northfield, MN, to David Choate, West Barnet, VT, 7/26/1883, CF Collection.

Sarah's parlor Northfield News (8/20/1964), "Way Furniture Goes to Smithsonian." Also obituary for granddaughter Lucile Way, *Northfield News* (2/17/1966). LAB is grateful to Rodris Roth, curator of Domestic Life at the Smithsonian, for her tour of the Way artifacts.

"*Sent 1 pail*" CAC, Diary, 4/22/1889, CF Collection. He listed the "Freight on Sugar" as two dollars.

CHARLES

"*Lyman & Charles are about the same size*" ChW to HSG/MWG, Jackson, MI, 1/18/1846, WG Family Papers.

choice of Monticello The Piatt County historian, Emma C. Piatt, states simply that Charles Watts came to Monticello about 1855 and taught school the first year (Piatt, pp. 162, 331).

Charles Choate's teaching CAC, Diaries, 1856 and 1860, CF Collection. These are the only Choate diaries surviving from this period. Rock Island County is on the western border of the state, and Sangamon County is in the middle of the state. Chatham is located southwest of Springfield. Recommendations from A. Boutelle and Wm. D. Harriman, 10/19/1855; CF Collection.

Piatt County schools Piatt, pp. 154, 161.

"*I would never advise*" CW, Monticello, IL, to AW, 3/9/1856, excerpted by EAC, WC Collection.

"*Piatt Co. is one of the greatest stock Counties*" CW, Monticello, IL, to unidentified person, 10/26/1856, ibid.

law and surveying Ibid., 5/30/1857, 3/19/1857; RBWW to HSG/AG, unidentified place, 7/27/1856, WG Family Papers.

"*I am now staying in the office*" CW, Monticello, IL, to unidentified person, 11/24/1856, excerpted by EAC, WC Collection. H. C. McComas was one of the first lawyers located in Piatt County (Piatt, p. 149).

"*I was called to attend*" CW, Monticello, IL, to unidentified person, 1/8/1858, excerpted by EAC, WC Collection.

lawyers in Monticello For information on lawyers in Monticello and Charles's practice, see Piatt, pp. 242–43, 290–91, 306–7, and *Piatt County Quarterly* 2, no. 2 (1981): 17.

lawyer or farmer CW, Monticello, IL, to unidentified person, 1/29/1865, excerpted by EAC, WC Collection.

fourteen Spencer children Watts and Choate, p. 281. The Spencer farmhouse on East Hill no longer stands.

Phebe is "just as little" AW to AG, unidentified place, 2/22/1861, WG Family Papers.

"a first rate good girl" RBWW to HSG/AG, unidentified place, 7/5/1854, ibid.

Jewish peddler Story told to LAB by Thelma White, summer 1989, corroborated by Rita Lodoska Bole's undated notes on family history sent to the authors by Helen Watts Richter, 1991.

"make a wife of her" RBWW to AG, unidentified place, 9/29/1856, WG Family Papers.

"Quite a family" AW to AGM, unidentified place, 7/4/1865, ibid.

accidentally drowned Helen Watts Richter, Wheaton, IL, to LAB, 2/1/1994.

Isaac worked in Charles's office INW, Diary, 1/2/1868, INW Family Papers.

Charles's public service Piatt, pp. 243, 331.

"had robbed the till" Helen Watts Richter, Wheaton, IL, to LAB, 8/16/1993.

Charles came "after her" AW to AG, unidentified place, 2/22/1861, 11/18/1867, WG Family Papers.

"Bro. Charles came here" INW, Diary, 10/24 and 26/1868, INW Family Papers.

Henry Bodwell U.S. Census, 1860, Piatt County, Monticello Township, IL. Phebe and Henry were married on September 13, 1863 (Watts and Choate, p. 281); INW, Diary, 3/4/1868, INW Family Papers.

"lungs were feeling quite strong" Lodoska Spencer Watts, Monticello, IL, to AW, 10/6/1866, excerpted by EAC, WC Collection.

Charles's death INW, Monticello, IL, to LW, 2/4/1875, excerpted by EAC, WC Collection; INW, Monticello, IL, to SWW, Northfield, MN, 2/8/1875, JB Collection; obituary in *Piatt County Republican,* 2/7/1875.

"Lodosky's about worn out" INW, Monticello, IL, to LW, 2/4/1875, excerpted by EAC, WC Collection.

Lodoska's attempt to collect fees Lodoska (Dottie) Watts Strawn, St. Petersburg, FL, to Helen Watts Richter, Wheaton, IL, ca. 1960; copy of letter given to authors, summer 1993.

"While I was [in Monticello]" EAC, Minneapolis, MN, to Charles [Chub] A. Choate, Brightlook Hospital, St. Johnsbury, VT, 4/10/1903, CF Collection.

"We were always delighted" Rita Lodoska Bole (1895–1989) in notes prepared for her cousin, Helen Watts Richter, ca. 1960. In 1927 Rita Bole became principal of State Normal School at Lyndon Center, VT, which evolved into what is now Lyndon State College; in 1947, she was appointed president, a position she held until her retirement in 1955. Schlereth points out that at the turn of the century girls spent leisure hours at needlecrafts, drying flower arrangements, and wood-burning or "pyrography" (p. 210).

obituary for Lodoska *Piatt County Republican,* 2/21/1918. LAB is grateful to Elsie Buech Watts of San Francisco for showing her pieces of Lodoska's lace and embroidery, passed down to her husband, J. Lyman Watts, grandson of Charles and Lodoska. Also among the Watts family materials are a set of Shakespeare and a Bible, both once owned by Charles. Helen Watts Richter claims that a set of Waverly novels was also part of Charles's collection (Helen Watts Richter, Wheaton, IL, to LAB, 8/16/1993).

CHASTINA

"*a verry prudent . . . girl*" RBWW to HSG/MWG, Jackson, MI, 9/24/1843, WG Family Papers; R Journal, biographical pages. See chapter on Clarissa for fuller description of teaching in Vermont.

Burlington College Daniels, p. 9. Dates of Alfred's attendance and graduation at the University of Vermont, Goodrich, p. 87. Alfred noted his college debts to Thaddeus Stevens, R Journal, 3/18/1850. ASR, Burlington, VT, to Thaddeus Stevens, Lancaster, PA, 3/18 and 10/22/1845, Thaddeus Stevens Collection. The authors wish to thank Beverly Wilson Palmer for pointing out these letters.

"*On the . . . occasion*" R Journal, biographical pages.

"*The spring & summer*" Ibid. Often in the diary, Chastina is referred to as "C."

wedding described Ibid.

marrying in church By the mid-nineteenth century, public weddings had become common, partly as a way for the community to demonstrate its interest in the union, although the concept of a honeymoon as a time isolated from others, was not in vogue until the 1860s. (Rothman, pp. 170, 175).

"*with Mr. Bruce's horse*" R Journal, 7/30/1849.

Alfred's description of Chastina Ibid., biographical pages. In view of the apparent rapport between Chastina and her mother, as expressed in the letters, we are puzzled by the word "neglected," but it may refer to the troubled years after Daniel died.

activities in their new home Ibid., 8/17–25 and 9/7/1849, 1/1/1850.

prepare "herself to teach" Ibid., 8/30/1849; Caledonia County Grammar School, *Catalogue*, 1849, p. iii.

"*Our salary*" R Journal, 1/1/1850. The handwriting in the original diary is difficult to read; the salary appears to be listed as $300, which we have corrected to $800. The 1849 *Catalogue* lists the student tuition at $2 "per quarter of eleven weeks" for "Common English Studies" and $3 for "Higher English Studies and Languages," meaning Latin, Greek, and French. Two hundred and ninety-two students spread over four quarters were named.

Chastina "is . . . industrious" R Journal, 9/12/1849.

sexual activity in nineteenth-century New England Rothman, p. 45. Osterud notes that "married women and men seldom even alluded to their sexual lives" (pp. 113–14).

"*After life's fitful fever*" R Journal, 7/30/1849. Alfred plays on words from Shakespeare's *Macbeth:* "Duncan is in his grave, After life's fitful fever he sleeps well" (III, ii, 22).

menstrual periods R Journal, 9/24, 10/21/1849. In later years Chastina wrote "Had company!" and her younger sister Alice noted in her diaries most months "my *sick* day." Ibid, 4/17 and 7/13/1852, 8/12/ 1853. See AWC, Diaries, 2/14/ 1873, 4/7/1874, and others, CF Collection. Delaney, Lupton, and Toth note that it was common in the nineteenth century to use euphemisms such as "sickness" or "unwell" (p. 116). Chastina and Alfred appear to be practicing birth control by limiting sexual intercourse to days before and after her period.

November through April R Journal, 11/18 and 12/13/1849, 1/9, 4/1 and 29/1850.

"We are . . . family way" Ibid., 6/2 and 10/1/1850.

"got a loose dress" Ibid., 10/23 and 25/1850.

Description of birth Ibid., 12/29–30/1850. For information on midwives in eighteenth- and nineteenth-century New England, see Ulrich, *Midwife's Tale,* pp. 46–49. For accounts of who might be in attendance at a birth, see Osterud, p. 117.

Roxana was "on the ground" and baby's growth R Journal 1/1/1851, 12/31/1850, 1/19/1851. Roxana must have walked the two miles from the Watts farm to the Corner.

Alfred's activities Ibid., 3/7/1850. He passed the state examination on December 6, 1850. Born in Peacham, ca. 1818, William Mattocks was the son of Governor John Mattocks (1777–1847), the lawyer who helped Thaddeus Stevens "read" law (Korngold, pp. 10, 25). William practiced in Peacham from 1844 to 1854 (Bogart, p. 284).

speeches from Washington R Journal, 1/11, 2/28, 3/4, 12, and 16, 4/13, 7/9 and 13/1850.

Wilmot Proviso Ibid., 10/14/1849, 1/19/1850. The Wilmot Proviso, proposed by antislavery leaders of Congress, would have excluded slavery from any territory acquired from Mexico. It passed the House but was narrowly defeated in the Senate.

Fugitive Slave Law and *"admission of California"* Ibid., 6/14/1850. Under the Fugitive Slave act, passed in 1850, Congress made a major concession to the southern states. The act secured the return of runaway slaves to their masters and increased penalties on antislavery leaders who aided fugitives. Free-soilers were people who were opposed to the extension of slavery to new states.

"long & wearisome" Ibid., 10/8/1851, 9/2/1852, 10/26/1851.

Mrs. Marsh Ibid., 2/17–21/1852.

Chastina's home industry Ibid., 2/24 and 28, 3/30, 5/29, 6/1 and 16, 7/22 and 30/1852.

reading Ibid., 3/25/1852, 12/13/1851, 3/22, 4/16, 5/16/1852, and others. Gilmore gives a detailed analysis of reading in Windsor County from 1780 to 1835 (pp. 255–56). This covers a county south of Caledonia (where the Walbridge-

Wattses lived), which was closer to urban centers, and a time period before the Rix Journal but it is still a useful description of Vermont rural reading. Gilmore's research has corroborated the fact that Chastina was well read.

Uncle Tom's Cabin R Journal, 6/24/1852. See chapter on Clarissa for more on reading.

Alfred had "been sick" Ibid., 1/2/1852. For Alfred's version of his trip, see ibid., 5/11/1853 and his San Francisco letter to "Mr. and Mrs. Watts," 6/26/1852, EAR Collection.

"taking lessons in Spanish" R Journal, 6/14 and 7/18/1852. The early settlers in the area around Mission Dolores were Spanish speaking.

Alfred's invitation Ibid., 6/5 and 30/1852.

"He is well" Ibid.

"I may go" Ibid., 8/22/1852.

Julian weaned Ibid., 4/22, 23, 28, and 5/8/1852.

packed her box for California Ibid., 11/16/1852.

"endure" on the trip ChWR Journal, 1/30/1853: "O! Alfred, Alfred, you do not know how much I have to endure." The third version of the R Journal was dated May 1, 1853, but was actually written on July 10, 1853, on the pages they had left blank.

Steamer "Ohio" Kemble, p. 239. Kemble notes only 80 berths for steerage, which we assume is an error and have corrected to 800.

quotes from sea voyage ChWR Journal, 1/20–25/1853.

steerage passengers suffer ChWR on board *Ohio* to "Friends [Family]," 1/29/1853, EAR Collection.

from Aspinwall to Cruces ChWR Journal, 2/1/1853; Lewis, pp. 184–86.

"dreaded" by women For descriptions by other women travelers crossing the Isthmus, see Myres, pp. 3–4, and Bates, *Incidents on Land,* pp. 291–306.

"Such a room" R Journal, 5/1/1853.

"Golden Gate" Kemble, p. 228. Launched on January 21, 1851, from New York for the Pacific Mail Steamship Company, this was a wooden side-wheel steamer of 2,067 tons with three decks and three masts.

"a palace" ChWR Journal, 2/2/1853.

"From forty to fifty deaths" ClW, San Francisco, to "Friends [Family]," 2/27/1853, EAR Collection.

newspaper report on "Golden Gate" St. Johnsbury (VT) Caledonian, 4/2/1853.

fourteen days In 1855 the *Golden Gate* set a record, making the trip on the Pacific from Panama to San Francisco in eleven days and four hours (Kemble, p. 228).

"Feb. 19" R Journal, 5/1/1853. The *San Francisco Herald,* 2/19/1853, printed the *Golden Gate* purser's report, which noted that the steamer "brings a very large mail, also a large number of passengers, among whom are 120 ladies and 50 children," also "725 in the steerage."

Alfred's view ASR, San Francisco, to "Friends [Family]," 2/27/1853, EAR Collection.

"The girls" Alfred used this expression often, R Journal, 5/10 and 17, 6/13 and 21, and 12/13/1853 and others.

order from a local church Ibid., 7/23/1853.

Vermont "boys" Ibid., 7/3, 22, and 24, and 11/12/1853, 4/2/1854.

Alfred elected justice of the peace Ibid., 9/7 and 26/1853. Alfred was one of five citywide justices, 1853–1857. He also served as associate judge of the Court of Sessions for a brief period.

Chastina and Alfred's activities Ibid., 12/18/1853, 1/29/1854, 3/5/1854, 6/18/1853, 7/9/1853, 6/12/1853, 1/29/1854.

"saw Hamlet played by Mr Murdock" Ibid., 12/30/1853; the entry went on "The play was very interesting, but Mr M. was not so pleasing to us, as his reputation as an actor lead us to hope to find him." The Metropolitan Theatre, located at Montgomery Street near Jackson and "said to be surpassed by none of its size in the Union," opened Christmas Eve 1853, with James E. Murdock in *The School for Scandal*. The *San Francisco Herald,* 12/31/1853, ran this review of *Hamlet:* It "was produced at this popular establishment with great effect last night. The house was well filled to the roof. Mr. Murdoch sustained the character of Hamlet, in an earnest and forcible style, equally remote from ranting or lack of the proper degree of excitement . . . " (Theatre Scrapbook, 1853).

"went to the Musical Hall" R Journal, 4/12/1854. The local newspapers carried ads for the Musical Hall located on Bush Street near Montgomery. It was a "spacious and elegant Hall" rented out for concerts, balls, lectures, and religious activities, (Theatre Scrapbook, 1854).

events they recorded R Journal, 9/3 and 25 and 11/2/1853.

the journal stopped The last entry was 4/22/1854 although there were few entries after 2/3/1854. Alfred wrote a final summary 5/21/1857 after Chastina died.

religion in San Francisco Ibid., 7/10, 8/28, and 12/4/1853.

reading aloud Ibid., 11/9, 16, and 27 and 12/6/1853.

Alfred bought land ClWR, Petaluma, CA, to AG, unidentified place, 9/18/1858, WG Family Papers. In the fall of 1853, the financial situation of the Rixes had begun to improve through Alfred's successful law practice and investments supplemented by Chastina's cottage industry.

"our house" ChWR, San Francisco, to RBWW [January 1855], EAR Collection.

"the particulars [of Chastina's death]" RBWW to AG, unidentified city, MI, 2/18/1858, WG Family Papers. Robertson and Robertson point out the custom at this time of describing the details of death for relatives and friends who were not present (p. 103).

Alfred's letter to granddaughter ASR, San Francisco, to Genevieve Rix, San Mateo, CA, 11/2/1901, R Family Papers.

CLARISSA

"to tend Baby" and other quotes RBWW to HSG/MWG, Jackson, MI, 9/24/1843, 6/23 and 9/27/1844, WG Family Papers.

"Clarissa is teaching" ChW to HSG, Janesville, WI, 8/6 and 9/12/1847, ibid.

"I arrived home last evening" ClW to SW, Lowell, MA, 12/2/1847, LAB Collection.

"Mr Joshua Gilfilen keeps our school" ChW to HSG/MWG, Jackson, MI, 1/18/1846, WG Family Papers.

Clara sent her "love to all the folks" ClW, San Francisco, to "Dear Friends [Family]," 2/27/1853, EAR Collection.

"Tell Clarissa I wish she had about a score" ChW, Topsham, VT, to SW, 7/23/1847, LAB Collection.

teachers . . . "boarded about" Wells, *Barnet,* p. 174. Chastina wrote in 1847 she had "changed my boarding place six times since I came here. found all good boarding places too," ChW, Topsham, VT, to SW, 7/1/1847, LAB Collection. See also Nelson, "Schoolteachers," pp. 8–9.

women teaching Bogart describes the Vermont scene (pp. 140–58); Cott, the larger New England experience (pp. 34–35).

"In all I have had 54 scholars" ChW, Topsham, VT, to SW, 7/23/1847, LAB Collection.

Vermont certification of teachers Bogart, p. 145. In Peacham, the principal of the academy examined the potential teachers. Huden places the first state legislature act for examining teachers in 1827, although this was not carried out until the law of 1845 (pp. 33, 71–72).

Clara received two dollars a week RBWW to HSG, unidentified place, 12/27/1850, WG Family Papers. For an analysis of female teachers' wages, see Nelson, "Schoolteachers," pp. 12–13.

"Mr. Bickford of Cabot" R Journal, 11/18/1851.

"because we disturbed him" Ibid., 9/24/1852.

"something fashionable & pretty" ChW to SW, Lowell, MA, 11/8/1847, LAB Collection.

"Many [women] were so modest" ClW, San Francisco, to "Dear Friends [Family]," 2/27/1853, EAR Collection.

"It cost the girls" RBWW to HSG/AG, unidentified place, 5/29/1853, WG Family Papers.

"as plump and gay" ASR, San Francisco, to "Dear Friends [Family]," 2/27/1853, EAR Collection.

"Clara tells me she does not take any comfort" R Journal, 7/28/1853.

"I do wish I could have some new sugar" ClW, San Francisco, to "Dear Brothers & Sisters," 5/22/1853, LAB Collection.

Clara at the mission Clara received her California teaching certificate on August 8,

1853, copy in R Family Papers; *Alta California* (San Francisco), 11/6/1852, lists
the teachers and their monthly salaries. We are grateful to Hazel Mills for giving
us the citations of this and other *Alta California* articles.

"[School] is somewhat different" ClW, San Francisco, to HSG, 2/26/1854, WG
Family Papers. For information on Mission Street, see Lotchin, pp. 43, 71, 76.
The mission school was located at the corner of Dolores and Fifteenth Streets
and was built of Mexican mahogany ("San Francisco Streets.")

Clara teaching ASR, San Francisco, to "Dear Friends [Family]," 12/15/1853, EAR
Collection; *Alta California,* 5/18/1855.

"As far as I am concerned" ClW, San Francisco, to HSG, 2/26/1854, WG Family
Papers.

she slept "on a bunk" ClW, San Francisco, to "Dear Brothers & Sisters," 5/22/1853,
LAB Collection.

shopping trip, R Journal, 12/16/1853.

second-floor room, ASR, San Francisco, to "Dear Friends [Family]," 1/14/1855,
EAR Collection.

courting of Clara ChW to HSG/MWG, Jackson, MI, 1/18/1846, WG Family
Papers; ChW to SW, Lowell, MA, 10/18/1847, LAB Collection; ClW to SW,
Lowell, MA, 12/2/1847, ibid.

"I like the climate and country" ClW, San Francisco, to "Dear Brothers & Sisters,"
5/22/1853, ibid.

need of chaperons Rothman, pp. 207–8.

Clara's activities R Journal, 1/2/1854, and others. Lotchin describes New Year
open houses where women welcomed their gentlemen friends (p. 287).

Clara "dont care for any one" ChWR, San Francisco, to "Dear Friends [Family],"
2/15/1855, EAR Collection.

special events Pickwick Assemblies were dances open to the public where Chastina
and Clara had "a very good time," R Journal, 3/5, 17, and 31/1854.

   Their Spanish friends, the Ruffinoes, gave parties where the guests stayed up
all night eating and talking, ibid., 1/3 and 3/5/1854. Lotchin describes the
ethnic neighborhoods in San Francisco in the late 1850s, noting, however, that
segregation was not a public policy (p. 120). There is little documentation of
Yankee-Spanish social mixing of the sort mentioned in the Rix Journal. As
well, we found no expression of hostility so common among Yankee forty-
niners (and—later in the century—of workers known to attack the Chinese
immigrants), who objected to all "foreigners," seeing them as economic com-
petitors. The social mixing in which Clara, Chastina, and Alfred participated
was family-to-family and a natural extension of community values they had
learned in Peacham.

"I do not know whether" ClW, San Francisco, to RBWW, 5/14/1854, LAB Collection.

attention to fashion Ibid., 5/14/1854, 5/22/1853.

interests of the individual Lotchin, pp. 344–45.

Clara and Russell's marriage Unidentified news clipping found in the WG Family Papers; RBWW to HSG/AG, unidentified place, 9/28/1856, ibid.

Russell's work ChWR, San Francisco, to "Dear Friends [Family]," 2/15/1855, EAR Collection.

"I have been mining" Russell K. Rogers, Placerville, CA, to unidentified person, 6/23/1853, copy, R Family Papers. The original of this letter is in the Mildred Maurer Brown Collection.

"Our house is situated on Pine St." ClWR, San Francisco, to SWW, Northfield, MN, 11/2/1856, JB Collection.

She "had a long confinement" RBWW to AG, unidentified city, MI, 2/18/1858, WG Family Papers; Clara's view, ClWR, Petaluma, CA, to AG, unidentified place, 9/18/1858, ibid.

we "keep cows" ClWR, Petaluma, CA, to AG, unidentified place, 9/18/1858, WG Family Papers.

"We have been having a regular California rain storm" Ibid., 2/1/1859; ClWR, San Francisco, to AGM, Mt. Sterling, WI, 8/26/1896, ibid.

"We live . . . for the past three years" ClWR, San Francisco, to AGM, unidentified place, 2/22/1863, ibid.

"now live at the Mission" ClWR, San Francisco, to SWW, Northfield, MN, 9/1/1865, JB Collection.

evaluations of Russell ASR, San Francisco, to RBWW, 9/17/1860, ASR Folder, PHA; DAW, San Francisco, to AW, 5/28/1862, excerpted in Bogart, p. 228; DSW, Fort Totten, Washington, DC, to AW, 4/9/1864, JWT Collection.

Rogers' family trip Edward A. Rix's Journal kept during the summer of 1871 and titled, "A Trip East," EAR Collection.

Russell Rogers's death obituary in *Alta California,* 11/1/1886. The authors are indebted to Wilber Leeds for locating this obituary although we had no death date. Russell made a last trip to Vermont which Charles A. Choate noted in his diary on 8/7/1886: "Chubby [his son] and I went to Boltonville to see Russ Rogers . . . the poor man looks bad." In his entry for 11/13/1886, Charles noted, "heard of Russell Rogers death which occurred October 30th," CF Collection. Rogers was born in 1827 in Boltonville (now part of Newbury) and his mother lived there until her death in 1892 (Wells, *Newbury,* p. 679). Wells incorrectly lists him as a lawyer.

"A mothers anxiety is not at rest" ClWR, San Francisco, to AGM, Mt. Sterling, WI, 8/26/1896, WG Family Papers.

"Isn't this a terrible war?" ClWR, San Francisco, to SWW, Northfield, MN, 7/8/1898, JB Collection.

"it was wonderful how Mother [Clara] stood it all" Nellie Rogers Halstead, San Francisco, to SWW/JSW, Northfield, MN, 8/16/1906, JB Collection.

Clara's obituary San Francisco Chronicle, 9/1/1917.

Julian

changes in child rearing McPherson, pp. 34–35, Evans, pp. 74, 92, 95, and Cott, pp. 58, 84. The shift to children being the center of a mother's activities was primarily an urban middle-class phenomenon. Maternal affection and gentle persuasion balanced patriarchal authority.

Alfred and Chastina's reports on Julian R Journal, 1/19, and 26, 2/1, 3/6 and 16, 5/24, and 6/29/1851.

Bronson Alcott Stickland, pp. 5–6.

Alfred took care of the baby R Journal, 3/30 and 5/12/1851.

Julian's growth Ibid., 6/22, 7/18–19, 8/30, and 12/24/1851, 3/22 and 8/22/1852.

Julian sick Ibid., 3/4/1852.

"he will be spoiled" Ibid., 3/4 and 4/8/1852.

"began to wean" and other activities Ibid., 4/22, 5/7, 12, 14, and 27, 6/21, and 9/25/1852.

"making bub's clothes" Ibid., 11/4 and 13/1852.

trip to California ChWR Journal, 1/17, 18, and 22, and 2/2/1853.

Alfred's first letter ASR, San Francisco, to "Friends" [Family], 2/27/1853, R Family Papers.

"There is hardly a day passes" ChWR, San Francisco, to "Friends" [Family], 4/20/1853, ibid; ChWR, San Francisco, to JSW/SWW, Hardwick, VT 8/31/1853, LAB Collection; ASR, San Francisco, to "Friends" [Family], 12/15/1853, EAR Collection.

Julian's "first attempt at shopping" ClW, San Francisco, to SWW, Hardwick, VT, 11/29/1853, JB Collection.

"I wish from my heart" ASR, San Francisco, to RBWW, 3/15/1854, EAR Collection.

Julian "enjoyed himself" R Journal, 7/21/1853.

"Julian is well" ChWR, San Francisco, to RBWW, 8/31/1854, LAB Collection.

"Julian thinks a good deal" ChWR, San Francisco, to "Friends" [Family], 2/15/1855, EAR Collection.

he "has seen to much" RBWW to AG, unidentified city, MI, 2/18/1858, WG Family Papers.

educate children in the East ASR, San Francisco, to "Friends" [Family], 1/14/1855, EAR Collection. Alfred wrote: "There is one consideration which alone would compel us to move to the East as soon as we can, that is 'the unfitness of this place for educating our boy.'"

"Mr. Rix broke up housekeeping" RBWW to AG, unidentified city, MI, 2/18/1858, WG Family Papers.

letters that Alfred wrote Roxana ASR, San Francisco, CA, to RBWW, 9/17 and 10/25/1860 sent in one envelope, Watts-Choate Genealogy Records.

Julian attended Peacham Academy The issue of *The Students Record* that lists him as editor (vol. 1, no. 6 [1867]) also contains the line: "as water is to the river, so is Laura Calder to Julian Rix" (PHA).

Two drawings CF Collection.

Dustan from the Civil War DSW, Fort Totten, Washington, DC, to ClWR, San Francisco, 12/28/1862, JWT Collection.

"The Step Mother" JWR, San Francisco, to LEW, 11/14/1868, JB Collection.

he had trouble finding the site Ibid. Lone Mountain Cemetery, established well outside the city of San Francisco in 1853, echoed the East Coast's concept of a "rural cemetery," as represented by Mount Auburn, near Boston. Through time its fifty-seven acres became a showplace of vistas with twenty miles of wide avenues and winding paths. In 1868 the cemetery was renamed Laurel Hill. As the city grew, the fact that Laurel Hill was the final resting place of its pioneers did not save it from pressure by developers and investors; finally in 1937 the citizens of San Francisco voted to move the bodies from the cemetery, which had been long neglected and where many of the graves had been desecrated. Teams of grave diggers working by hand took two years to move the more than 35,000 bodies to other selected sites. Chastina's body was reburied in Oakland with her son Edward.

Most of the Laurel Hill gravestones were dumped, some at Ocean Beach and others to form the seawall on the bay at the St. Francis Yacht Harbor and Aquatic Park. If Julian had a gravestone made for his mother, it would today be a part of the seawall of this Bay (Culbertson and Randall, pp. 256–57).

apprenticed to Charles Hopps Alta California, 2/27/1875; "Studio Notes," *San Francisco Chronicle*, 11/30/1903.

"has great merit" San Francisco Bulletin, 9/4/1872.

his father refused to help him Interview by LAB with Elizabeth Rix Fairfax, Julian's niece, spring 1988; "Studio Notes," *San Francisco Chronicle*, 11/30/1903.

Alfred visited his sister, Adeline Rix Bierstadt R Journal, 5/15/1850, 8/4/1851. No newspapers of the time noted the Bierstadt-Rix connection.

Albert Bierstadt There are several biographies of Bierstadt (1830–1902); see especially Anderson and Ferber. The authors are indebted to Alfred C. Harrison, Jr., of the North Point Gallery for allowing us access to newspaper clippings on JWR.

Edward and Adeline Bierstadt in San Francisco In EAR's photograph album, "Mental Photographs, An Album for Confessions of Tastes, Habits, and Convictions," ed. Robert Saxton there are pages for Addie Bierstadt, 8/6/1872, and for Edward H. Bierstadt, 8/7/1872, indicating that they were in San Francisco on those dates, EAR Collection.

Bohemian Club Founded in 1872, the Bohemian Club functioned as an artists' clique. According to Van Der Zee, "Originally a club for men with talent but no money, the Bohemian Club [soon became] . . . the reverse" (p. 21).

Peacham visits AWC, Diary, 6/7–8 and 7/17/1874, and CAC, Diary, 2/16–17/1883, CF Collection.

"*There is a picture*" *Alta California*, 2/27/1875.

"*At Morris & Schwab's*" "Art Notes," *San Francisco Chronicle*, 8/27/1876.

"*the Adonis of the Profession*" *San Francisco Chronicle*, 4/22/1877.

"*a little masculine fun*" Ibid.

illustrated note to an art student Lorenzo Palmer Latimer (1857–1941), Santa Cruz, CA, to Mabel Harvey, San Francisco, 8/23/1878, CaHS; Jules Tavernier (1844–1889), Kirk, pp. 37–38, 41–44; "Painter and Palette," *San Francisco Evening Post*, 4/22/1877.

"*San Francisco, though only a little over twenty-five*" Harrison, "Albert Bierstadt," p. 83.

"*Summer Morning*" *San Francisco Chronicle*, 3/16/1879. Change in taste of art buyers of San Francisco (Harrison, "Haggin," p. 18).

William T. Ryle Information on Ryle (b. 1845) was kindly provided by Andrew F. Shick of the Passaic County Historical Society, Paterson, NJ: letters to LAB, 1/7 and 5/31/1990. See also Stote, p. 190.

"*You must understand*" *San Francisco Bulletin*, 4/28/1883.

"*You are very much mistaken*" JWR, Paterson, NJ, to ClWR, San Francisco, copy, 6/12/1885, R Family Papers. The original of this letter is in the Mildred Mauer Brown Collection.

a failed love affair Telephone conversation between LAB and Betty Hoag McGlynn, Tavernier biographer, 6/6/1994. Nellie Hopps (1856–1956) was the daughter of Julian's former employer, Charles Hopps, an early San Francisco artist. She sketched with Julian. (*San Francisco Chronicle*, 12/8/1879). In 1884 Nellie Hopps married B. Chandler Howard, an agent for the Pacific Mail Line, and they lived in the Far East for the next fifty-seven years.

Julian Rix "got rid of his sideburns" This quote was sent to LAB in a letter from Betty Hoag McGlynn, 4/21/1977.

Julian's will New York Times, 12/4/1903.

"*not in the most robust health*" "Studio Notes," *San Francisco Chronicle*, 11/30/1903.

"*I was born in Peacham Vermont*" JWR, New York City, to F. B. McGuire, Corcoran Gallery, Washington, DC, 2/5/1903, Registrar's Records, Corcoran Gallery.

report on Julian's estate New York Times, 12/4/1903.

Julian's obituary New York Times, 11/25/1903; San Francisco Examiner, 11/25/1903.

DUSTAN

"*in Marshfield at his trade*" RBWW to HSG, unidentified place, 12/27/1850, WG Family Papers.

"*We were waiting this time*" ChWR, San Francisco, to "Dear Friends [Family]," 4/20/1853, LAB Collection. Family members spelled Dustan's name several different ways.

"*he can make the nicest waggon bodies*" Ibid., 8/31/1854.

"*I hope John wont go west*" DSW, San Francisco, to RBWW, 11/13/1854, ibid.

"*Large brick buildings*" DSW, San Francisco, to LSW, unidentified place, 9/13/1853, ibid.

"*Leckshun is just over*" Ibid.; Lotchin describes this kind of "politicking" by quoting Milo Hoadly's diary entry for 3/30/1850: "Candidates for office must treat every one out of ten" (pp. 214–15).

"*Today is the* glorious fourth" DSW, San Francisco, to INW, 7/4/1856, LAB Collection.

"*It seemes . . . you have . . . found the Eden*" DSW, San Francisco, to JSW, Northfield, MN, 7/30/1855, ibid.

"*I can hardly realize it now*" DSW, St. Johnsbury, VT, to ClWR, San Francisco, 11/3/1861, JB Collection.

Army enlistment records for Dustan Provided to the authors by John W. Turner, a Civil War collector, these records are preserved at the National Archives, Washington, DC. See the chapter on Isaac for additional stories about Peacham soldiers.

"*We came here*" DSW, camp near Fort Lincoln, Washington, DC, to ClWR, San Francisco, 9/15/1862, JWT Collection.

"*We had a pretty hard time*" Ibid.

"*I enlisted as a* private" DSW, Fort Totten, Washington, DC, to SWW, Northfield, MN, 3/14/[1863], ibid. Not all Americans were carried away with the tide to eliminate Indians. Bowen gives Theodore Bost's view (pp. 211–12).

"*Our Mother is gone*" DSW, Fort Totten, Washington, DC, to ClWR, San Francisco, 12/28/1862, JWT Collection.

"*You tell me to study the Bible*" DSW, Fort Totten, Washington, DC, to LSW, East Calais, VT, 4/3/1863, ibid.

"*I think now that a girl*" DSW, Fort Totten, Washington, DC, to ClWR, San Francisco, 5/31/1863, ibid.

"*Abbie has done everything for me*" DSW, Fort Totten, Washington, DC, to AW, 6/28/1863, ibid.

"*Our little Nellie*" DSW, Fort Totten, Washington, DC, to ClWR, San Francisco, 5/31/1863, ibid. "Eddie" is Edward A. Rix, son of Alfred and Chastina Rix, born in San Francisco in 1855.

"*All the men that are not detailed*" DSW, Fort Totten, Washington, DC, to DAW, unidentified place in California, 5/17/1863, ibid.

"*You are terrible on ducks*" DSW, Fort Totten, Washington, DC, to JSW, Northfield, MN, 6/3/1863, JB Collection.

"*I suppose you get the news*" DSW, Fort Totten, Washington, DC, to ClWR, San Francisco, 5/31/1863, ibid.; DSW, Fort Totten, Washington, DC, to DAW, unidentified place in California, 5/17/1863, ibid.

"*It is rather a pleasant Country*" DSW, Fort Totten Washington, DC, to DAW, unidentified place in California, 5/17/1863.

"*I am . . . making a Topographical map*" DSW, Fort Totten, Washington, DC, to
   ClWR, San Francisco, 5/31/1863, ibid. See McPherson for his account of the
   lack of accurate maps of the South. (p. 313).

"*I shall always remember him*" Sophia Way to JSW/SWW, Northfield, MN, 6/26/
   1864, JWT Collection.

"*Marched a short distance*" INW, Diary, 6/2/1864, INW Family Papers.

confusion over name of Cold Harbor Benedict, 1: 459.

no veteran ever expressed a desire to revisit Catton (p. 149), based this evaluation on
   Following the Greek Cross, or, Memories of the Sixth Army Corps, by Brevet Brig-
   adier General Thomas W. Hyde (Boston, 1894), p. 214. For a description of the
   battle at Cold Harbor as fought by the Vermont Brigade, see Benedict 1: 462–
   69. Bogart notes that 30 percent of the soldiers from Peacham lost their lives in
   the war: eight were killed in action or died as the result of wounds received in
   battle; four died in prison; and twenty died of disease (a total of thirty-two). On
   July 4, 1870, at the dedication of the Peacham Soldiers Monument, Isaac Watts
   read the names of forty-one soldiers enlisted from Peacham who died and two
   others, including Dustan, who had enlisted from St. Johnsbury, VT. (Dustan's
   name is inscribed on the St. Johnsbury Soldiers Monument next to the courthouse. He was one of eighty who died from that town.) We cannot account for
   the difference in numbers between Bogart and Isaac Watts. INW, Dedication
   Speech, 7/4/1870, INW Family Papers.

"*I regret this assault*" McPherson, p. 735.

"*The fight was pretty warm*" INW, Diary, 6/2/1864, INW Family Papers.

only one surgeon Charles Harvey Brewster, cited in Blight p. 308. At this time
   surgeons were able to stop gangrene only by amputation and were ignorant
   about the connection between unsterilized instruments and infection (Catton,
   pp. 101, 106, 163; McPherson, pp. 482–86).

transportation of injured At Cold Harbor, on June 3, seven thousand Union soldiers
   were killed in the first half hour of battle, and thousands more were wounded.
   The latter were carried by stretcher-bearers from the field and transported to
   makeshift hospitals by ambulance wagons, which Catton describes as having no
   springs and going over rough roads (pp. 101–7). From the field hospital, Dustan
   was probably taken by steamer to Douglas Hospital in Washington.

"*had good accommodations*" AW to SWW, Northfield, MN, 7/9/1864, JWT Collection.

"*I hardly know how to write*" Sophia Way to JSW/SWW, Northfield, MN, 6/26/
   1864, ibid. Sophia Edsen Way's husband, Jacob Way, was John S. Way's
   uncle.

Dustan's gravestone The inscription reads, "Lieut. D. S. Walbridge died in Douglas
   Hospital Washington, DC of wounds received in battle at Coal Harbor June 3,
   1864 aged 32 yrs." Dustan actually died on June 19, 1864.

AUGUSTUS

"I think he is more of an enigma" INW to LEW, Northfield, MN, 10/14/1878, INW Family Papers.

letters from Augustus Two fragments dated 11/20/1852 and 12/11/1859 are quoted in Bogart (pp. 227–28). Six short excerpts were made by Elsie A. Choate where it is difficult to tell which words are quoted exactly and which are paraphrased: 1/17/1855, 11/30/1861, 5/28, 8/23, and 12/10/1862, 11/9/1864, WC Collection.

"I wish you could see Aug" ChW to HSG/MWG, Jackson, MI, 8/3/1843, WG Family Papers.

"Augustus met with quite an accident" RBWW to HSG/MWG, Jackson, MI, 6/23/1844, ibid.

"Augustus is large of his age" RBWW to HSG, State Center, WI, 4/22/1850, ibid.

"sober boy" ChW to HSG/MWG, Jackson, MI, 1/18/1846, ibid.

Brattleboro Retreat, or "Insane Hospital" R Journal, 10/25/1851. For a good history of the treatment at the Retreat, see Swift and Beach, esp. pp. 2–3. The authors wish to thank Kurt A. Isaacson for sending us a copy of this history.

Alvah Watts Son of Lyman's brother Thomas Watts and Jane Bailey Watts, Alvah was born in Peacham in 1822, attended the University of Vermont, graduating in the class of 1849. He died at the Brattleboro Retreat in 1877 (Goodrich, 89).

"crazy" and other quotes R Journal, 4/10/1850, 4/21 and 27/1851.

"Augustus . . . is gone to sea" RBWW to HSG/AG, unidentified place, 5/29/1853, WG Family Papers.

"Augustus did not get" Ibid., 7/5/1854.

"Augustus has got so that he is a good work man" Ibid., 7/27/1856.

"I have always calculated" DSW, San Francisco, to JSW, Northfield, MN, 12/16/1855, LAB Collection.

wheelwright trade in St. Johnsbury A town larger than Peacham, St. Johnsbury in 1860 had a population of 3,470 and much more industry. Bogart identifies in Peacham one "wheelwright's establishment in Ewell's Hollow" in 1860 and notes that of the thirty-seven persons listed with "industrial occupations" in the census of that year, there were "2 blacksmiths and 2 millwrights and wheelwrights" (pp. 264, 269). No more were needed. We have not been able to identify Mr. Miller from whom Augustus learned his trade.

set out for California DAW, New York to AW, 11/30/1861, excerpted by EAC, WC Collection. In a later letter from San Francisco, Augustus wrote Alice that he was working very hard and not making much more than he had at home (5/28/1862).

"I suppose that Augustus starts" DSW, St. Johnsbury, VT, to ClWR, San Francisco, 11/3/1861, JB Collection.

"the healthiest place in Calif." DAW, Mountain View, CA, to unidentified person, 12/10/1862, excerpted by EAC, WC Collection. Casebolt was apparently a former employer.

"I am glad if Augustus has come down" DSW, Fort Totten, Washington, DC, to AW, 11/5/1863, JWT Collection.

"Augustus has been here" ClWR, San Francisco, to AW, 11/24/1864, JB Collection.

Augustus in California as late as 1869 JWR, San Francisco, to AWC, West Barnet, VT, 12/12/1868, ibid.

Centennial Exposition Gales and Loewenson pp. 22–23.

the stump of an oak McPherson, p. 730 n. Another version of this episode at Spotsylvania is given in Blight, p. 298.

"How are you enjoying" INW to LEW, Baltimore, 9/17/1876, INW Family Papers.

"Agustus is the same" EBW to LEW, Northfield, MN, 4/8/1878, ibid.

Vermont law on married teachers It was customary for women who married to leave the profession although there were no Vermont laws against married women teachers. The authors wish to thank Vermont State Archivist, D. Gregory Sanford, for checking the laws.

"Agustus is still here" EBW to LEW, Northfield, MN, 10/27/1878, INW Family Papers; INW, Montpelier, VT, to LEW, Northfield, MN, 10/14 and 12/12/1878, ibid.

"Your kind letter" DAW to ClWR, San Francisco, 9/23/1881, JB Collection.

"Augustus and Ella down" CAC, Diary, 10/14/1881, CF Collection.

Augustus's suicide Several people who read this chapter in manuscript asked whether Augustus was impotent or perhaps homosexual. We have no answers to these very modern questions. It seems clear from the material available that although his fits of melancholy and his final sense of having taken on more than he could handle might have made him impotent in his marriage, it was clinical depression that ruled his life and caused his death. Significantly, many years later, Marietta was buried next to Augustus in the Peacham cemetery, rather than in the plot of her third husband, Jacob Trussell.

"Alice David and I attended" CAC, Diary, 11/10/1881, CF Collection.

"I went to East part" and other quotes Ibid., 11/14–30/1881.

baby Nelson Watts and Choate incorrectly list Nelson's death date (p. 73). He died May 12, 1881.

"a most shocking affair" ChW to HSG/MWG, Jackson, MI, 2/9/1844, WG Family Papers; Brown, pp. 11–12. The authors are indebted to Edmund A. Brown for giving us a copy of his speech, "John Mattocks: Governor of Vermont," ca. 1989.

LYMAN

ministers held positions of power Bogart describes the great influence of Peacham's first minister, Leonard Worcester, who served from 1799 to 1839 (p. 177). Bogart also generalizes the power of the clergy. Keene wrote that "ministers were . . . the most influential men of the town" in eighteenth- and nineteenth-century Vermont (p. 7).

"made a profession of religion" Obituary for LSW, *St. Johnsbury (VT) Caledonian,* 6/14/1872.

Rev. David Merrill Minister at Peacham (1841–1850), was born in Peacham in 1798 and died there in 1850. For more information on this noted minister, see Pearson. The quote on his preaching style is from Bogart as told by Merrill's daughter (p. 180).

"You will recollect that my health" LSW, St. George, ME, to Ashbel Martin in White Rock, CA, 12/25/1852, Ashbel Martin Papers. The authors are grateful to Martin's great-granddaughter, Maxine Martin Long, for a copy of this letter.

"Both before and during his college course" Wells, *History of Barnet,* pp. 660–61.

Lyman persuading his father to let Alice go to Castleton LSW, Middlebury, VT, to LW, 8/4/1859, RCG Collection.

book "as an offering . . . of Friendship" Students at Castleton, VT, "to our dear teacher and friend" [LSW], 7/31/1860, CF Collection.

seminary catalog [Andover Theological Seminary], pp. 16–20.

"Dear Brother, I received a letter from you" DSW, Fort Totten, Washington, DC, to LSW, East Calais, VT, 4/3/1863, JWT Collection.

"It seems Lyman has mad another of his . . . visits" DSW, Fort Totten, Washington, DC, to LEW, 4/5/1863, ibid. East Calais, Vermont, is located about twenty-five miles northeast of Montpelier, about fifty miles from Peacham.

minister and superintendent, a common combination In neighboring Barnet before the beginning of official supervision of schools, Rev. David and Thomas Good-willie, father and son (David served 1790–1850, Thomas, 1833–1866), made it part of their ministerial duty to visit annually all the schools in town (Wells, *History of Barnet,* p. 176). Other historians have pointed out the great influence of clergy on education (Bogart, p. 124, and Keene, p. 7).

U.S. Christian Commission Printed on Commission Record No. 5049 and signed by LSW, 5/24/1865, LW folder, PHA. Lyman's commission appointed him as a delegate "to serve without remuneration from or expense to the Government; distributing stores, circulating good reading matter; visiting sick and wounded, to instruct, comfort, and cheer them, and aid them in correspondence; aiding Surgeons on the battlefield and elsewhere, in the care and conveyance of the wounded to hospitals; helping Chaplains in their ministrations and influence." For a description of some soldiers' evaluations of the Christian Commission clergy, see Catton, pp. 215–16. McPherson writes the Christian Commission was "founded by YMCA leaders in November 1861 to provide blankets, clothing, books, and physical as well as spiritual nurture to Union soldiers" (p. 483).

Sarah Chamberlain Wells, *History of Barnet,* p. 660; Watts and Choate, pp. 66, 304.

Of the four sisters Jane (b. 1831), Sarah (b. 1838), Abby (b. 1840), and Laura (b. 1843), only Sarah married.

"*She is real good*" AW to AGM, unidentified place, 11/18/1867, WG Family Papers.

"*more than usually energetic*" Obituary for Sarah Chamberlain Watts, *St. Johnsbury (VT) Caledonian,* 7/29/1870.

"*We all went to Barnet*" INW, Diary, 10/11/1867, INW Family Papers.

"*He hasn't got a heart*" Schuyler Choate, St. Louis, MO, to CAC, West Barnet, VT, 8/2/1868, CF Collection.

Lyman's busy schedule LSW, Diary, 1869, passim, ibid.

"*A very spiritual man*"; "*extreme conscientiousness*" Wells, *History of Barnet,* p. 165.

"*I believe 28 rose for prayer*" LSW, Diary, 1/13–26/1869, CF Collection. In the transcription of these entries, the authors have spelled out the word "Christ" in place of the Greek symbol used by Lyman.

"*Had good attention*" Ibid., 1/31 and 2/3/1869.

"*Went into Factory*" Ibid., 1/13, 20/1869. See Wells, *History of Barnet,* pp. 206–8, for a description of industry in Barnet at the time. For patent to C. E. Norris for machinery for boring bobbins, see Bogart, p. 269.

And the sermons! Because none of his sermons has survived, it is impossible to do more than guess at his preaching style, but to judge from the biblical passages chosen for them, as listed in his 1869 diary, they were a combination of close reasoning and a strong appeal to the consciences of his parishioners. They would be today called evangelical, and perhaps owed something to the Methodist preaching style of his day.

"*Rose at quarter before 5*" LSW, Diary, 7/10/1869, CF Collection.

"*Sarah did not sleep*" Ibid., 8/5/1869.

"*This morn went with Ella*" Ibid., 12/21/1869.

"*a hard fire*" Ibid., 12/15–16/1869. Wells writes, "It was the fate of nearly all the woolen mills in this part of New England to be burned, sooner or later. . . . The mill on the hill was burned Dec. 15, 1869. The loss was about $50,000 fully insured" (Wells, *History of Barnet,* p. 206).

God is our refuge Psalms 46:1–4.

Although the fig tree shall not blossom, Habakkuk 3:17–18.

"*never recovered from the death of his wife*" Obituary for LSW, *St. Johnsbury (VT) Caledonian,* 6/14/1872.

tuberculosis More often called consumption at that time, tuberculosis was the most common cause of death in the United States throughout the nineteenth century. Although it was thought to be "the result of hereditary predisposition, aggravated in some unfortunate way by a bad environment or improper living," people contracted the infection from other human beings with active pulmonary tuberculosis (Bates, *Bargaining for Life,* p. 328).

spent the . . . winter in Florida LSW, Haynes Landing, FL, to INW, 2/28/1872, RCG Collection. See also AWC, Diary, 1/29, 2/7, 3/18, 5/4, 5/18–6/3/1872,

CF Collection. Bates reports that those suffering from consumption "often traveled in search of a better climate" (*Bargaining for Life,* p. 329).

"*They left in good spirits*" LSW, Diary, 12/29–30/1869, CF Collection.

"*the smiles of the Savior*" Ibid, 3/26/1857.

ISAAC

"*Does Isaac make a good teamster?*" LSW, Richmond, ME, to LW and Friends [Family], 11/1/1852, RCG Collection.

"*how do you like out west*" INW to Edgar and Martha Way, Northfield, MN, 1/19/1856, LAB Collection.

"*Isaac has tried*" RBWW to JSW/SWW, Northfield, MN, 1/19/1856, ibid.

change of name RBWW to AW, Castleton, VT, 9/25/1859, excerpts by EAC, WC Collection. Isaac Watts (1674–1748) wrote *Hymns and Spiritual Songs* which introduced hymn singing into the Congregational churches. Isaac Newton (1642–1727) formulated the law of gravitation.

"*The Patent Office*" INW, Fort Bunker Hill, Washington, DC, to AW, 3/30/1864, excerpts by EAC, WC Collection.

"*In his youth*" Obituary for Isaac Newton Watts, *St. Johnsbury (VT) Caledonian,* 3/11/1881.

"*he is a little white head*" ChW to HSG/MWG, Jackson, MI, 1/18/1846, WG Family Papers.

Peacham "boys" Bogart notes that a total of 122 Peacham men enlisted; only 7 in 1863 when Isaac joined and when the town's quota was 14 (pp. 321, 323). See chapter on Dustan for further description of Vermont boys in the Civil War.

"*When ready for college*" Obituary for INW, *St. Johnsbury (VT) Caledonian,* 3/11/1881.

commutation Bogart, pp. 322–23. A man subject to compulsory enlistment could hire a substitute or be excused on payment of $300. Bogart reports that two Peacham men hired substitutes, none paid the $300.

"*Does Father have any one*" DSW, Fort Totten, Washington, DC, to LEW, 5/10/1863, JWT Collection.

Isaac enlisted AW, Diary, 8/15/1863, CF Collection. August 15: "Ike went to Brattleboro to enlist." August 16: "Ike's birthday." August 26: "Ike started for a soldier's life this morn. Rained like any thing."

"*Abe's pet lambs*" INW, Diary, 5/10/1864, INW Family Papers.

"*I[t] blew all the morning*" INW, Fort Slocum, Washington, DC, to AW, 11/6/1863, JWT Collection.

Describing Christmas Day Ibid., 12/30/1863.

"*Sunday in the army*" INW, Diary 1/3 and 3/27/1864, INW Family Papers. See chapter on Alice for description of the home scene during the Civil War.

"*I have not seen Isaac*" DSW, Fort Totten, Washington, DC, to AW, 11/5/1863, JWT Collection.

"*Abbie got here all safe*" INW, Fort Bunker Hill, Washington, DC, to AW, 4/4/1864, ibid.

Battery M and the regiment For information on Isaac and Dustan's regiment, see Dyer, 3: 1648–49.

"*I can't see the use of marching*" INW, camp near Harpers Ferry, W. VA, to AW, 7/30/1864, added note to letter, 8/1/1864, JWT Collection. Catton gives a description of "the series of aimless marches and countermarches [which] showed clearly that Washington did not know what it was doing" (pp. 267–68).

"*I can hardly make myself believe it*" INW, Diary, 6/24/1864, INW Family Papers; INW, camp near Petersburg, VA, to LEW, 7/3/1864, RCG Collection.

"*I do not care to see any major generals*" Driscoll, p. 25.

"*We . . . marched through Md*" INW, camp near Harpers Ferry, W. VA, to AW, 7/30/1864, JWT Collection.

"*Last night I made a raid*" INW, camp near Harpers Ferry, W. VA, to LEW, 8/7/1864, ibid.

"*I'm pretty sure*" INW, camp near Harpers Ferry, W. VA, to AW, 7/30/1864, ibid.

"*Yesterday morning our pickets were attacked*" INW, camp near Cedar Creek, VA, to AW, 10/20/1864, INW Family Papers.

"*Yesterday we passed back*" INW, camp near Kernstown, VA, to AW, 11/10/1864, ibid; INW, Camp Russell, VA, to AW, 12/2/1864, ibid.

"*We had a very quiet election*" INW, camp near Kernstown, VA, to AW, 11/10/1864, ibid. The election took place on November 8. Historian G. G. Benedict reported that "the Vermont soldiers in their camps . . . [gave] Lincoln a majority in the brigade of 416, out of 1,112 votes cast. The Second and Fourth regiments gave majorities for McClellan, who was still a favorite with many veterans" (1:566–67). At home in Peacham, the vote was 155 for Lincoln's Union ticket electors Kellogg-Simpson and 52 for Chamberlain-Noyes, McClellan's Democratic electors (Book No. 1, Peacham Town Records). The party of the electors was identified for us by the Vermont state archivist, D. Gregory Sanford, in a letter to LAB, 3/3/1993.

"*It seems a little singular*" INW, Strasburg, VA, to AW, 11/5/1864, INW Family Papers.

"*A bullet went through*" AW to AGM, Rawsonville, MI, 12/7/1864, WG Family Papers.

"*I dont know the number*" INW, camp south of Petersburg, VA, to AW, 12/18/1864, JWT Collection.

"*Made about 23 miles*" INW, Diary, 4/23–27/1865, INW Family Papers.

"*I suppose . . . the President*" INW, camp in the field, VA, to LW, 4/19/1865, RCG Collection.

"*Lyman told me*" INW, unidentified place, to AW, 6/25/1865, INW Family Papers.

"*Returning home*" Obituary for INW, *St. Johnsbury (VT) Caledonian,* 3/11/1881.

"*Everything is the same*" INW, Diary, 9/2 and 10 and 12/31/1865, INW Family Papers. At the Watts farm everything might have been the same to Isaac, but other Vermonters were experiencing profound changes. For one thing, 5,128 young men did not return from the war, and of those who did return, many went west to farm or to industrial jobs in cities, creating labor shortages in the state (Barron, "The Impact of Rural Depopulation," pp. 327–30, 334). By 1864 the mowing machine gained popularity, butter production increased, and state dairy associations were being organized (Russell, pp. 245–55).

farm work in 1860s Bogart, pp. 311–17; Wilson describes the decline in sheep raising and the rise of the dairy industry (pp. 81–89, 185–94).

"*the blues*" INW, Diary, 6/1/1868, INW Family Papers.

"*As I did not go to bed*" Ibid., 2/15/1867.

go west for the winter In one letter, Isaac admitted that he thought of going to Iowa "to get a farm," INW, Northfield, MN, to AW, 12/15/1867, MHS. Under the Homestead Act, Isaac, as a Civil War veteran, could purchase 160 acres of public land for a small payment and only one year's residency.

Father Lyman had died Lyman Watts died on August 31, 1875. The only personal documentation on his death comes from Alice's diary, August 31, 1875: "Chas [Charles Choate, her husband] washed & sowed the wheat & grass seed and had the Dea[con] horse to harrow part of the day. Excessively hot and very hard work. I have made bread & donuts. Chas went up to Fathers and stayed over night. He died at 11 this eve." Two days later "Marion [hired girl] came & worked today. Made pies & churned in little churn & she pared some of the peaches. We started for Fathers funeral a little past noon very warm. A storm of wind & rain came up at 4 o'clock. Stopped at the Corner [Charles's parents] a little while" (CF Collection). Less than two months later Alice had a baby whom they named Lyman Watts Choate; he lived only six months.

Father Lyman can be described as a silent, stern, nineteenth-century patriarch; but he was a good provider. His will, written in 1872 after his oldest son, Lyman, had died, left $1,200 to each of his children, Charles (because he died after the will was written, his share went to his children), Isaac, Alice, and Ella, with an extra $100 to Ella "for her services" taking care of him in his last years. To his late son's daughter, Jennie Chamberlain Watts, Lyman left $300, knowing full well that she would be taken care of by the Chamberlains. The will does not mention the Walbridge stepchildren (Copy of Probate Record, 11/2/1875, CF Collection).

"*Just six years ago*" INW, Diary, 1/20/1876, INW Family Papers.

"*Should like to feel better*" Ibid., 8/24/1876.

"*most all day getting deeds*" Ibid., 8/16/1876. The basis of the home farm was what Lyman had bought in 1830: 60 acres. In 1842 he doubled the size of the farm and in 1848, he added the summer pasture. When he died in 1875, in addition to real estate and farm animals, he had personal property listed at $1,482, including bank stocks of $960. At the time Isaac had no real estate although he was listed as having $800 in personal property. In 1877 Isaac was $600 in debt; 1878, $500; 1879, $1,000; 1880, $700 (Peacham Town Records, Grand List, 1876–1880).

letters to Ella INW to LEW, Northfield, MN, 11/1/1877, 5/30/1878, INW Family Papers. See chapter on Lucy Ella for quotes from EBW's letters.

"My Dear Wife" INW, Montpelier, VT, to EBW, [probably mid-October 1878], ibid.

Meroe's upbringing Way family legend disputes this, saying Isaac changed his mind on his death bed and left Meroe to her grandfather Way to be raised by her aunt (Merrill, "What I Know About the Ways").

ALICE

"Alice, three & a half years old" ChW to HSG, Janesville, WI, 8/6/1847, WG Family Papers. Date is puzzling because in 1847 Alice would have been only two and a half.

"I have just written to Alice" LSW, Middlebury, VT, to LW ("Dear Father"), 8/4/1859, RCG Collection.

"At Castleton" AW, Diary, 1/1–6/1860, CF Collection. Few Peacham girls boarded at private secondary school. Among them were Sarah Chamberlain, who graduated in 1860 from Lasell Female Seminary, Auburndale, MA, and Augusta Merrill, who attended Bradford Female Seminary in Massachusetts in 1848–49 and kept a diary, a copy of which is at the Vermont Historical Society.
    Founded in 1787 as Castleton Academy, it became Castleton Seminary in 1833, State Normal School at Castleton in 1867. Today it is known as Castleton State College (Barrick, pp. 9, 75, 205). The authors wish to thank Bob Buckeye, archivist at Middlebury College, for pointing out Barrick's manuscript history of Castleton.

cruel phrases AW, Diary, 1/29, 2/21 and 25/1860, and passim, CF Collection.

"She goes Monday" Ibid., 1/13 and 16/1860. Many historians, notably among them Carroll Smith-Rosenberg, have documented nineteenth-century schoolgirl attachments.

singing school Ibid., 1/28/1860. See Keene for a discussion of Vermont singing schools (pp. 10–35).

Alice's health AW, Diary, 2/10–15/1860, CF Collection.

"Came home this morning" Ibid., 5/5/1860.

"Before Mother died" DSW, Fort Totten, Washington, DC, to AW, 6/28/1863, JWT Collection.

"Lyman has just been preaching to me" AW, Diary, 2/12 and 19/1860, CF Collection.

"Clear sweet moonlight" Ibid., 7/31/1860.

"There is a thunder shower" Ibid., 8/10/1860.

"*Mother's death has made a vacancy*" AW to AGM, unidentified place, 11/30/1862, WG Family papers.

"*I am 'boss and all hands'*" Ibid., 3/18/1863.

"*I had a nice visit*" Ibid., 12/7/1864.

women's war work Ibid., 2/22/1861; DSW, Fort Totten, Washington, DC, to LEW, 5/10/1863, JWT Collection; AW to AGM, Rawsonville, MI, 1/6/1864, WG Family Papers.

high prices and wages AW to AGM, Grass Lake County, MI, 5/6/1862, ibid. She wrote: "All sorts of goods are pretty high here. Calico's a shilling 16⅔ or more. . . . Tea all the way from .75 to 1.25 per pound." In another letter, Alice wrote: "They are haying now and next week we are to have work folks Wages are $2.00 per day and laborers are scarce at that" (AW to SWW, Northfield, MN, 7/9/1864, JWT Collection).

Civil War deaths AW, Diary, 2/25, 3/13 and 19, and 4/28/1863, Memorandum page at end of diary, PC Collection. This is the year her brother Isaac enlisted.

"*It is hard for the girls*" INW, camp near Charlestown, VA, to ClWR, San Francisco, 8/29/1864, JB Collection.

"*I know you are not happy*" DSW, Fort Totten, Washington, DC, to AW, 11/5/1863, JWT Collection.

Mount Holyoke Seminary The school opened in 1837, and the 1865–66 catalog calls it "Mount Holyoke Female Seminary." Of the 287 girls listed for the year, 100 were first-year students. We have identified six Peacham girls who attended Mount Holyoke Seminary from 1850 through 1866 including Elsie Choate, Alice's future sister-in-law (exchange of letters between LAB and Patricia J. Allbright of the Mount Holyoke College Archives, 1/22, 2/26, 3/9, and 6/30/1988).

Mary Lyon writing on cornerstone Crawford, p. 72; general information from Woody, 1:358–62.

"*I never had two such hard lessons*" AW, South Hadley, MA, to LEW, Lowell, MA, 5/14/1866, PC Collection.

"*Lessons went hard*" AW, Diary, 2/5/1866, ibid. Bogart gives a detailed listing of Alice's expenses at Mount Holyoke using two account books which are no longer part of the family archives (p. 347). Not counting tuition, board, or travel, Alice spent $64.31 from October 1865 to June 1866.

"*You were the only Christian*" E. P. Bowers, East St. Johnsbury, VT, to AW, 3/1/1867, PC Collection. The Mount Holyoke College *Directory* lists Ellen Priscilla Bowers, class of 1858 (p. 90). The authors are grateful to Patricia J. Allbright for having loaned us a copy of the *Directory*. "Rix" was sixteen-year-old Julian Walbridge Rix, Alice's nephew.

"*Father froze his feet*" AW to AGM, Mt. Sterling, WI, 2/17/1868, WG Family Papers.

"*Alice's wedding day*" INW, Diary, 11/19/1868, INW Family Papers.

"*from my new home*" AWC, West Barnet, VT, to AGM, unidentified place, 1/23/1869, PC Collection.

"*Things my nurse*" There is no identification of the author, date, or place of this note; on the verso is written, "For Alice's private reading," CF Collection.

"*It takes so much of the day*" AWC, Diary, 1/28/1872, ibid.

Alice's activities Ibid., 4/18 and 27/1872, 2/24, 5/5, and 6/2/1873. The buttery was a pantry or larder in New England, usually a small room next to the kitchen.

Charles's activities Ibid., 5/4/1872, 3/14 and 15/1872, 1/14 and 16/1873, 1/18/1872, 1/6/1873.

Charles was sociable Ibid., 1/29, 2/3, and 5/12/1873.

"*I finished Middlemarch*" Ibid., 11/15/1873.

"*The last call for them*" Ibid., 1/21/1876.

"*They put a lot of mullein leaves on baby*" Ibid., 5/21/1876. Maine midwife Martha Ballard gave "Syrrup of mullin" to an unwell infant in 1791 (Ulrich, *Midwife's Tale,* p. 357). Barbara Swan of Stamford, VT, had a medicinal garden at the middle of the nineteenth century in which was "mullen," among other plants from "the sandy uplands" (Lawrence, pp. 36–37). The women who came to help Alice were her mother-in-law, her sister-in-law, and her sister. We have not been able to identify "Aunt Margaret" as a member of either the Watts or Choate family. Later, on July 30, 1876, when Charles was sicker than usual, "Aunt Margaret came down & nursed him an hour or two." She may have been a local midwife and "Aunt" may have been a sign of respect for her medical knowledge.

butter molds Van Vuren describes the butter mold carvers in Peacham beginning in the 1880s (pp. 78–82).

Butter earned $518.94 AWC, Diary, memorandum at end of 1878 diary, PC Collection. Butter sold from twenty to thirty-five cents a pound. This was the year that Alice and Charles began stamping their butter rather than selling it in tubs.

Alice died Charles made no entries from September 12, 1882, when Isaac was born, through the year, CF Collection. Alice died on September 19, 1882.

ELLA

tuberculosis "ran in families" Conversations with Helen Watts Chase, remembered by her daughter, MCM.

haying schedule According to the diaries kept by Isaac, haying was always right after the Fourth of July; he recorded "commence mowing": July 13, 1866; July 10, 1867; July 8, 1868; July 8, 1876, INW Family Papers.

"*We decided to be married*" Chase, "Memoirs," p. 18, MCM Collection.

"*Meroe [sent] . . . the enlarged*" LEWC, Northfield, MN, to Helen Watts Chase, Passumpsic, VT, 1/14/1906, MCM Collection. Helen's first child, Stephen Chase, Jr., was born in 1904.

"*Mr. Sargeant of North Dakota*" Ibid. Charles and Huldah Moody Sargeant left

Peacham "for Dak[ota]" in the spring of 1878, EBW to LEW, Northfield, MN, 4/8/1878, INW Family Papers.

"*Go on the street*" AW, South Hadley, MA, to LEW, Lowell, MA, 5/14/1866, PC Collection.

Ellen's letters EBW to LEW, Northfield, MN, 1/12 and 4/8/1878, INW Family Papers.

plants and flowers Ibid., 4/28, 7/13, and 8/25/1878.

"*Has anyone written you*" Ibid., 10/27/1878.

farm women's flower gardens Reiter presents a photograph of a flower box "as evidence of a woman's decorative touch" (p. 69); Carty describes house plants "lined up indoors on window sills and 'stands'" giving "color to dull winter days" (p. 77).

treatment of single women in a family By the late nineteenth century the view toward singlehood was changing and the benefits of not marrying were being discussed (Chambers-Schiller, pp. 10–18, 24–25). For a warm reminiscence of a "dear old maiden aunt" from the 1840s, see Fairbanks, pp. 357–58.

"*such good boys and men*" LEW, Northfield, MN, to David and "Chub" Choate, West Barnet, VT, 9/24/1882, PC Collection.

"*It is useless to say*" CAC, West Barnet, VT, to LEW, Northfield, MN 1/1/1883, ibid.

Ella's knowledge of the deaf From local lore Ella may have been aware of two Peacham sisters who lost their hearing from sickness at an early age. Considering the length of the obituary in the *Caledonian* of the oldest, Hannah Varnum, who died on October 6, 1840, it appears that the sisters made quite an impact on the county. *St. Johnsbury (VT) Caledonian,* 10/27/1840.

assistant matron J. L. Smith, p. 111. The official history of the school, published in 1963, lists Lucy in the column for "Housemothers" (Lauritsen, p. 261).

"*Miss Watts has had experience*" Minnesota School for the Deaf, p. 45.

"*Dear Aunt Ella*" Helen and Meroe Watts to LEW, Faribault, MN, 3/29/1889, PC Collection.

Lucy Ella's work J. L. Noyes, Superintendent, Minnesota School for the Deaf, Faribault, MN, to LEW, Northfield, MN, 7/20/1889, ibid.

it was God's will Interview by MCM with Paul Choate, grandson of Charles and Alice, 9/4/1992, Cabot, VT. The house east of the church that Ella came to is owned by Nancy Bundgus at the time of this writing.

Charles's diary entries CAC, Diary, 11/7–16/1889, 6/29 and 8/10/1891, CF Collection. Charles had trouble with the name of Ella's niece, Helen Watts, and called her sometimes "Ellen" and other times "Hellen."

"*the children will start*" LEWC, West Barnet, VT, to CAC, Peaks Island, ME, 8/19/1900, CF Collection. By "the children" she meant David, who worked on the railroad out of Minneapolis, and Isaac, who was attending the University of Minnesota.

Brightlook Hospital This St. Johnsbury hospital was temporarily established in 1899 in the former executive mansion of Gov. Erastus Fairbanks. It was not until 1908 that the new building was dedicated (Fairbanks, pp. 328–30). At the present time, this "new" building is used for apartments and another new hospital has been built across town.

"*Don't worry about us*" LEWC, West Barnet, VT, to CAC, St. Johnsbury, VT, 2/9/1901, CF Collection.

He went to Peacham Elsie Choate Merrill lived with her niece, Elsie A. Choate, Charles's daughter, at the Corner in the Choate house, which is presently owned by Ina and Charles Wallace. The Choate family began living there in the late 1840s and bought the house in 1856. They owned it until 1959 when Elsie A. Choate died. In 1931 Elsie and Alzina Esden opened the Choate Inn, which took in guests off and on for twenty years, although it closed officially during World War II (Bogart, p. 380). A 1933 hand-painted flyer by Sylvia Hunter called it "a Hostelry of Early American charm," Chris Choate-Raible Collection. See also a typed two-page obituary for EAC, author unknown, found in the CF Collection. Stories from the first half of the twentieth century were fondly told on August 12, 1993, at a program at the Peacham Historical House. The tape "Remembering Elsie Choate" is available from the Peacham Historical Association.

his daughter later reported EAC, autobiography, 8/16/1904, RCG Collection.

"*not quite the thing*" Charles A. Choate III, grandson of Charles and Alice, in conversation with authors, summer of 1989, West Barnet, VT.

"*a large, forceful, slightly bear[d]ed lady*" Chase, "Memoirs," p. 104, MCM Collection.

Bibliography

I. Primary Sources

A. Manuscript Collections and Public Records

Barilla, Jack. Private collection.

Barnet Town Records. Town Clerk's Office. Barnet, VT.

Bonfield, Lynn A. Private collection.

Brown, Mildred Maurer. Private collection.

Bryant, Sarah Snell. Diaries, 1795–1847. Houghton Library, Harvard University, Cambridge, MA.

Cabot Town Records. Town Clerk's Office. Cabot, VT.

Caledonia County Court Records. Probate records, wills, guardianship papers, and household inventories. Courthouse. St. Johnsbury, VT.

Chamberlain, Jane. Letters. LaRie Jensen (private collection).

Choate, Paul. Private collection.

Choate Farm Collection. Private collection.

Choate-Raible, Chris. Private collection.

Fairfax, Elizabeth Rix. Private collection.

Gaudette, Roberta Choate. Private collection.

Martin, Ashbel. Papers. Maxine Martin Long (private collection).

Merrill, Augusta. Typed copy of diary, 1848–1849. Vermont Historical Society, Montpelier.

Morrison, Mary Chase. Private collection.

Peacham Historical Collections. Peacham Historical Association, Peacham, VT.

Peacham Town Records. Records Books; Grand List for 1800–1916; Vital Records; and Cemetery Records. Town Clerk's Office. Peacham, VT.

Piatt County Court Records. Courthouse. Monticello, IL.

Rice County Court Records. Courthouse. Faribault, MN.

Rice County Historical Society. Notes from directories and death records. Faribault, MN.

Rix, Edward A. Collection. The Bancroft Library, University of California, Berkeley.

Rix Family Papers. Includes "Daily Journal of Alfred and Chastina W. Rix," 1849–
1854; and Chastina W. Rix, "Journal of My Journey to California," 1853.
California Historical Society, San Francisco.

"San Francisco Streets." News clippings by E. G. Fitzhamon. The article on the
Rix House is in volume 2, p. 3. California Historical Society, San Francisco.

Stevens, Thaddeus. Papers. Manuscript Division, Library of Congress. Washington, D.C. Two Alfred Rix letters, 1845–1848.

Theatre Scrapbook, 1853, 1854. The San Francisco Performing Arts Library and
Museum, San Francisco.

Trunzo, Roberta Garry. Private collection.

Turner, John W. Private collection.

Walbridge-Gregory Family Papers. California Historical Society, San Francisco.

Watts-Choate Collection. Material gathered by Jennie Chamberlain Watts and
Elsie A. Choate, mainly excerpts, used by Ernest Bogart. Vermont Historical
Society, Montpelier.

Watts-Choate Genealogy Records. Responses to Jennie Chamberlain Watts and
Elsie A. Choate's inquiries. Peacham Historical Association, Peacham, VT.

Watts, Isaac Newton. Letter, 12/15/1867. Minnesota Historical Society, St. Paul,
MN.

Watts, Isaac N. Family Papers. Special Collections, Bailey/Howe Library, University of Vermont, Burlington.

Way, Chris. Private collection.

Wolcott Town Records. Town Clerk's Office. Wolcott, VT.

B. Manuscripts

Barrick, W. Boyd. "Vermont's First College: A Chronicle of the First One Hundred Years of Castleton State College, 1787–1887." Typescript, 1988. 209 pages.
Special Collections, Middlebury College.

Brown, Edmund A. "John Mattocks: Governor of Vermont." Typescript, ca. 1989.
12 pages. Lynn A. Bonfield collection.

Butler, Josephine. "The Thomas Watts Family." Typescript, 1990. 5 pages. Lynn A.
Bonfield collection.

Chase, Stephen. "Memoirs." Typescript, 1958. 343 pages. Mary C. Morrison
collection.

Choate, Elsie A. "Life Sketch Written for Miss Wheelock's Kindergarten School."
Handwritten, 8/16/1904. 9 pages. Peacham Historical Association.

Ferraro, William Michael. "Lives of Quiet Desperation, Community and Polity
in New England over Four Centuries: The Cases of Portsmouth and Foster,

Rhode Island." Ph.D. diss., Brown University, 1991. UMI Dissertation Services. Microfilm of typescript. 694 pages.

Long, Harold M. "Early Schools of Peacham." A paper read at the Peacham Historical Association meeting, 8/29/1971. Typescript. 22 pages. Peacham Historical Association.

Merrill, Evangeline Way. "What I Know about the Ways." Transcript, ca. 1960. 16 pages, not numbered. Susan A. O'Brien collection.

C. Newspapers

Alta (San Francisco) California. 11/21/1853; 5/18/1855; 2/27/1875.

Faribault (MN) Republican. 1/13/1909; 2/10/1909.

New York Times. 11/25/1903; 12/4/1903.

Northfield (MN) News. 8/20/1964; 2/17/1966; 3/31/1966.

Piatt County (Monticello, IL) Republican. 2/7/1875; 2/21/1918.

San Francisco Bulletin. 9/4/1872; 5/2/1904.

San Francisco Chronicle. 8/27/1876; 4/22/1877; 3/16/1879; 12/8/1879; 11/30/ 1903; 9/1/1917; 8/28/1928.

San Francisco Evening Bulletin. 11/29/1858; 4/28/1883.

San Francisco Evening Post. 4/22/1877.

San Francisco Herald. 2/19/1853; 12/31/1853.

St. Johnsbury (VT) Caledonian. 1837 to 1909.

St. Johnsbury (VT) Caledonian-Record. 9/29/1990.

II. PUBLISHED SOURCES

Abbott, Susie A. "Place Names in Peacham." *Vermont Quarterly* 20, no. 4 (October 1952): 291–94.

Abel, Emily K., and Margaret K. Nelson, eds. *Circles of Care: Work and Identity in Women's Lives*. Albany: State University of New York Press, 1990.

Anderson, Nancy K., and Linda S. Ferber. *Albert Bierstadt: Art & Enterprise*. New York: Brooklyn Museum and Hudson Hills Press, 1990.

[Andover Theological Seminary]. *Catalogue of the Officers and Students of the Theological Seminary, Andover, Mass., 1863–64*. Andover, MA: Printed by Warren F. Draper, 1864.

Barron, Hal S. "The Impact of Rural Depopulation on the Local Economy: Chelsea, Vermont, 1840–1900." *Agricultural History* 54, no. 2 (April 1980): 318–35.

———. *Those Who Stayed Behind: Rural Society in Nineteenth-Century New England*. Cambridge: Cambridge University Press, 1984.

Bartlett, Richard A. *The New Country: A Social History of the American Frontier, 1776–1890*. New York: Oxford University Press, 1974.

Bates, Barbara. *Bargaining for Life: A Social History of Tuberculosis, 1876–1938*. Philadelphia: University of Pennsylvania Press, 1992.

Bates, Mrs. D. B. *Incidents on Land and Water or Four Years on the Pacific Coast*. Boston, 1860.

Benedict, G. G. *Vermont in the Civil War: A History of the Part Taken by the Vermont Soldiers and Sailors in the War for the Union, 1861–65*. 2 vols. Burlington, VT: The Free Press Association, 1886.

Blight, David W., ed., *When This Cruel War is Over: The Civil War Letters of Charles Harvey Brewster*. Amherst: University of Massachusetts Press, 1992.

Bogart, Ernest L. *Peacham, the Story of a Vermont Hill Town*. Montpelier: Vermont Historical Society, 1948.

Bonfield, Lynn A. "Diaries of New England Quilters Before 1860." *Uncoverings, 1988*. 9:171–97. San Francisco: American Quilt Study Group, 1989.

———. "The Production of Cloth, Clothing, and Quilts in 19th-Century New England Homes." *Uncoverings, 1981*. 2:77–96. Mill Valley, CA: American Quilt Study Group, 1982.

Boorstin, Daniel J. *The Americans: The National Experience*. New York: Random House, 1965.

Bowen, Ralph H., ed. and trans. *A Frontier Family in Minnesota: Letters of Theodore and Sophie Bost, 1851–1920*. Minneapolis: University of Minnesota Press, 1981.

Bowman, John S., ed. *The Civil War Almanac*. New York: World Almanac Publications, 1983.

Bushman, Richard L. "Family Security in the Transition from Farm to City, 1750–1850." *Journal of Family History* 6, no. 3 (Fall 1981): 238–55.

Butterfield, C. W. *History of Crawford and Richland Counties, Wisconsin*. Springfield, IL: Union Publishing Co., 1884.

Caledonia County Grammar School. *Catalogue of the Officers and Students*. Peacham, VT: 1839, 1843, 1845–46, 1846–47, 1848, 1849, 1850, 1851.

———. *100th Anniversary of the Caledonia County Grammar School, Peacham, Vermont, Report of the Commemorative Exercises, August 11–12, 1897*. The Alumni Association, 1900.

Carty, Margaret Durick. "Garden Traditions of Vermont." *Vermont Quarterly* 20, no. 2 (March 1952): 71–88.

Catton, Bruce. *The Army of the Potomac: A Stillness at Appomattox*. Garden City, NY: Doubleday, 1953.

Chambers-Schiller, Lee Virginia. *Liberty A Better Husband, Single Women in America: The Generations of 1780–1840*. New Haven, CT: Yale University Press, 1984.

Coffin, Howard. *Full Duty: Vermonters in the Civil War*. Woodstock, VT: The Countryman Press, Inc., 1993.

Colt, George Howe. *The Enigma of Suicide*. New York: Summit Books, 1991.

Cott, Nancy F. *The Bonds of Womanhood: Woman's Sphere in New England, 1780–1835*. New Haven, CT: Yale University Press, 1977.

Cott, Nancy F., and Elizabeth H. Pleck, eds. *A Heritage of Her Own: Toward a New Social History of American Women*. New York: Simon and Schuster, 1979.

Crawford, Mary Caroline. *The College Girl of America*. Boston: L. C. Page & Co., 1905.

Culbertson, Judi, and Tom Randall. *Permanent Californians: An Illustrated Guide to the Cemeteries of California*. Chelsea, VT: Chelsea Green Publishing Co., 1989.

Cummins, Ella Sterling. "Art in California: A Sketch of Miss Nellie Hopps." *The Golden Era* (October 1885):368–69.

Curtiss-Wedge, Franklyn. *History of Rice and Steele Counties Minnesota*. Vols. 1 and 2. Chicago: H. C. Cooper, Jr. & Co., 1910.

Daniels, Robert V., ed. *The University of Vermont: The First Two Hundred Years*. University of Vermont. Distributed by Hanover, NH: University Press of New England, 1991.

Darroch, A. Gordon. "Migrants in the Nineteenth Century: Fugitives or Families in Motion?" *Journal of Family History* 6, no. 3 (Fall 1981):257–77.

Davis, Allen F. "The Girl He Left Behind: The Letters of Harriet Hutchinson Salisbury." *Vermont Quarterly* 33, no. 1 (January 1965):274–82.

Degler, Carl N. *At Odds: Women and the Family in America from the Revolution to the Present*. New York: Oxford University Press, 1980.

Delaney, Janice, Mary Jane Lupton, and Emily Toth. *The Curse: A Cultural History of Menstruation*. Rev. ed. Urbana: University of Illinois Press, 1988.

Demeritt, David. "Climate, Cropping, and Society in Vermont, 1820–1850." *Vermont History* 59, no. 3 (Summer 1991):133–65.

Doan, Ruth Alden. *The Miller Heresey, Millenialism, and American Culture*. Philadelphia: Temple University Press, 1988.

Driscoll, Jeff. " 'Put the Vermonters a head . . . ' A History of the 1st Vermont Brigade." *Military Images* 13, no. 2 (September–October 1991):16–29.

Dublin, Thomas. *Women at Work: The Transformation of Work and Community in Lowell, MA., 1826–1860*. New York: Columbia University Press, 1979.

Dublin, Thomas, ed. *Farm to Factory: Women's Letters, 1830–1860*. New York: Columbia University Press, 1981.

Dyer, Frederick H. *A Compendium of the War of the Rebellion*. 1908. Rev. ed.: Dayton, OH: Morningside Bookshop, 1978.

Evans, Sara M. *Born for Liberty: A History of Women in America*. New York: Free Press, 1989.

Fairbanks, Edward T. *The Town of St. Johnsbury, VT, a Review of One Hundred Twenty-five Years to the Anniversary Pageant 1917*. St. Johnsbury, VT: Cowles Press, 1914.

Gales, Ruth L., and Diane F. Loewenson, *Bicentennial Philadelphia*. Philadelphia and New York: J. B. Lippincott, 1974.

Gilmore, William J. *Reading Becomes a Necessity of Life: Material and Cultural Life in Rural New England, 1780–1835*. Knoxville: University of Tennessee Press, 1989.

Goodrich, John E., comp. *General Catalogue of the University of Vermont and State Agricultural College Burlington, Vermont, 1797–1900.* Burlington, VT: Free Press Association, 1901.

Guy, Tirzah, M., comp. *Caledonia County Grammar School, Peacham, Vermont, 1797–1897.* St. Johnsbury, VT: Caledonian Press, n.d.

Harrison, Alfred C., Jr. "Albert Bierstadt and the Emerging San Francisco Art World of the 1860s and 1870s." *California History* 71, no. 1 (Spring 1992):74–87.

———. "The Haggin Museum." *Art of California* 1, no. 2 (December/January 1989):10–19.

Himelhoch, Myra. "The Suicide of Sally Perry." *Vermont Quarterly* 33, no. 1 (January 1965):283–89.

Hoffert, Sylvia D. *Private Matters: American Attitudes Toward Childbearing and Infant Nurture in the Urban North, 1800–1860.* Urbana: University of Illinois Press, 1989.

Holliday, J. S. *The World Rushed In: The California Gold Rush Experience.* New York: Simon and Schuster, 1981.

Horowitz, Helen Lefkowitz. *Campus Life: Undergraduate Cultures from the End of the Eighteenth Century to the Present.* Chicago: University of Chicago Press, 1987.

Hubbell, Seth. *A Narrative of the Sufferings of Seth Hubbell and Family, in His Beginning a Settlement in the Town of Wolcott, in the State of Vermont.* Danville, VT: Ebenezer Eaton, 1824. Reprint, Bennington, VT: Vermont Heritage Press, 1986.

Hubka, Thomas C. *Big House, Little House, Back House, Barn: The Connected Farm Buildings of New England.* Hanover, NH: University Press of New England, 1984.

Huden, John C. *Development of State School Administration in Vermont.* Montpelier: Vermont Historical Society, 1943.

Jensen, Joan M. *Loosening the Bonds: Mid-Atlantic Farm Women, 1750–1850.* New Haven, CT: Yale University Press, 1986.

Keene, James A. *Music and Education in Vermont 1700–1900.* Macomb, IL: Glenbridge Publishing Ltd., 1987.

Kemble, John Haskell. *The Panama Route, 1848–1869.* Berkeley: University of California Press, 1943.

Kirk, Chauncey A. "Bohemian Rendezvous, Nineteenth-Century Monterey: Sanctuary and Inspiration for Early Western Artists." *American West* 16, no. 6 (Nov./Dec. 1979):34–44.

Korngold, Ralph. *Thaddeus Stevens: A Being Darkly Wise and Rudely Great.* New York: Harcourt, Brace, 1955.

Larkin, Jack. *The Reshaping of Everyday Life, 1790–1840.* New York: Harper and Row, 1988.

Lauritsen, Wesley. *History of the Minnesota School for the Deaf, Faribault 1863–1963.* Faribault: Minnesota School for the Deaf, 1963.

Lawrence, Marion B. "Cure-alls of the Past." *Vermont Quarterly* 20, no. 1 (January 1952):35.

Lee, Edward B., Jr. *East Village Portrait: Based on the Autobiography of Arthusa Hibbard Ayer, 1824–1904.* "To Commemorate the 75th Anniversary of Old Home Day in East St. Johnsbury, Vermont." [1988].

Levy, Jo Ann. *They Saw the Elephant: Women in the California Gold Rush.* Norman: University of Oklahoma Press, 1992.

Lewis, Oscar. *Sea Routes to the Gold Fields: The Migration by Water to California in 1848–1857.* New York: Knopf, 1949.

[Long, Harold M.] *A Profile of Peacham.* Published in commemoration of the bicentennial of the signing of the Charter of the Town of Peacham 1963.

Lotchin, Roger W. *San Francisco, 1846–1856: From Hamlet to City.* New York: Oxford University Press, 1974.

Ludlum, David M. *Social Ferment in Vermont, 1791–1850.* New York: AMS Press, Inc., 1966.

Lystra, Karen. *Searching the Heart: Women, Men, and Romantic Love in Nineteenth-Century America.* New York: Oxford University Press, 1989.

McFarland, Gerald W. *A Scattered People: An American Family Moves West.* New York: Penguin Books, 1987. Reprint, Amherst: University of Massachusetts Press, 1991.

McGoren, Constance M. "The Insane, the Asylum, and the State in Nineteenth-Century Vermont." *Vermont History* 52, no. 4 (Fall 1984):205–24.

McPherson, James M. *Battle Cry of Freedom: The Civil War Era.* New York: Oxford University Press, 1988.

Matthews, Glenna. *"Just a Housewife": The Rise and Fall of Domesticity in America.* New York: Oxford University Press, 1987.

Meier, Peg, collector. *Bring Warm Clothes, Letters and Photos from Minnesota's Past.* Minneapolis: Minneapolis Tribune, 1981.

Merchant, Carolyn. *Ecological Revolutions: Nature, Gender, and Science in New England.* Chapel Hill: University of North Carolina Press, 1989.

Minnesota School for the Deaf. *Annual Report, 1887–88.* Faribault: Minnesota School for the Deaf, [1888].

Mount Holyoke College. *One Hundred Year Biographical Directory, Mount Holyoke College, South Hadley, Massachusetts, 1837–1937.* South Hadley: The Alumnae Association, 1937.

Mount Holyoke Female Seminary. *Twenty-Ninth Annual Catalogue of the Mount Holyoke Female Seminary in South Hadley, Mass., 1865–66.* Northhampton, MA: Bridgman & Childs, 1866.

Myres, Sandra L., ed. *Ho for California! Women's Overland Diaries from the Huntington Library.* San Marino, CA: Huntington Library, 1980.

Nelson, Margaret K. *Negotiated Care: The Experience of Family Day Care Providers.* Philadelphia: Temple University Press, 1990.

——. "Vermont Female Schoolteachers in the Nineteenth Century." *Vermont History* 49, no. 1 (Winter 1981):5–30.

[*Northfield News*]. *All About Northfield, Minn.: Directory of Names and Business Firms, Information in Regard to the City.* Northfield, MN: Steam Printing House, 1889.

Osterud, Nancy Grey. *Bonds of Community: The Lives of Farm Women in Nineteenth-Century New York.* Ithaca, NY: Cornell University Press, 1991.

Paul, Rodman W. *California Gold: The Beginning of Mining in the Far West.* Cambridge, MA: Harvard University Press, 1947.

[Peacham Congregational Church]. *Anniversary Exercises of the Congregational Church, Peacham, VT, April 14, 1894.* St. Johnsbury, VT: I. W. Rowell, 1894.

[Peacham Congregational Church]. *Manual of the Congregational Church, in Peacham, Vermont.* Jericho, VT: Roscoe Publishing House, 1890.

Pearson, Thomas Scott, comp. *Sermons by the Late Rev. David Merrill, Peacham, VT. With a Sketch of His Life.* Windsor, VT: Vermont Chronicle Press, 1855.

Peck, Lt. Col. Paul R. *Landsmen of Jackson County.* Clark Lake, MI: Liberty Town Press, 1977.

Piatt, Emma C., *History of Piatt County.* Chicago, IL: Shepard & Johnston, n.d.

Piatt County Quarterly 2, no. 2 ([Spring] 1981):17 [Deaths].

Premo, Terri L. *Winter Friends: Women Growing Old in the New Republic, 1785–1835.* Urbana: University of Illinois Press, 1990.

Preston, Jo Anne. "Female Aspiration and Male Ideology: Schoolteaching in Nineteenth-Century New England." In *Current Issues in Women's History,* edited by Arina Angerman et al. New York: Routledge, 1989.

Reiter, Joan Swallow. *The Women.* Alexandria, VA: Time-Life Books, 1978.

Riley, Glenda. *Divorce—An American Tradition.* New York: Oxford University Press, 1991.

Robertson, James Oliver, and Janet C. Robertson. *All Our Yesterdays: A Century of Family Life in an American Small Town.* New York: HarperCollins, 1993.

Robinson, Harriet H. *Loom & Spindle or Life among the Early Mill Girls.* Kailua, HI: Press Pacifica, 1976.

Roth, Randolph A. *The Democratic Dilemma, Religion, Reform, and the Social Order in the Connecticut River Valley of Vermont, 1791–1850.* Cambridge: Cambridge University Press, 1987.

Rothman, Ellen K. *Hands and Hearts: A History of Courtship in America.* Cambridge, MA: Harvard University Press, 1987.

Russell, Howard S. *A Long, Deep Furrow: Three Centuries of Farming in New England.* Abridged ed., 1976. Hanover, NH: University Press of New England, 1982.

Ryan, Mary P. *Cradle of the Middle Class: The Family in Oneida County, New York, 1790–1865.* Cambridge: Cambridge University Press, 1981.

———. *Womanhood in America from Colonial Times to the Present,* 2nd ed. New York: New Viewpoints, 1975.

San Francisco Directory for the Year 1852–1853. San Francisco: James M. Parker, 1852.

Schlereth, Thomas J. *Victorian America: Transformations in Everyday Life.* New York: HarperCollins, 1991.

Schlissel, Lillian. *Women's Diaries of the Westward Journey.* New York: Schocken Books, 1982.

Sears, John F. *Sacred Places: American Tourist Attractions in the Nineteenth Century.* New York: Oxford University Press, 1989.

Smith, Daniel Scott, and Michael S. Hindus. "Premarital Pregnancy in America, 1640–1971; An Overview and Interpretation." *Journal of Interdisciplinary History* 5, no. 4 (Spring 1975):537–70.

Smith, J. L., comp. *History of the Minnesota School for the Deaf.* Faribault, MN: School for the Deaf, 1893.

Smith-Rosenberg, Carroll. "The Female World of Love and Ritual: Relations between Women in Nineteenth-Century America." *Signs: Journal of Women in Culture and Society* 1 (Autumn 1975):1–29.

Stilwell, Lewis D. *Migration from Vermont.* Montpelier: Vermont Historical Society, 1948.

Stote, Amos. *The Bookman* 30 (October 1909):190.

Strasser, Susan. *Never Done: History of American Housework.* New York: Pantheon, 1982.

Strickland, Charles. *A Transcendentalist Father: The Child-Rearing Practices of Bronson Alcott.* Cambridge, MA: Charles Warren Center for Studies in American History, Harvard University, 1969.

Suitor, J. Jill. "Husbands' Participation in Childbirth: A Nineteenth-Century Phenomenon." *Journal of Family History* 6, no. 3 (Fall 1981):278–93.

Swift, Esther Munroe, and Mona Beach. *Brattleboro Retreat, 1834–1984, 150 Years of Caring.* Brattleboro, VT: Book Press, 1984.

Theriot, Nancy M. *The Biosocial Construction of Femininity, Mothers and Daughters in Nineteenth-Century America.* New York: Greenwood Press, 1988.

Thompson, Zadock. *History of Vermont, Natural, Civil, and Statistical.* Burlington, VT: Chauncey Goodrich, 1842.

Toensing, W. F., comp. *Minnesota Congressmen, Legislators, and Other Elected State Officials, An Alphabetical Check List, 1849–1971.* St. Paul: Minnesota Historical Society, 1971.

Ulrich, Laurel Thatcher. *Good Wives: Image and Reality in the Lives of Women in Northern New England, 1650–1750.* New York: Knopf, 1982.

——. *A Midwife's Tale: The Life of Martha Ballard, Based on Her Diary, 1785–1812.* New York: Knopf, 1990.

U.S. Bureau of the Census. Illinois, 1860, 1870; Michigan, 1840, 1850; Minnesota, 1860, 1870, 1880; Vermont, 1850, 1860, 1870, 1880.

Van Der Zee, John. *The Greatest Men's Party on Earth.* New York: Harcourt Brace Jovanovich, 1974.

Van Vuren, Barbara. "A Lasting Impression: The Delicately Carved Butter Molds of Peacham, Vermont." *Yankee* 58, no. 1 (January 1994):78–82.

Wallbridge, William Gedney, comp. *Descendants of Henry Wallbridge Who Married*

Anna Amos December 25th, 1688, at Preston, Conn. Litchfield, CT: William Gedney Wallbridge, 1898.

Warner, Robert M. "A Document of Michigan Pioneer Life: A Letter from Ann Arbor, Mrs. Elijah William Morgan." *Michigan History* 40, no. 2 (June 1956): 215–24.

Watts, Jennie Chamberlain, and Elsie A. Choate, comp. *People of Peacham.* Montpelier, VT: The Vermont Historical Society, 1965.

Weisberger, Bernard A. "The Working Ladies of Lowell." *American Heritage* 12, no. 2 (February 1961).

Wells, Frederick. *History of Barnet, Vermont, From the Outbreak of the French and Indian War to Present Time, with Genealogical Records of Many Families with Some Corrections.* 1923; Second Printing, With Some Corrections. Privately printed, Burlington, VT: Free Press Printing Co., 1975.

——. *History of Newbury, Vermont, From the Discovery of the Coös Country to Present Time.* St. Johnsbury, VT: Caledonian Company, 1902.

Welter, Barbara. "The Cult of True Womanhood: 1820–1960." *American Quarterly* 18 (1966):151–74.

Wertz, Richard W., and Dorothy C. Wertz. *Lying-In: A History of Childbirth in America.* Expanded Ed. New Haven, CT: Yale University Press, 1989.

Wiley, Bell Irvin. *The Life of Billy Yank, The Common Soldier of the Union.* Garden City, NY: Doubleday, 1971.

Wilson, Harold Fisher. *The Hill Country of Northern New England: Its Social and Economic History, 1790–1930.* Morningside Heights, NY: Columbia University Press, 1936.

Winsor, Justin, ed. *The Memorial History of Boston, including Suffolk County, Massachusetts, 1630–1880.* Vol. 1. Boston: James R. Osgood, 1881.

Woody, Thomas. *A History of Women's Education in the United States.* 2 vols. Vol. 1: New York: Octagon Books, 1914; Vol. 2: New York: Science Press, 1929.

Yale, Allen R., Jr., *While the Sun Shines: Making Hay in Vermont, 1789–1900.* Montpelier: Vermont Historical Society, 1991.

Zonderman, David A. "From Mill Village to Industrial City: Letters from Vermont Factory Operators." *Labor History* 27, no. 2 (Spring 1986):265–85.

Index

Numbers in italics refer to pages having illustrations.